Whiff!

The Revolution of
Scent Communication
in the Information Age

C. RUSSELL BRUMFIELD
WITH JAMES GOLDNEY
AND STEPHANIE GUNNING

Quimby Press
New York, New York

First Quimby Press hardcover edition June 2008.

For information about special discounts for bulk purposes, please contact Quimby Press Special Sales at sales@quimbypress.com.

ISBN 978-0-9817460-0-5

Cover Design by Andrew Newman

Book Design by 1106 Design

Book Cover Scent Design by International Flavors & Fragrances

Book Cover Scent Delivery by Scentisphere

Manufactured in the United States of America

10 9 8 7 6 5 4 3 2 1

For my mother Patricia and my late father Chuck "Sonny" Brumfield.

A perfect marriage of Old Spice and Persian Wood.

You are the essence of my life.

Praise for *Whiff!*

"Whiff! unveils what all of us already knew and ignored: Scents ignite pictures, memories, and emotions within us like no other marketing tool ever invented."

—David Angelo, Chairman and Chief Creative Officer, David & Goliath

"Scent marketing is one of the more powerful recent additions to the mix of assets in the portfolio of the effective CMO. It does and will make a positive difference for those who learn to manage its power."

—Joe Cronin, DDB Worldwide, Former Vice Chairman
of Saatchi & Saatchi Worldwide

"Whiff! provides valuable insight into the importance of scent in marketing and ways to unleash its powerful effect."

—Ken Perich, Vice President, Sales and Marketing,
Rolls-Royce North America

"We all want a magic formula for attracting a customer's loyalty and love. Who knew it would be as simple as appealing to their olfactory gland?"

—Fulton Smith-Sykes, President of the Fulton Group,
Former Vice President of Marketing, Outback Steakhouse

"Scent is the final frontier in which to weed out the clutter of advertising in the marketplace, and gain the consumer's attention."

—Harald Vogt, Founder of The Scent Marketing Institute

"I've known Russell Brumfield for over a decade, and he is a genius. He never ceases to amaze me with his limitless fountain of ideas and never-ending creative entrepreneurial spirit."

—Nancy L. Altenburg, Sponsorship Marketing, FedEx

Success is a great deodorant.
It takes away all your past smells.
—Elizabeth Taylor

Contents

Part Three
How to Play the Game   159

Part Four
Winning Strategies for a New Century   225

Acknowledgments

After a lifelong career of bringing concepts to life in other ventures, I was rather amiss in my estimation of the measure of effort that this particular quest would entail. I have since come to understand why a certain prolific novelist has avowed to forever avoid works of non-fiction. It is simply a matter of facts, and his utter aversion to sourcing, noting, and checking them. And this book is chock full of them. It is also awash in concepts that were derived from these facts, and I owe a debt of gratitude to all of those folks who helped to bring these facets together along the way.

I am most indebted to my coauthor, business partner, and friend James Goldney, who spent countless days and nights researching many of the facts, as well as contributing some of the pioneering ideas contained in this book. I am equally indebted to his wife Debby for her faith and constant sacrifice during the process. I also want to thank my coauthor and editor Stephanie Gunning for her expert guidance, ideas, and direction. Her enthusiasm for this project only grew with each new concept we revealed.

Thanks to Liz Broom for her comments and suggestions about the manuscript. Props to my literary agent Peter Miller for his tireless efforts, and for seeding the idea of a companion documentary. Mega-props to my speaking agent Mike Taubleb for his enthusiasm, diligence, and patience during my sabbatical. A grateful salute goes to Rich Roher, Phillip Bergman and Janet Appel, our dedicated PR team, to Michele DeFilippo and Andrew Newman for their talented designs, and to Ronda Rawlins for her expert proofreading.

I owe my initial inspiration to the revelations of Piet Vroon and the endeavors of David Martin and my passionately creative friend, Chris Jones. I am much obliged to Martin Lindstrom, Chandler Burr, and Dr. Alan Hirsch for their affability and generosity of time over the course of many meetings. Infinite thanks to my friend and colleague Harald Vogt for harnessing this new industry, and introducing me to so many of its players.

I would like to acknowledge the folks at IFF, especially Steve Semoff for his invaluable assistance and ability to explain the science in layman's terms (he was also the force behind the book's scent). Kudos also go to Melissa Sachs for managing the interviews, and to Nicolas Mirzayantz, for his zeal and enthusiasm for our project. Thanks to Bob Bernstein and Scentisphere for the scent delivery of the *Whiff!* cover.

I am also grateful to Professor Valerie Edwards-Jones and Dr. Anna Doran of the Manchester Metropolitan University, for their time and support for this book. An added mention of gratitude is due to Roy and Pam Jackson for their friendship and hospitality.

Special thanks go to my friends and colleagues Fulton Smith-Sykes, Jacquelyn Huppi, Joan Wavpotich, Citron Arbel, Spence and Marc Levy, John Van Roemburg, Yvan Regeard, Dr. J.D. Megargel, Tom Conroy, Mark Peltier, Juan Miguel Antoñanzas, Matt Saravay, Yolanda Diaz, Nancy Altenburg, Dave, Larry and Ken Perich, and to Ritch Crawford for his endless cheerleading.

I couldn't have accomplished this task without the aid, comfort, encouragement and inspiration of my friends and loved ones. Heartfelt thanks especially to Jason Fortner, Lawanna Rine, Kristen Paulin, Ida Rudom, Deb Berhle, Lorraine Montgomery, Sheryl St. John, James Welsh, Russ and Leddy Hammock and JoEllen Farnham. I wish to express my endless gratitude to my friend, angel, and ally, Linda Neidzwiecki, who I playfully regard as my biggest fan.

I owe my final praise and gratitude to my mother, Pat Brumfield, for her undying love and support, and infinite belief in my potential.

Introduction: A Whiff of the Future

Can you smell it? There's a tsunami of scent on the horizon that's about to make landfall. It will be of historical significance, transforming every aspect of business and life around the globe. Whether or not you are keen about the idea, at this point it's an unstoppable phenomenon. There hasn't been a wave of this magnitude in the fields of marketing and advertising since the onset of photography. It's all due to new discoveries and our growing understanding of the subtle influence that scent has upon the human mind and body.

The sense of smell has existed since the humble beginnings of life on Earth (there's evidence that even the earliest life forms emitted and could sense aromas), but only in the recent blink of history have we begun to study scents and their physiological and psychological effects upon human beings to determine the different ways that they may be of significant benefit to us. Among other discoveries, we have learned that the sense of smell is the quickest way to tap into someone's emotional responses and memory. This makes scent an excellent tool for many different kinds of communication.

Our relatively recent understanding of the prominence and influence of scent in our lives is rapidly changing the paradigm of how we market, sell, and deliver products and services to consumers. This insight also has created entire industries that have sprung up to offer us scent-based solutions to age-old problems. As leading edge companies integrate revolutionary new devices and concepts into their operations and products, and realize extremely encouraging results, other companies are following suit, embracing the promise of scent.

In the coming years, scent will be used in countless ways to influence decisions and moods for every conceivable purpose. Strategies will change in branding, product manufacturing, and packaging. High schools, colleges, and training institutes will use scent environmentally to enhance learning, recall, alertness, and even safety. Aromas will be used to calm groups in public spaces, such as banks, post offices, and airports, and in hospitals, nursing homes, prisons, courts, and other government buildings. They also will be used as a navigation aid, to help eliminate infectious airborne diseases, and to combat theft and counterfeiting. Odors will alert people of danger through recognizable signals related to specific emergencies and disasters. Scents also will inform and alert us to the safety issues and maintenance needs of our vehicles and appliances, and apprise workers of dying batteries and impending worn parts in heavy industrial equipment. All these revolutionary applications for scent are covered in *Whiff!*

An exciting new science of scent and its applications is only beginning to waft across the landscape. As you will see, much about this innate pathway leading directly to our emotions and instincts has yet to be explored. Although its applications to marketing and branding are relatively straightforward, the cognitive and physiological benefits of scent open a door to a range of possibilities that can take the breath away. Frankly, those who apply practical scenting methods in their businesses in the next few years will place themselves ahead of the curve of a significant trend.

Why This Book Exists

Yes, a richly scented tsunami is brewing in the distance. In *Whiff!* it is my intention to document the signs of the impending wave and make predictions about its ultimate landfall and impact. This book will offer you a simple understanding of how and why scent works, and also reveal as many applications in different fields and endeavors as room and good taste allow.

For many years, entrepreneurs have attempted to expand the use of aroma to encompass new areas of trade (I can lay claim to being among the earliest innovators, as can my coauthor and colleague James Goldney), but until recently the scent industry wasn't ready on a technological level. In *Whiff!* we'll chart some of the failed or mildly successful attempts at scent marketing as well as some very successful ones, and explain why we believe the situation has changed dramatically for the better.

A new army of entrepreneurs is in the making, ready to charge into this original and unknown territory, creating additional uses that are yet to be considered. Whatever your interest in reading this book, and whatever you believe about the possibilities for scent, you can be assured that the material covered in *Whiff!* will affect you, your friends and loved ones, our society at large, and the way we all do business in the years ahead.

The Dilemma of the Information Age

The only thing that is certain in life, besides death and taxes, is change. The way we do things is in a state of constant flux. The past half-dozen generations have each experienced amazing, life changing advances in transportation, communication, entertainment, health care, and living standards. In six short generations, we have almost doubled our life expectancy, we have traded a single horse for 400 simulated ones under the hood, and we have gone from sending scouts on horseback into unknown territory to dispatching rocket-propelled robot scouts to distant planets.

Our parents and grandparents have experienced wonders in their lifetimes that they never dreamed of as children, while today we live in a period of even more rapid innovation. So much of this is taken for granted that on a daily basis we may casually read news of human gene mapping, embryonic stem cell therapies, $100 laptops, intelligent robots, and alternative fuels, and then mindlessly turn to the entertainment page for stories that seem more interesting. We are jaded, cautious, well informed, and knowing. We are so inundated with new information, that we must use technology to help us store, catalog, and search for the information that personally concerns us.

In an era of flowing information and high-speed digital technology, we have few doubts about the vast potential of the future. We have grown to expect great things of our inventors, knowing that someone, somewhere "out there," is working to improve every product and service that has ever been conceived, and design new ones to do the extraordinary. The problem is that it is hard to capture our attention.

True, some of us pine for the days of old, when things seemed to be simpler and less complicated. People of my generation, at the tail end of the Baby Boom, look back to a time of rotary phones that accorded us only as much privacy as the length of the cord allowed. We can recall an age of IBM Selectrics, telex machines, and service stations that actually provided service. We would bellyache about our scratched record albums or our eight-track tapes being eaten up by our players. We sometimes watched movies from behind a steering wheel, and we actually had to move our bodies if we wanted to turn the TV dial to switch from one to another of only a half-dozen channels. The term "mouse" was used to refer to either an unwanted rodent visitor or an iconic cartoon character. Candles were generally reserved for emergencies and special romantic dinners.

During my childhood, Kmart was king and tennis shoes were cheap—and only came in a few styles. We could actually work on our own cars, for they were built using purely mechanical parts. But those times are gone now, paved over by progress and innovation. My generation might fondly recall a time when a phone at the dinner table signaled that you were at a *very* fancy restaurant, and store clerks actually knew how to count change. But we do not miss many of the old, more arduous ways. We wouldn't trade our yesterdays, and we're happy with almost all of the conveniences we've been granted.

Today we stand squarely in the middle of the information age, an era of world shrinking, time shrinking, and constant, instantaneous contact. Ours is a Silicon Valley world of Apple, Dell, Intel, X-Box 360, and PlayStation. We think nothing of diving headlong into the surf of the World Wide Web, as we zap pictures through our cell phones and listen to our favorite songs on our iPods. It is an era where legal drugs come in multi-sized cups with Italian sounding names, in every flavor from mocha and caramel, to pumpkin and banana. Our Sport Utility Vehicles cost the price of our childhood homes. We ride crowded tin airbuses through the clouds to see clients and friends.

Generation Xers and Millennials, having been raised in the midst of the digital revolution, cut their teeth on computers and the Internet. Their minds have been honed to shift gears more quickly than those of their elders, and their attention spans and patience levels are commensurately shorter. They've seen practically everything, are wise beyond their years, and they have little tolerance for hype. They want what they want now—without waiting. And they are the most "connected" generation the world has seen. The era of scent communication ultimately belongs to these ingenious crafters of tomorrow.

Contemporary Westerners are the most privileged, wealthy, well-kept people in the history of the world. Even our poorer folks live lives of which ancient kings could only dream. The more that we consume, the more we want to taste what else life has to offer. As consumers we have become demanding and faithless. It's all about us and what can be done for us.

Adroit companies and marketers understand this phenomenon ("What's in it for me?"). They know that they cannot rest upon their laurels for even one second, for their customers will switch loyalties at a whim in response to a glitzy advertising campaign, the latest design, a cheaper-this, a better-that, or whatever the competition has cooked up. Companies are cognizant of basic facts: If they're not growing, they're dying. If they grow too big and sluggish, they risk losing market share. If they are not on the cutting edge, they risk profitability, or even worse, they can become obsolete like the corporate dinosaurs of a past era. They are not only on a fervent search for solutions—they need them for their very survival.

As we become more accustomed to the ease and easy access in our lives, the more difficult it becomes for advertisers to reach us. Product and service providers work overtime to bring us the next big thing, and frequently we don't give their offerings the time of day. In order to succeed, the question we must ask ourselves is: How can a business, a product, or a professional stand out when consumers are overwhelmed with a daily glut of messages and seemingly infinite emails, while simultaneously being inundated by TV, radio, and print ads? The question is how do we get their attention as they continue to tune out and turn off these messages in a newly insulated world of iPods and perpetual text messaging? We once believed that connection was communication, and that getting in front of them would make an "impression," but now more than ever we know that this just isn't true.

Today's consumers have relegated advertising to a faint background hum, and developed an instinct specifically to filter out slush ads and solicitations. We don't blink at scam emails offering million-dollar payouts from "widows" in Nigeria or proposing "free sex" with coeds. Startling tactics that work one week seem passé and ineffectual the next. The average consumers only pay attention to what moves them. Like pretty girls in a nightclub full of would-be Lotharios, they will keep their gaze downward and distant until something or somebody triggers their interest. Only when the right message, nuance, or gesture makes it onto their radar screen, will they take notice and respond.

Communication is on overload, yet advertisers and salespeople keep pouring out message upon message, impression upon impression, in the hope of connecting with consumers. Most have overzealously exhausted traditional forms of communication, achieving increasingly poor results from print, TV, radio, and online advertising. These elements still work, but only to a continually lessening degree. Although marketers and advertisers have reaped great rewards from newer digital communication tools, they have just about milked the cow dry. Most companies inadvertently ignore or have not yet become enlightened to this secret, ancient tool of communication; the silent key that unlocks the inner recesses of our mind, breaking through our fortified barriers with its eloquently muted message. Yes, most have yet to learn and employ this seemingly foreign language of scent. But that will soon change.

Scent: The Communication Solution

Bold, forward-thinking companies have begun to embrace the subtle influences of scent to reach out and touch the emotions of their customers. These innovators have come to realize that the simple element of scent is in itself a very dynamic form of information, so they are studying, testing, and implementing ways to use scent to communicate more effectively with consumers. Some are fully immersed in the scent dimension already, and others are still testing the waters, taking note of what works and what doesn't. In *Whiff!* you will see that an overwhelming trend has emerged. Hundreds of scent-savvy companies have found insightful new ways to use scent that you've probably never imagined.

After reading this book, no matter what business you are in or what role you play in your business, you will discover innumerable applications of scent, and an entirely new, exciting world of possibilities. With the curtain unveiled, and a new paradigm of thinking in place, there's little doubt that you're going to want to try them out for yourself!

The Origin of Scent Marketing

Who knew we would ever see scented phones, bowling balls, slippers, paintings, and A-list feature-films? Emotional clothing and intelligent spaces, scented mirrors and Scratch 'n' Sniff windows, aren't these the musings of science fiction writers? Well, yes. Speculation is kind of how it all started—in the mind of a freethinking literary dreamer.

What do a well-known science fiction writer, a major communications company, and an icon in the themed entertainment business have in common? That's right, scent. In searching for the ground zero of many modern technological breakthroughs and innovations, we frequently discover the Walt Disney Company at its epicenter. Disney was one of the earlier innovators in nontraditional uses of aroma. It was no accident that founder Walt Disney was a fan of science fiction writer Ray Bradbury. Likewise Bradbury was an avid fan of all things Disney, including the man. Contemporaries in the world of ideas, they were both futurists in search of a way to manifest their concepts. Long after Walt Disney passed into the virtual world, the Disney Company contracted Bradbury to write the original storyline for their flagship attraction, Spaceship Earth, in the newly constructed Epcot Center in the early 1980s. This wasn't the first time that Bradbury had conceived of a scent-related story, for in his 1953 novel *Fahrenheit 451* (see Bibliography) he concocted robotic smelling hounds that searched for their prey by way of scent.

Bradbury's Spaceship Earth storyline was the impetus for the invention of a scent delivery system called the "Smellitzer" that emitted the smell of smoke during the ride's "Roman Ruins" scene. Disney inventor and imagineer Bob McCarthy receives credit for this invention.[1] It also seems serendipitous that a major communications company—AT&T—sponsored the debut of this modern-era scent device.

Since the invention of the Smellitzer for use in multisensory entertainment, Disney has adapted it to many other rides and attractions, including Pirates of the Caribbean, Tower of Terror, Pooh's Adventure, Haunted Mansion, and A Bug's Life. The success of the Smellitzer spawned other delivery systems and other uses of scent. A particularly brilliant Disney employee had the bright idea to use the Company's scent device as a marketing tool. As a result, for years now, one has been able to stroll up Disney World's Main Street and encounter the waft of enticing smells in the air. Coffee or cookies may draw us in to one shop or another. The faint smell of peppermint lingers outside the door of a candy store. During the Very Merry Christmas Parade, the Chip n' Dale's Bakery Float sends out intoxicating aromas of baked cookies and ginger, as it hovers past the viewing guests.

At my company Whiff Solutions, we would love to see the sales figures, but no one's talking. The smart folks at the Walt Disney Company have been silently using scent marketing for years. No one is complaining either. Although other entrepreneurs previously had made stabs at scent marketing, it took this giant entertainment company with the means and wherewithal to get the ball rolling. Now there is no looking back.

My Own Adventure in the Scent Dimension

I have followed the path of environmental scent delivery and other innovative uses of aromas since the 1990s. After reading Piet Vroon's book *Smell* (see Bibliography), I was hooked. As the "Wizard" of a company called Wizard Studios, I was an avid collector of all things related to wizards: collectibles, stories, and quotes. When I serendipitously came across the following Helen Keller quote, I felt destined to integrate aroma into my business. "Smell is a potent wizard that transports you across thousands of miles and all the years you have lived." [2] Agreeing that no truer statement exists in dealing with the psychology of an audience, I set out to find an avenue where I could employ this "potent wizard" in my business. Reading Vroon's relatively obscure, short science book that explained the amazing impact of scent on the human brain immediately reinforced my interest in the vast possibilities of aroma in marketing, and opened my mind to various additional applications of scent.

Soon after I read the book, I met an inventor and former Disney Imagineer named David Martin, who happens also to be a former engineer for Lockheed Martin Corporation. Martin had invented a scent delivery system while working out of his garage. At the time he approached me as a possible partner, he had rented a small workshop and created a company called Fragrance Technologies. He claimed that this big toolbox-sized machine was the first portable unit on the market. It consisted of dispensing fragrance from a paste-type medium, and had a fan that blew the scented air out of a nozzle. Pretty simplistic, it worked for smaller environments, but needed a lot of tweaking. Its key problem was that the concentration of scent was not delivered consistently over a period of time. After a good six months of discussions and negotiations on how to improve the machine, I passed on the technology and Martin recruited one of my salespeople to assist him in marketing.

Convinced that there was a better technology out there, I traveled the U.S. and Europe in search of a product that I could bring to market. I was looking for a portable machine that could be used in retail and hospitality environments. I had pitched the idea to several Fortune 500 companies, and they were open to experiment, while I searched for the Holy Grail of delivery systems. My journeys took me on a two-day trip to the North of England, where I purchased a dozen scent machines without ever seeing the actual product—only a prototype. Several thousand dollars later I received the shipment. To my dismay, I discovered that the 12 waffle iron-sized black metal boxes were made up of no more than a hollow case with a switch and a fan, and a sliding tray that held an oil-soaked SOS-style pad. It was another fruitless journey.

At a later juncture, I had a covert roadside meeting with a nervous British scientist who, after surveying our surroundings in search of spies, looked me in the eye and uttered with a solemn, straight face, "You, my friend, know what I know." In this comical cloak and dagger meeting in 1998, he was intimating that we both understood that a billion-dollar industry was about to be born. Why he wanted to keep it a secret was a mystery to me. Little did he know that his secret was quite safe. So safe, in fact, that even with a troop of entrepreneurs out hawking scent marketing, it would be another decade before the idea would gain a foothold in mainstream business.

All the while I was making inquiries about the birth of this technology, my primary business, Wizard Studios, was growing by leaps and bounds, opening up offices internationally, and taking on more and more clients. I eventually put my scent technology quest on a back burner, sold many of my business interests, and took a sabbatical. I returned to discover that the scent marketing industry was finally taking off. My enthusiasm was reignited and I jumped headlong back into the swirl. Forming a new company, Whiff Solutions, with my coauthor, business partner, and friend James Goldney, and some other smart folks, we started sourcing all types of new technologies and began to spread the word.

Two years later, I walked into the headquarters of International Flavors and Fragrances to meet an executive named Steve Semoff for the first time. He took me into a testing room, and revealed a long table filled with machines. He pointed to each one, as he commented on the individual machines gathered for testing from the various companies in the field. "We've taken a look at each of these machines—their output, efficiency, and quality—and that one on the end there, is the best damn system on the market," he exclaimed. The system was manufactured by an Australian firm called Air Aroma International. I had met with the founder many months earlier to discuss their entry into the U.S., and received confirmation of my own feelings with IFF's evaluation. I traveled to Australia to meet the company's founder, and eventually both James Goldney and I became passive minority shareholders in the North and South American operation called Air Aroma America. With true entrepreneurial spirit, we have since become shareholders in other scent marketing companies, as we continue to discover the merits of new emerging technologies.

Our mission at Whiff Solutions is to change the paradigm of contemporary marketing and communications by providing organizations with solutions that incorporate scent. Whiff Solutions works with companies at every phase in the process to develop and implement highly effective multisensory branding strategies. In addition to strategic planning and research, Whiff Solutions provides advice and direction on quality aroma development and fragrance media systems for advertisers, manufacturers, retailers, hoteliers, entertainment, healthcare and other industries. Many of the systems and methodologies that you'll find here were formulated through our experience. Our group is also rolling out a series of new and exciting products for a variety of applications. We are actively developing some of the innovations that you will read about in this book.

It is only recently that multisensory marketing has begun to be studied and formalized. When marketing guru Martin Lindstrom described the results of a study by marketing research firm Millward Brown in his highly acclaimed book *Brand Sense* (see Bibliography), he popularized the concept and has led the way to making multisensory branding practices *de rigueur* in the marketing world. His concepts have been implemented by businesses across the globe.

The concept of multisensory marketing is an outgrowth of experiential marketing, a revolutionary business approach that was hot in the late 1990s, wherein businesses communicate and interact with their customers through their senses, feelings, and creative associations. In his seminal book *Experiential Marketing* (see Bibliography), thought leader Bernd H. Schmitt, cofounder and CEO of the Ex Group, describes how important it is for businesses to design and create holistic experiences for their customers.

In *The Experience Economy* (see Bibliography), authors Joseph B. Pine, II, and James H. Gilmore take a similar tack by describing how a company's brand and services are similar to a theatrical performance, where the customer should be cast as an audience member who needs to be entertained and engaged emotionally. Both of these categorical, breakthrough books motivated companies and brand managers to re-examine and redesign their products and services through storytelling and multisensory measures. In an area of my own field (themed environmental design), we had been working with these principles for years, as well. The phenomenon they were describing was the marriage, first, of design and marketing, and, second, of design and theater.

I was thrilled to encounter all three of the aforementioned books when I did, because they validated my personal business philosophy and methods, and made it easier to relay them to my customers. In my own company, Wizard Studios, we began using experiential design a decade before the marketing industry discovered the impact of multisensory storytelling with scripting, choreography, entertainment, special effects, lighting, video, sets, sounds, and scent. I cut my teeth producing thousands of events, sales meetings, business meetings, corporate messaging, and custom shows for the Fortune 500 from the late 1980s to the turn of the century. We also took our live theatrical expertise and experience, and incorporated it into a successful division that designed environments and entertainment for restaurants, theme parks, nightclubs, and retail centers. By the mid-90s, these industries came to realize that they were in the business of entertainment as well as in the business of providing goods and services.

Wizard Studios excelled in the experiential design genre—and still does. In the fields of corporate communications, product rollouts, and messaging, its directive is to bring products and corporate messages to life in the form of entertainment. Wizard's illustrious creative team of writers, designers, choreographers, technicians, artisans, and producers is challenged to make simple products intriguing, interesting, and entertaining. That's easy with a pill called Viagra or a car named Lexus, but try making a dog's heartworm drug or a garbage truck into a star performer. For this team, it's all in a day's work.

In the early years, we used incense, sprays, candles, and a variety of crude technology to scent our environmental designs (there's nothing better than damp Spanish moss or wet burlap to lend authenticity to a pirate shantytown or swamp scene). But while the lighting and sound fields were rolling out amazing new technologies, very few inventors were working on scent technology. For a long time, sophisticated scent delivery technology remained elusive.

Then, after years of searching, the time and technology finally arrived and, as you can see, the entire world is now beginning to enter the scent dimension. I do not approach this field as a branding expert or a marketing guru, but as an expert in developing multisensory and experiential design around a corporate message. In the process of entertaining hundreds of thousands of people, I've learned a thing or two about human nature. At Wizard Studios we have used scent to enhance everything from our own Cirque-style shows, to avant-garde parties and large corporate meetings. We have found that scent adds a magical element, from creating realism at an event to even elevating the moods of the guests. We have used thematic scents in myriad events from the essence of tea and cake at a Mad Hatter's Ball to delivering a Valentine's Day scent of chocolate and roses in New York's Grand Central Station.

At large-scale business meetings and product rollouts, scent can emotionally stamp the event into the attendees' brains and offers a more vivid recall of not only the products introduced, but also of the information delivered.

Mastering the Information in This Book

With a simple understanding of how this book is organized, you can easily navigate your way through the information. The material is offered in four progressive sections. Even though you may wish to jump to certain sections of the book, I highly recommend that you read the first two sections in their entirety, in order to fully understand the applications described in the later material.

We hit the ground in running in Part One, "The Powerful Influences of Scent," with a comprehensive panorama of exciting discoveries on how scent affects the human brain. It is important for us to understand how this ancient, silent language influences our perceptions, memory, sensuality, security, health, and decision-making faculties. Along with the hard science, we show how the information can be used innovatively in business and marketing, and to enhance people's lives.

Once we connect the dots on scent's powerful role on consumers and its vast implications for industry, we'll do reconnaissance of the scent marketplace in Part Two, "Entering the Scent Dimension." You'll learn how industry forces have arrived at their present strengths, what is driving them today, and what may motivate them in the future, especially in the realms of advertising and entertainment. You'll ascertain how to talk the talk and walk the walk of the 20-billion dollar fragrance industry, with an insider's view of some of the industry's movers and shakers. Along with this comprehensive overview, we discuss societal and ethical considerations connected to the use of scent, including ominous governmental strategies that could affect our lives and our privacy in the future.

In Part Three, "How to Play the Game," we equip and mobilize you to brand your business, product, or service with scent in a step-by-step process of scent strategy evaluation and application. We'll show you how to identify your Whiff Factor, create the perfect signature scent for your needs, and deliver it using the appropriate fragrance medium—print, plastic, fabric, or environmental.

In Part Four, "Winning Strategies for a New Century," we offer an in-depth discussion of specific applications in a diverse array of market categories. From healthcare and safety to retail, restaurants, and entertainment, we study the underlying motivational factors of each business, and how scent can play a large role in improving sales, customer impressions, crowd control, and offer an improved working and living environment.

What Can We Expect in the Future?

As you'll soon learn, the future applications of scent are practically limitless. While certainly not as consequential as the Internet, scent communication in its current form can be compared with the Internet when it was in its incubation stage. The early Internet concept was viewed as a cool, but limited communication device between participating universities. We had no idea in the beginning how many millions of applications and benefits would be derived from the medium. Eventually, however, it transformed all aspects of communication on the planet. Similarly, scent communication will eventually impact and transform our lives in ways we cannot yet imagine. But innovative minds first must grasp its potential.

Initially the applications of scent communication will be almost entirely motivated by material and commercial interests. Then, as we become accustomed to the pecuniary uses of aroma, we'll include its other powerful applications, and entire new industries will work to harness its benefits for all of mankind. Among other things, we'll be trained to rely on scent to increase our comprehension and recall while we study. We will also see a shift in how we use scent to control our own behaviors, moods, and health. Tired of the predatory marketing of magic pills-for-whatever-ails-you and their unwanted side effects (both physical and financial), we'll return to developing scent-based solutions to the root causes of many of our health problems. The holistic application of naturally based scents shows great promise in this area.

We can anticipate using odors to control our moods, enhance or decrease our appetites, invigorate our workout routines, shield us from infections, and boost our learning and memory. The goldmine of remedies has been derived from nature's plants for the pharmaceutical industry. Plants' naturally emitted essences can be equally tapped without many of the complications and middlemen.

Aroma's impact on the next generation of commerce will be broad and diverse. The understanding of the significance of scent as a language and communication tool will become commonplace. Over the coming decades, as science and technologies evolve, the entertainment industry will gradually incorporate scent into its presentation of theater, film, television, and video games, as awareness, technology and affordability dictates. Public safety, security, and loss prevention agencies will debut scent as a means to communicate with the masses. Consumers will be able to authenticate the branded products they purchase with a sniff. Safety will improve with the scent diagnostics of worn and defective products. Embedded scent triggers will inform us when to replace our worn tires, batteries, water heaters and other important possessions. Governments and security organizations will use people's unique organic scent prints as a means of identity verification. Forensic investigators will be able to track perpetrators of crimes via their unique scent signatures, a much simpler solution than DNA.

Most importantly, transformation of consumer consciousness will change the way products are designed, manufactured, and delivered. First will come an unfolding awareness of the scent-related research, studies, and technological applications. Then ingenuity will be responsible for applications of the research across a wide range of markets. Your own creativity and resourcefulness could make you a leader in an application of scent in your field of expertise!

Public awareness of the powerful influence of scent on the human brain is approaching a tipping point. The meteoric rise in the sales of scent related products over the past few decades has demonstrated that a large portion of the public already has a strong positive interest in aroma. Once the public has become aware of the beneficial uses of scent, an entire paradigm shift will take place in our society. As our collective awareness of its physiological impact on us grows, smell will transform from its place as the redheaded stepchild of the family of senses to being recognized as a key sense that everyone uses for differentiation, evaluation, judgment, and response to external circumstances.

What does the future hold in the deep waters of the scent dimension? Only the innovative minds of inventors, marketers, and industry can foresee the true depth and scope of the commercial use of scent. The future is rich with a bounty of yet-to-be-discovered applications. From where I sit, the water looks good, and there are treasures to be uncovered in the depths below.

Let's jump in.

Part One

The Powerful Influences of Scent

A wedding is a funeral where you smell your own flowers.

—Eddie Cantor

Everything smells—and that's a good thing! Scent is a biological mechanism used for recognition, communication, and signaling. Some scents alert us to danger. Other aromas contribute to our sexual arousal. Applied correctly, under the right conditions, scent also promotes health and improves cognitive functions, like memory, learning, and alertness.

If you are fascinated by brain research and the science of the mind, you'll love the information in *Whiff!*. You only need to reflect upon your own personal experiences to appreciate how the tiny molecules of chemicals that humans perceive as aromas play a prominent role in your everyday life. Because scent is pervasive, you spend your days constantly encountering different smells that waft in and out with varying intensities and durations, however, you hardly notice how they influence you, reassure you, and assist in your decision making.

Until now, most of us have regarded the aromas in our lives to be of minimal influence, only intermittently noticing and reacting to the most obvious aromas, such as foods, sensual perfumes, the smells of our personal toiletry items, and our scented candle preferences. While some still consider the practice of aromatherapy as voodoo science, relegating it to the likes of phrenology, tarot cards, and UFO sightings, scientific research has now proven that aromas are integral to our lives, and have a powerful impact on our memory, perceptions, emotions, and even our physiology.

New scientific insights have brought aromas to the forefront to be viewed in a new light as a communication tool. Researchers continue to decode the ancient Rosetta Stone of scent, as pioneers in every industry learn to speak its language and to integrate it into everyday products and services. Even the fragrance industry has had to create a new category to identify these new applications. Where in the past scents were either termed fine fragrances (perfumes) or functional fragrances (such as those that are used in laundry detergent, household products, and kitty litter), these new applications of aromas are classified as non-traditional or communication scents, tools that can be used to deliver a powerful and intricate message, and evoke a desired response.

Once you understand more about the subtle influences of scent, you will become more aware of its possible applications. You'll discover new applications in your own life, how it could drive your business in new directions, and you'll probably identify several new ways to use scent to strengthen the emotional bond with your consumers. Understanding scent's physiological and psychological powers may be your key to marketing excellence and excelled performance. They are also the key to an unexpected and compelling way of communicating because they are biologically ingrained in us. As you study these powerful influences, keep your own business, product, or service in mind, and you might just find the one element needed to surpass the competition. In any event, knowledge is power, and your knowledge of the power of scent will benefit you for years to come.

Chapter 1
The Nose Knows

Every living creature on our planet has an aroma, a chemical signal by which it may be differentiated from the rest of creation. Each smells with a varying degree of intensity. Flowers, plants, trees, animals, fish, birds, and ants can be identified by scents that are unique even within their own species. Sure, dogs smell like dogs and daisies smell like daisies, yet each also has a scent that represents its own individual identity. We do, too. Trillions upon trillions of animals, fish, plants, and people have signature scents. This may seem incredible, but it's true.

Long ago, mankind started identifying and classifying the Earth's inhabitants. Foragers, naturalists, and biologists have tended to use precise visual observations to recognize and describe the physical features of countless creatures, recording them for posterity. Until now, scent has played a secondary role. Only recently have modern devices enabled us to make use of scent much as animals do—consciously and for the purpose of identification.

Odor is the tool that most animals instinctively use to investigate, identify, and classify each other.[1] Yes. Animals bow their heads, wink, bristle their fur, flash their wing colors, and use body movements for communication. They chirp, bark, growl, and gobble in order to make their points known. But for many, scent is the main way they communicate. With scent, an animal or insect is able to send a message where the eye cannot see and the ear cannot hear. Scent helps them identify a newcomer as friend or foe—or food. A male moth can pick up the scent of a female from miles away.[2] Ants follow scent traces to valuable food sources.[3] Dogs know when females are fertile. In the animal kingdom, smells are utilized to mark territory, spread gossip, initiate mating, and sense danger.

Despite scent's secondary role in our conscious communication systems, if you believe that ordinary people are not highly influenced by the sense of smell, you are mistaken. As mammals, *Homo sapiens* unconsciously incorporate smells into all phases of our lives, in the same manner as other species around us. Smells are tightly interwoven into our everyday lives, however, we remain unaware of most of them, even as they make their way into our brains and assist us with our survival and everyday activities.

What Makes Smell Special?

Unlike the other four physical senses, scent takes an express route directly to the right side of the brain, leaving all of the other senses in its dust. When information gathered by the other senses reaches the brain's receptors, these signals are first routed through the interpretive reasoning centers of the left-brain before circuitously making it to the emotional centers of the right hemisphere. Although this happens in a nanosecond, sights, sounds, tastes, and textures need to be assimilated and sorted logically by the brain in order for us to perceive the information we took in. Along with the logic and reasoning of the left-brain, these senses go through a sort of cognitive filter that adds our prejudices and preconceived notions to the sensory stimuli, and therefore taints the information.

Scent is not subjected to a cognitive, judging, analyzing, prejudiced filter. It doesn't matter if we are eating, drinking, making love, having an argument, or simply shopping for shoes. Whenever the olfactory bulb in the brain detects a smell, a chemical message is immediately sent directly to the limbic system, an enigmatic, primordial part of the right hemisphere of the brain. The limbic system contains the keys to our emotions, our lust, our perceptions, and our imaginations. The result is immediate: When we smell, we feel. The limbic system needs no reasoning interpreter to decode the results. The process of smelling is unadulterated by thought, translation, or editing. But it does communicate a message.

Smell can trigger memory, nostalgia, and mental pictures before any left-brain analysis muddies the waters. As Diane Ackerman states in *A Natural History of the Senses* (see Bibliography), "When we give perfume to someone, we give them liquid memory." [4] And the memory of smell is a long one. What we see and hear slowly grows dim in memory, but what we smell lives on and can be easily recalled.

Memory, Nostalgia, and Mental Imagery

A simple examination of our own experiences with smell is revealing. We may find it hard to gather a memory of our third grade classroom. But if we encounter the actual smells of chalk, old books, and a musty atmosphere, a vibrant picture of the place—perhaps not retrieved since childhood—appears in our mind's eye, along with the return of our feelings about that picture. Encounters throughout our lives form indelible imprints upon us, replete with emotional significance. In real time, the scene is experienced through all of the senses, then stamped in our memory centers through smell.

Where a picture of a deceased loved one may bring tears to our eyes while we reflect upon our loss, if we smell old clothing or perfume of that loved one an emotional and visual picture comes to mind instantly, re-creating or mimicking an actual prior experience of being in the presence of that individual. The picture, the clothing, or the perfume is triggering a feeling-memory, an imprint.

Within our psyche and memory centers, each of us has stored a vast catalogue of imprinted feelings and responses to specific aromas. These scents are as innumerable and diverse as our life experiences. Try right now to recall the feelings that are summoned as you reflect upon a few of the many scents in your brain's vast registry. Perhaps the distinct aromas of freshly laundered linen, baked apple pie, a salty ocean breeze, a forest rain, your mother's perfume, a summer carnival, an Italian bistro, a dentist's office, a new car interior, propane gas, a baby's hair, a Thanksgiving meal, a room full of books, your father's workshop, and a relative's deathbed are among the many imprinted memories associated with the more than ten thousand smells that you can actually identify.[5]

Many of us have a "nose" for identification. We are able to pinpoint exactly what we smell as well as any perfumer or wine connoisseur worth their salt. But as much as we can identify and classify a smell, we have a difficult time describing that smell to someone who has never smelled it before. The smell of damp carpet, the exhaust from a paper mill, or the scent of burning olive pits from a ceramic factory in Fez. The instinctive sense of smell often leaves us dumb or inarticulate, for we have an inefficient vocabulary when it comes to describing odors. What we see, hear, taste, and touch has been analyzed, described and catalogued over the tide of our history, for those senses are routed first through the brain's translation centers. Yet what we smell, we automatically feel, so we absently acknowledge that feeling and move on, often without ever naming it.

When we observe a dog, we describe it as such. When it barks, we acknowledge its communication as a bark. When we touch it, we identify that it is furry. But when we smell the dog, we can only state that it "smells like a dog." We actually describe most smells with a simile precursor, saying that it smells "like" something. Your room smells *like* a pizza factory, your car smells *like* cigarettes, or the sofa smells *like* an old lady. Although we don't usually notice how we phrase descriptions of smells, if you spend a little time observing yourself and others around you, you will quickly realize that aromas are like feelings, which we describe circuitously, if not vaguely.

We have been living with these subtle truths about smells for all of our lives, never paying much attention to their meaning, just taking them for granted, as we would treat a jilted mistress who waits in anticipation for the phone to ring. We call them up as needed and desired, ignoring them the rest of the time, assured that they are there in the background, circulating around us. We don't really acknowledge smells unless they are overwhelmingly positive or negative, like the aroma of chocolate chip cookies baking, or a bathroom that was recently visited by a stranger.

As Henry David Thoreau once wrote: "We perceive and are affected by changes too subtle to be described." [6] Most smells pass through our olfactory system and travel directly to our brain, checking in with the limbic guard, where, if no alerts or emotions are triggered, they melt into the background. They act as just another indicator in our daily mix of senses, reassuring us that all systems are go, and that we are safe and secure. It is only when omnipresent smells are combined with life's experiences (especially ones that move us either positively or negatively), that they are imprinted in our memory.

Researchers have been studying how scents stir and trigger memories, emotions, moods, desires, cravings, perceptions, and the brain's warning systems. At first you may consider their discoveries and the facts of how smells affect the human psyche merely to be interesting insights on the workings of the brain. Yet, when you consider how these facts and revelations relate to marketing, branding, advertising, and environmental and product design, the implications are astounding.

The Nose Knows

Recognition plays a substantial part in olfactory communication. We recognize the people, places, and things in our lives by the aromas they radiate. Even though it pales in comparison to the snout of man's best friend, the human nose has over a million receptors and can identify as many as 10,000 different smells.[7] That's pretty impressive considering we ignore most of what we smell. Yet our ancestors used scent recognition more intentionally than we do in their daily struggle for survival. They would search out the smell of an oncoming individual and identify upon a whiff of the wind whether friend or foe approached. Mating rituals involved smells, much as they do today. And wild game could be identified downwind when searching for the evening meal.

Not only does scent play an integral part throughout every scene in our lives, researchers now think that scent plays a role in every phase of our reproductive process. We all realize that scent plays a part in our sexual attraction, and that sex itself is an aromatic event, yet this is merely the beginning in how scent plays a role in the way we come to be. The event of conception is now thought to be a fragrant one. A 2003 study revealed that a smell receptor was present in human sperm.[8] Scientists now think that sperm make their way up through the vaginal canal in search of a fragrant egg. They also think that fetuses can smell in the womb. At birth, we come out with the ability to smell—and smelling. A baby quickly imprints upon the mother's scent and the scent of her milk.[9] A newborn infant smiles the first time that it recognizes the mother's smell. A mother also can recognize the smell of her brand-new baby after only an hour.[10]

As a child grows older, scent communication and recognition is in full swing. Children can differentiate their siblings from other kids of the same age through smell alone.[11] While children play, invaluable scent memories are being made for recall in later life. Emotional imprints are created with each and every new experience, as we shall explore in depth in the next section of this chapter, "How Scent Imprints Influence Us."

The smells of home, mother's cooking, father's cologne, summer flowers, holiday cider, carnivals, libraries, and favorite pets are all being filed away for a lifetime of use as memories and for future recognition. Good times and bad, happy and sad are stocked away complete with an emotionally scented connection.

At puberty, the ability to smell increases. Between the ages of 20 and 40 the capability of both genders to perceive smells is at an optimum, although women are much better at smelling than men.[12] Scent originally may have been a factor in mating. When women ovulate or are pregnant, their smell capabilities increase even more.[13] Yet when on birth control pills or menstruating, the olfactory sense is more muted.[14]

Call it intuition or the smell of emotion, but women seem to have the upper hand over men when it comes to scent detection. In a test, a panel of women sniffed underarm swabs and could tell the difference between smells of people who had watched "sad" or "happy" movies.[15] Men could not distinguish between the two types of smells.

Studies show that, on average, men's body odor and breath are perceived as more unpleasant than women's body odor and breath.[16] According to Noam Sobel, Ph.D., associate professor of psychology at Stamford University, people can detect a single drop of androstenedione (a compound found in human sweat) in an Olympic-sized swimming pool filled with water.[17] Now that's an amazing example of our olfactory capability.

As we age, our sense of smell declines. This also affects our sense of taste for reasons previously mentioned. By age 80, approximately 80 percent of people have some major smell dysfunction and 50 percent are close to anosmic (odor-blind). [18] Not only do we lose our sense of smell, we also lose our ability to differentiate between smells. Women's sense of smell diminishes with age, but in all trials, they outperform the sniff test over men.[19] Early stage Alzheimer's patients often show a loss of smell, and may eventually become anosmic.[20] Old people can also suffer from olfactory hallucinations.[21]

Olfactory aging seems to align with the rest of our senses. As we get older we tend to lose our hearing, our eyesight fades, and coincidentally, our memory begins to experience outages. Could memory loss and olfactory loss be connected? Research is being conducted currently, with findings that difficulty in identifying odors predicts subsequent development of mild cognitive impairment (MCI), which is often a precursor to memory-debilitating Alzheimer's disease.[22]

Here's another interesting fact: Contrary to popular opinion, blind people do not have a better sense of smell.[23] Yet they can certainly recognize more smells than most sighted people. And if we view scent as the recognition and communication system that it is, the newly blind probably become more attuned to smells, as they do to sounds.

How Scent Imprints Influence Us

What elements do we encounter daily that most influence our judgments and decisions? Most of us would put little real thought into answering this important question. We might reply, "I think, therefore I am—and therefore I decide." Yet while human beings are busy with their human doings, their decisions are most often based upon their own personalized worldviews. An individual's perspective on the world is usually based on that person's experiences and environment. Historical experiences from childhood and exposure to new events, ideas, and encounters, color a person's worldview and give that individual a unique perspective. Our perceptions and our judgments are created through learning and past experience, and our decisions are made accordingly.

In other words, how you feel about men, women, authority figures, cars, cellular phones, music, romance, furniture, and the sea is directly related to your personal history and experience with these subjects. In relation to the senses, past interactions while viewing, hearing, tasting, touching, and smelling these objects and people are the key factors to establishing your worldview and responses. In addition, your worldview is shaped by the intensity of the emotions experienced during your encounters with a specific subject.

How you feel about your mother will be determined by your interactions (positive and negative) with her in early childhood. Childhood and adolescent learning from your family and culture will determine how you feel initially about your sexuality. The same can be said for dogs, salesmen, food, and the forest. Our perceptions are created by the tone of our initial contact with a person, place, or thing, and are also shaded by warnings, musings, and encouragement by our parents and authority figures in early childhood.

These early encounters that we speak of are imprinted upon us, as if burned into our emotional and perceptual composition. Imprints that create our worldviews are truly the basis for, and the root cause of what influences us. One dictionary definition of influence describes it as "the capacity or power of persons or things to be a compelling force on or produce effects on the actions, behavior, opinions, etc., of others." [24] In essence, these early imprints (or feeling-memories, if you will) determine how we feel about things upon re-encountering them, and therefore how we feel compelled or influenced to respond.

While visual, auditory, tactile, and taste imprints have quite a significant influence upon our behavior, studies have shown that aromatic imprints (meaningful scents that reach directly into our limbic system from the get-go) have an even more compelling effect on our perceptions, emotions, opinions, and behaviors.

For example, most of us love "new car" smell. The fact is that a fragrance factory manufactures much of that smell. My sources state that over two million dollars worth of liquid leather is used each year in Detroit alone. While some manufacturers completely deny using fragrance enhancers—Lexus states, for example, that their scent comes from the rich leather interior of their cars, and Volkswagen has been working to erase all of their cars' smells—in reality many of the new cars rolling off of the assembly line are marketed using an enhanced scent because of people's fondness for the aroma.

Some carmakers have been open about it. In 2003, Cadillac generated a buzz when they rolled out a signature scent called Nuance.[25] They tested manufactured scents for a decade while their brand was in decline. When they finally thought that they had gotten it right, they brought 340 Cadillac owners together for a blindfold test of six cars. The winning scent came to be their new signature fragrance. Considering that the resuscitation of the brand roughly coincided with this new scent—sales of the Cadillac Escalade really took off—could it be that it was more than just the physical design that was responsible?

When Rolls-Royce buyers began complaining in the mid-1990s that the new cars just didn't live up to their earlier models, the company went to work to track down the problem. They found that the smell was the issue. They returned to a 1965 Silver Cloud for their inspiration, and deconstructed its aroma identifying 800 separate elements. They reconstructed the classic scent, and now spray it under the seats of new vehicles.

There is nothing new or groundbreaking about the connection between our automobiles and the field of scent marketing. But isn't it interesting that one of the largest purchases people make has such a large stake in how it smells? G. Clotaire Rapaille, M.D., founder of Archetype Discoveries Worldwide, a consumer research firm in Florida that serves as an advisor to automakers and scent makers, acknowledged that while smell would not be the first impression that a potential car buyer would have, it could be a deal breaker nonetheless.[26]

The Cultural Significance of Smell

There has been an ongoing debate in the scent field as to whether or not we are so-called blank slates when it comes to how aromas affect us at birth, and how hereditary and cultural aspects play a part in the process of scent responsiveness. We do know that aromatic imprints are dynamic, and that our responses to smells and their associated emotions can change. We also know that certain smells are pleasant to the population as a whole, [27] capable of elevating and decreasing our moods, changing our brain waves, and stimulating certain responses in us, including sexual arousal and alarm. We also know that different populations react differently to specific scents.

Since smells imprint feeling-memories on people, it is only natural for separate families, communities, ethnicities, and cultures to share separate responses to varying types and strengths of smells. Within diverse cultures, the sense of smell plays a different role.

Americans and British are culturally similar yet sometimes react to certain smells (and associated flavors) very differently. For example, while Americans in general enjoy the scent of wintergreen, which in the U.S. is found primarily in wintergreen candy and gum, many of the British find this particular aroma unpleasant.[28] To elderly Britons, it smells like an analgesic rub that was used during World War II. Over a half-century later, they have passed on this feeling-memory and an aversion to their descendants.

What might smell good to the Germans does not necessarily smell good to the Japanese. At the University of Tsukuba in Japan, when German and Japanese subjects similar in age and background tested a wide variety of aromas and were asked to grade them as pleasant or unpleasant, the results were eye opening. The three aromas that the Germans disliked the most (cypress oil, fermented soybean, and dried fish flakes) were indigenous Japanese products. As if in some quarrelsome tête-à-tête, the three most displeasing aromas to the Japanese (church incense, sausage, and blue cheese) were all German in origin.[29]

Interestingly, some ethnicities have a keener sense of smell than others. Asians lead the way in the ability to detect odors and have the lowest level of body odor production. The Japanese and Koreans smell better than most Westerners. When it comes to perspiration, only half of the Vietnamese and Korean populations have apocrine (sweat) glands under their arms. Of the Japanese, only 10 percent have detectable body odor. The Chinese barely hit 2 percent as a body odor-producing "race." [30]Another tidbit: until recently young Japanese men that belong to the tiny 10 percent of the odiferant population could be disqualified from military service due to their undesirable underarms.[31]

In many cultures, scent has great meaning and importance. The Ongee people of the Andaman Islands off the coast of India have integrated smell into every aspect of their lives. When a local refers to himself, he touches the tip of his nose—referring to his being and his odor. The Ongee also construct their calendar on the basis of floral aromas that come into bloom in certain seasons. Each season is dubbed with the name of an aroma and is thought of in terms of smell more than in terms of time. When greeting one another they ask, "How is your nose?" The traditional response to this greeting is either "I am quite odiferous," which obligates the questioner to take a big whiff of the acquaintance, or "I am not too smell-strong today," which invites the greeter to blow some of his own scent onto the deficiently aromatic friend.[32]

The Bororo of Brazil and the Serer-Ndut of Senegal also associate personal identity with smell. For the Bororo, body odor is associated with the life force of a person, and breath-odor with a person's soul. The Serer-Ndut believe that two different scent-defined forces animate each individual. One is physical, associated with body and breath odor; the other spiritual scent is claimed to survive the death of an individual to be reincarnated in a descendant. The Serer-Ndut can tell which ancestor has been reincarnated in a child by recognizing the similarity of the child's scent to that of the deceased person.[33]

In India, a traditional affectionate greeting, equivalent to a Western hug or kiss, is to take a whiff of a newly greeted friend. An ancient Indian text declares, "I will smell thee on the head, that is the greatest sign of tender love." [34] Similar traditions are found in many Arabic countries, where standing close together and breathing on a compatriot signals friendship and good tidings. To deny someone your breath conveys avoidance and is considered a bit rude.

The Desana of the northwest Amazon region in Brazil believe that all members of the same tribe share a like-smelling odor.[35] Marriage is only allowed between people with different odors, ensuring that spouses will be chosen from among unrelated tribes. The tribes also have a tradition and ritual to exchange goods with different odors. One group offers a gift of meat, for example, while another offers a gift of fish. They have even been known to exchange differently scented ants.

Whether the reasons scent affects us in the ways it does are hereditary, cultural, or learned is under investigation. One conclusion is certain: Smell is a complex and highly effective communication device. And communicate it does, 24 hours a day, for it is a sense that never sleeps. As a result, the scent dimension of our lives plays a role in almost every decision we make.

Biology Brings Us Back to Our Senses

Imagine a world in which everyone was more aware and knowledgeable about the silent language of scent. It would make sense to disseminate information to a scent-aware population through a range of aromatic media. We would not only judge products, logos, advertisements, and everyday situations through our eyes and ears, but also by seeking out and giving credence to the scent of the objects and environments around us. In every area of our lives, we would base our decisions consciously on how things smelled.

In the future world I'm describing, the decision to buy a new grocery item will be determined by gently rubbing its packaging. For example, a toothpaste package may smell like peppermint. A tomato sauce with garlic may smell like an Italian grandmother's home cooking. When you buy cinnamon, thyme, or curry you will simply rub the label to smell those spices. But this technology will not be limited to foods. When opening a bottle of medicine, you will first smell the cap to tell if it is counterfeit or if it has been opened previously. You will be able to make the same distinction before opening any new product.

In the future, if your automobile acts up, you'll be able to sniff out and accurately identify the problem. You will immediately know if your tires are worn, or if there's a leak in the valve or a nail embedded in the rubber. Sight unseen you will detect the effects of wear and tear in your car's brake pads, fan belts, and a variety of other engine parts.

Olfactory recognition will not just be relegated to the world of inanimate objects. It's easy to imagine a world in which our signature scents are used to help authenticate our identities quickly in the course of banking, business, and other types of official dealings with authorities and institutions. This form of technology already exists; it's just a mater of time before it gains widespread application. We'll explore this in more detail later on in this chapter, in a section called "Scent Identification Devices."

Today we stand upon the threshold of this newly fragrant-aware world. Although the physiological purpose of smell was slowly lost to us over millennia and generations, its comeback is well on the way. Soon we shall reintegrate into our cognition and lifestyle a forgotten form of intelligence that was well used and honed by our caveman ancestors, who depended on their olfactory abilities for their very survival. Theirs was an era in which every other human being, animal, and plant was sniffed, explored, and responded to on an emotional level. We still incorporate a portion of the scent communication used by our primal forebears when selecting our foods and when avoiding harmful products and situations. But our conscious awareness of scent and our skill in making decisions based on it has atrophied, so that aroma has faded into the background of our lives.

The implications of scent research upon education are profound. In his book *Fragrance* (see Bibliography), [36] Edwin T. Morris states, "When children were given olfactory information along with a word list, the list was recalled much more easily and better retained in memory than when given without olfactory cues."

Research is providing a fascinating insight into how scent can affect memory, and the role sleep plays in memory formation. In one study, although students did not notice the presence of a rose bouquet while they were sleeping, their brains were found to be paying attention. Subsequently these students retained an almost perfect memory of their subject material while undergoing tests accompanied by the scent of roses (97 percent), compared to 86 percent recall when no scent was used. Furthermore, a team of German neuroscientists reported that by spritzing research subjects with rose scent as they performed a memory exercise, then spritzing them again when they were sound asleep, the researchers could improve their subjects' recall by 13 percent.[37] That equates to a substantial grade point increase for both the struggling and the excelling student.

As our understanding of how scent impacts the brain and emotions develops, we're destined to begin applying the knowledge in myriad ways. In the years ahead, the unexpected applications that different industries find for aroma will reignite our reliance on the sense of smell. In general, we can all expect to be more conscious of the aromas of people, products, and services, including the smells we ourselves emanate. The person of the future will strategically design signature aromas to communicate personal style and elicit a desired response in a way that transcends the current use of perfumes, aromatherapy, and scented home candles.

Here's a scene that we may see in the future. Imagine meeting a professional. Upon being handed his business card, you automatically raise the card to your nose—perhaps even before reading the words printed on it. You also catch a faint whiff of his scented suit. Subtly you have received the strategically formulated message he wishes to convey to you about himself.

In the future, when selecting a cellular phone or personal handheld device, you will be as interested in its scent transmitters as you are in other features. Just as you can program your phone to ring with signature music that helps you identify your favorite callers, you will also program it to release signature scents to let you know if the caller is a spouse, child, best friend, or lover. Your new boyfriend's calls could be a multisensory blend of Beethoven's Fifth and musk, and the scent of fried chicken could mean that Grandma is on the line.

These are not unrealistic pipe dream visions. Sony Ericsson, Motorola, Nokia, and others have been playing a game of one-upmanship in the multisensory field for some time now. Originally scent was a value-added, non-strategic novelty feature on telephones. Now, as technology improves, the ultimate scented cell phone is close to being brought to market. One major manufacturer claimed that in the future, we would be able to see, hear, and smell the other caller.

So, let's take a look now at some of the other products being designed to take advantage of scent as a means of identification and differentiation, and explore the many exciting marketing opportunities being made possible by the power of scent imprinting—beginning with an exciting concept that I have formulated from all of the research studied.

A Brand New Idea—Endorphin Branding™

Before I move on to a discussion of specific industries that are making use of scent for authentication of identity and product verification, I'd like to propose an intriguing theory concerning the marriage of aromas and branding. Although no formal study has been done to directly demonstrate this theory, I have threaded together the results and substantive empirical evidence from research that has been done on the physiological effects of aromas on humans. My theory is that uniquely formulated branded scents will be able to induce a patterned physiological reaction in consumers after strategically introducing a scent during an emotional experience, and then repeating its delivery at the point of sale.

Here are the million-dollar questions. First, could a savvy marketer introduce a signature scent that would enhance the production of endorphins in the consumer's brain, thereby causing a mild high? Second, could another innovative marketer create a branded scent that would stimulate the release of adrenaline, in essence turning the consumer on? Third, and perhaps the most intriguing idea—would it be possible to imprint the consumer's brain with a signature scent while simultaneously triggering either of the aforementioned physiological responses, such as might happen during a stimulating event or experience? With new discoveries being revealed by science, we feel that certain scents can induce these effects, and can subsequently trigger a similar response when strategically released at a later time.

The research to-date shows that this may indeed be possible. It has been established that the sense of smell has a dynamic relationship to memory, meaning that we can perpetually create new memory associations as we smell already familiar scents during new and evocative events. In other words, we can connect new scent-based memory imprints with emotional experiences. Let's take a look at the supporting evidence.

To answer question number one, a body of evidence supporting this theory has been increasing as researchers continue to study the effects of odors. In 2006, the Sense of Smell Institute awarded the prestigious Science of Fragrance Award to Australian researchers John Prescott, Ph.D., and Jenell Wilkie, Ph.D., of James Cook University, in recognition of their investigation of odor and pain tolerance. These researchers showed that sweet smelling fragrances, such as the vanilla scents of vanillin, ethyl vanillin, and musk, have an analgesic effect.[38] Another study conducted by the Smell and Taste Treatment and Research Foundation found that the odor of green apple reduces pain in subjects who find the odor pleasant.[39] Both studies found that certain scents can alleviate pain.

The body's natural response to pain and stress is to bathe the brain with endorphins—opiate-like neuro-chemicals—to alleviate it. Endorphins induce a state of euphoria and well-being, and are responsible for the effect popularly known as the "runner's high." They are released during exercise, laughter, and sexual activity, upon overexposure to light, and after ingesting chocolate. If additional research confirms that certain odors (vanilla, green apple, and possibly many others) stimulate an endorphin release, the implications could be astounding. When I asked Dr. Hirsch, the researcher in the green apple study, if his results meant an actual release of endorphins, he replied that most likely yes, but endorphins were not measured in the study—only responses to pain.

What about question number two? Like endorphins, we have long known that adrenaline is released when a person is excited, stressed, frightened, during exercise, and after ingesting caffeine or sugar. Now we know its release also can be triggered by smell. Researchers at Shiseido, a giant Japanese cosmetics firm, investigated the effects of certain fragrances on the sympathetic nervous system, the body's auto regulator that produces the fight-or-flight response. They found that the studied fragrances stimulated the release of adrenaline in the subjects.[40] The findings revealed that certain essential oil aromas substantially increased the production and concentration of adrenaline in the body, while others (rose and patchouli) caused adrenaline to decrease.

So, the question of highest interest is: Could either of these two scent-based effects become paired with an imprinted feeling-memory? Could both effects be triggered simultaneously? Along with the release of endorphins, a rush of adrenaline would produce a powerful condition that is a fleeting simulation of real joy. The adrenaline-endorphin effect would not specifically be the result of joy, but it could possibly enhance and imprint an existing physiological condition induced while the subject was in a state of excitement at, for example, a concert, football game, or nightclub.

Now for the kicker, the most exciting bit of research news: A recent groundbreaking experiment has produced a literal Pavlovian (physiological) response in a group of healthy male subjects. These men experienced an expected glucose drop after being injected with insulin while simultaneously smelling a specific odor four days in a row.[41] On the fifth day, they were *only* subjected to the odor, yet their glucose levels dropped anyway! When subjected to the same odor, their bodies responded as if they had actually received a dose of insulin. This suggests that specific scents can be imprinted into the memory in tandem with induced physiological changes—and, most importantly, that physiological responses can be replicated through the presence of an odor alone.

For the purpose of marketing this concept, at Whiff Solutions we call this concept *Endorphin Branding*™. Our proposition is this: If a consumer attends an exciting event in which endorphin or adrenaline production is triggered, while a branded signature scent is simultaneously released along with the branded logo (colors and words can intensify scent memory) during the height of excitement, then perhaps that endorphin/adrenaline rush could be replicated at the point of sale at a later date. And if this hypothesis hits its mark in trials, Endorphin Branding™ will open an entire new field.

What would be a practical application of the endorphin branding theory? Let's look at a well-known brand like Federal Express, a company that has been in the experiential marketing game for years. Some of their efforts include sponsoring the National Football League, the Orange Bowl, and the Professional Golf Association, as well as a notable NASCAR racing team. Should FedEx ever decide to create a signature scent, they could permeate the air with that aroma during exhilarating moments at the sporting events they sponsor. At a strategic point while stakes are high and spectators are excited—and the FedEx logo is highly visible—their hypothetical branded scent could be released into the sporting venue. If our theory is correct, an endorphin/adrenaline imprint would be branded into consumers' brains, creating an exhilarating memory that would later be recalled in conjunction with smelling the FedEx signature aroma.

In order to capitalize upon a positive scent memory, FedEx would need to integrate their signature scent with their products and environments. The following are only a few of the ways the company might do so. A signature scent could be released whenever one of six million customers each day pulls the paper off the adhesive strip before sealing a FedEx package.[42] Another six million customers can take a whiff of FedEx while pulling the strip to open the same package on the receiving end. In essence, two whiffs are created for the price of one shipped package. To continue spreading the brand experience, the company can introduce their aroma to tens of thousands more customers each day as they walk into one of the 1,500 FedEx Kinko's stores around the globe.[43]

If scent research continues to reveal more results that support these suppositions, we may see an upsurge in the already booming sponsorship of sporting events. Who knows? FedEx may even return to sponsoring Walt Disney's Space Mountain. For even more so than sporting events, theme rides everywhere are capable of satisfying the cravings of adrenaline junkies in search of their next natural high.

Imagine locating portable motion simulator attractions (theme rides) in the food courts of suburban malls where they would fragrantly invigorate riders for free, as a company's brand is imprinted into their emotional memory banks. Envision a company brand-scenting nightclubs, carnivals, concerts, gyms, and anywhere else that provides an adrenaline rush to the consumer. Maybe endorphin branding is the real secret behind Starbucks' success? After all, nothing beats coffee for generating a quick adrenaline rush.

Scent Identification Devices

The future promises an entirely new way of eliminating identity theft and security breaches, with new discoveries being made and recording about the identification of each person's unique organic signature scent. Scent IDs will be captured without the invasive methods of DNA swabs, thumbprints, iris scans, or dental records, and will be recorded with a mere pass of a pen-sized wand. No longer will we need to keep track of a plethora of ever-changing passwords and codes, nor will we need to remember our childhood dog's name or the name of our mother's elementary school.

Our individual scent ID will be captured with a *Star Trek*-like device held just inches from our skin, recording volatile chemicals, amino acids, and the surfaces of our T-cells, to be registered in a scent ID registry database. This bodes well for use in protecting our finances, health records, and even for tracking missing children. Police will be able to track child molesters, terrorists, and serial rapists, and even be able to pick up the signature scent trail hours and maybe days after they've left the scene of the crime.

Scent ID technology is already in the making, with millions in funding from the government, and everyone from the CIA and the military, to the banking and security industries anticipating its arrival. A mere whiff of the essence of our skin will be one of the most radical changes to come in the new age of scent communication, and we hope that it will be used for the ultimate good of the public—for its misuse would represent a horrifying misstep.

In this case of science fiction becoming science fact, researchers from Purdue University have developed a portable instrument that can identify any substance in less than a second, much like the "tricorders" used by the crew of the Starship Enterprise.[44] The 20-pound, battery-powered unit is an advanced version of the mass spectrometers used today for airport security. Those larger units weigh up to 300 pounds and require target substances to be swabbed and inserted in the instruments' test chambers. But the desorption electrospray ionization (DESI) tricorder ejects a puff of ionized water vapor, which it then "inhales" for analysis. The entire procedure takes less than a second.

In addition to a whole range of forensic, security, and corporate applications, DESI has been used to accurately detect cancer in human livers, and is being used to test for explosives, chemical warfare agents, [45] bacterial contaminants in food, biomarkers that provide an early warning of disease, and the authenticity of drugs.[46] A great benefit is that it can determine the precise chemical composition of a substance non-invasively.

A Whiff of Authenticity

Governments and institutions spend millions of dollars every year combating counterfeiters who are flooding the market with forged currency, passports, birth certificates, securities, traveler's checks, and other assorted business documents. An entire industry is dedicated to defending against an onslaught of professional scammers in the document industry. As official agencies continue to use increasingly sophisticated inks, watermarks, striations, indentations, and high-tech stamps, covert rogues have kept pace with investments in equally impressive state-of-the-art technology made available to anyone with the means to acquire it. Radio frequency identification chips (RFIDs) are one new hope to combat these sharks, yet spreading the scanning technology to every corner of the globe is many years away and, as of yet, cost prohibitive.

With a little ingenuity and effort, all of these documents could incorporate scent technology, adding another level of protection to the mix, making it that much harder for a would-be counterfeiter to work from his hotel room in Accra or Milan. One can buy a ream of paper, a laminating machine, and a color copier most anywhere in the world. Yet reproducing a distinctly scented paper or plastic document would add a layer of difficulty to the process, and can be much more easily traceable. Where RFIDs can assist in the detection of counterfeits whenever a scanner is at hand, anyone with a nose can detect the scent of deception. RFIDs and scented varnish can be cheaply made and scanning equipment is limited and expensive, but noses are a no-cost line item.

Worldwide, counterfeit goods are said to account for 5 to 7 percent of world trade, costing the global economy well more than a trillion dollars each year.[47] Industries affected include clothing, footwear, toys, sports equipment, pharmaceuticals, cosmetics, CDs, and DVDs. There is also a thriving counterfeit perfume industry, driven by illicit under-the-radar perfumers replicating famous brand names. Even though aromas can be created and are available on the black market, counterfeit scents are merely a fraction of the world's underground trade. Given the limited supply and expertise in the fragrance market, it would take a global conspiracy network to integrate all of these factions, if all branded products emitted a signature scent. And it would not just involve creating aromatic oil mixtures, it would also imply that a new underground microencapsulation industry be cultivated. In essence, adding scent identification to any branded product makes it that much more difficult for the black market scoundrels. The entire counterfeiting industry could be radically challenged with a signature scent program. Additionally, uniquely secure scents can now be created to combat counterfeiting.

If globally branded products are scented in the future, it will create great difficulty for many counterfeiting enterprises. As it stands today, when a DVD or CD is released in the U.S., frequently the pirated version is made available on the street the same day. Scenting legitimate products may not reduce the demand for pirated copies, but it would certainly assist in detection of the fakes by the local constabulary.

There is also a broad market section of consumers that knowingly purchase counterfeit products, understanding that their friends and associates know full well that they could never afford a Rolex, Gucci bag, or some other luxury item. For this segment, the demand for counterfeit products would continue regardless of whether the item emitted a signature scent. However, another large segment of consumers are duped into believing that they are purchasing the genuine article, with the pitch that the item is somehow "hot" or was part of an unnoticeable "seconds" batch (slightly irregular or damaged). By using scent to identify authentic products, these folks could at least make an informed decision, regardless of the moral implications.

The final group of consumers that unknowingly purchase "discounted" mock brands is the largest target market to be affected by branded scent. They truly wish to buy and display/wear authentic products, and would be highly disappointed to be regarded as cheap or illicit. When a friend nonchalantly asks if that Coach Bag is the real thing, they could indignantly respond, "Why, of course! Can't you smell it?"

In essence, as long as marketers and leading manufacturers create a demand for their products, there will always be pirates, con artists, and bogus sellers to swoop in to take a slice of the pie. Communicating the brand to the consumer through the use of scent is just one more layer of protection against these culprits.

New, Used, or Pre-Owned?

Have you ever searched the shelves of a store for an item only to find half a dozen packages that look as though they've already been opened? This scenario seems more prevalent in home improvement stores and at electronics outlets. One large electronics chain has made it a store policy that a consumer cannot inspect the contents of a package without buying it. And if he wishes to buy it, and subsequently opens the package in the parking lot, only to be dissatisfied with the contents, he must pay a restocking fee for his trouble. This is merely one measure taken by retailers to avoid open packages that look like used or damaged goods. We have all bought something at one time or another that we suspected had been used, returned, and replaced on the shelf.

While there is not much we can do about opened packages and how to resell returned goods, quite a bit can be done to assure the consumer that the product has not been manhandled or used since leaving the factory. With the simple application of scent microencapsulation in the package sealing process, the manufacturer can offer a "freshness" guarantee that the goods are fresh from the factory floor.

An additional layer of scent in the packaging can assure us not only of the virginal contents, but also lend a hand in the emotional branding of the product—that is, if the package isn't so difficult to open that we become filled with negative energy and frustration in the process. Some children's toys are extremely difficult to open, with wires and ties run throughout, creating difficulty for the shoplifter, and resentment in the purchaser.

Some companies put a lot of thought into the overall experience of opening a package. Apple is a prime example. This company's designers have placed themselves in the shoes and hands of the consumer, managing the entire brand experience from the tactile interaction encouraged in the store, to the superb presentation experienced while unveiling the newly purchased product. Opening an Apple product is not only easy, but also pleasurable. Other smart companies are following Apple's lead and, as the trend of scent branding continues, it's just a matter of time before consumers everywhere will open up their newly purchased gadgets and toys, and breathe in a pleasing fresh scent. They'll be assuring themselves that they love the product, and feeling that they have made the right decision, for as you now know: What we smell, we feel.

Our feelings and emotions are usually based on the sensory input that we receive from the world around us. When receiving a phone call from a friend, for example, their mere tone of voice communicates the mood and disposition of the caller, and chances are that your own mood and disposition will follow suit. However, scent is a much more powerful form of communication than sound, because it bypasses our cognitive recognition centers and zeroes in on our emotional centers. Its message is subtle, yet specific, designed by nature to evoke a feeling response.

Chapter 2
Nostalgia, Mood, and Desire

Even though we are barely aware of most of the smells we smell throughout the course of the day, they are ever present—speaking to us, reminding us, and warning us—influencing us to seek that which we feel could bring us harmony and gratification. While we each have unique sensibilities and longings, emotion is the common theme underlying the mental activity that is the background music of our lives, and emotion is most easily triggered by scent. Let's take a look at three of the most important ways that aromas stir our emotions and influence our decision-making processes: nostalgia, mood, and desire.

Nostalgia

The word most of us associate with childhood memories and memories of good times is nostalgia. When a nostalgic occurrence takes place, a picture forms in our mind's eye and emotions are recalled from our past, representing mostly positive experiences. Nostalgia conjures up a wistful desire to return in time to a place or situation that was familiar or pleasant, or a sentimental yearning for the happiness of a prior occurance from the past.

We all have a massive catalogue of nostalgic smells filed away in our brains that can be recalled instantaneously with a whiff of something familiar. While growing up, for example, my mother wore a memorable perfume called Persian Wood. Every time that I smelled that scent, I felt comforted and recalled a clear picture of a classic red perfume bottle crowned by a gold cap. That little red bottle was my own symbolic vision of happier days. Avon eventually discontinued it. My father, a barber, was an Old Spice man like many of his era. I love the smell of Old Spice and, to this day, when I encounter it I have wonderful visions of myself as a little boy sitting in his barber chair while he chewed the fat with his customers. The scent brings back images of my father sweeping up the scattered remains of hair from the floor while making jokes and chuckling his familiar chuckle. It is amazing how scent can trigger one's memories.

Nostalgic smells cross a wide spectrum of memories, as you'll see if you try an experiment right now. What comes to mind when you ponder the smell of hot tar, Vick's VapoRub, a wet dog, leather boots, an old lover's perfume, frying bacon and eggs, or cotton candy? Do you automatically recall an experience or an emotion? It seems that most of us do. If you haven't done so already, pick one of these items and then stop for moment to daydream about it before you continue reading. When marketers are able to reproduce such nostalgic scents in the marketplace, they find that their influence increases dramatically. The trick is to know which smells to use.

Nostalgic recall from scent may also be called the "Proustian Effect," a phrase coined in reference to Marcel Proust's famed tome *In Remembrance of Things Past*, where he speaks of "involuntary memories" invoked by smells, tastes, and sounds.[1] A famous vignette portrayed in the book called "The Episode of the Madeleine" depicts a vivid memory that occurs while he is drinking tea and eating a small cake. He suddenly finds his thoughts returning to a similar occurrence in childhood. The episode is one of many instances in the novel where Proust describes his involuntary memories. "The whole of Proust's world comes out of a teacup," observed Irish novelist and poet Samuel Beckett.[2]

A recent study addressed so-called autobiographical memories by testing 93 older adults using different sensory cues. The test subjects were presented with one of three cues (a word, a picture, or an odor) and then were asked to relate any biographical event to the given cue. The results showed that autobiographical memories triggered by smells were older than memories associated with either verbal or visual information. More specifically, most odor-cued memories were traced back to the first decade of life (under 10 years), whereas verbally and visually evoked memories peaked in early adulthood (11-20 years). The odor-evoked memories were also deemed emotionally stronger and more evocative, even if they had been thought of less often than the visually and verbally-cued memories. The smells used in the study were campfire, fresh-cut grass, and popcorn.[3]

Dr. Rachel Herz of Brown University in 1995 asked research subjects to associate emotional paintings with odors or odor labels. When subjects were later presented with the odors or words and asked to describe the associated painting, the recollections of paintings cued by odors were more emotionally toned than those cued by words.[4]

Many studies over the past two decades have brought a better understanding of how the Proustian Effect is triggered in the brain. The combined results are pretty clear about a few things. Smells associated with events or encounters are recalled with more emotional intensity than other sensory cues. Experience, age, gender, and culture also must be taken into account when identifying nostalgic smells. The best advice, no matter what your business may be, is to please people by invoking comforting memories.

For years, those in the real estate business have known about the positive effects of comforting aromas, such as baked goods and vanilla. Lately, real estate sales agencies and homebuilders have been taking this advice to the next level, simulating smells of fresh-baked cookies and brownies while showing properties. D.R. Horton, who delivered over 53,000 homes in 2006, has implemented scent marketing strategies in some of their markets—along with Pulte, Beazer, Centex, and C.P. Morgan. Today, instead of making sure that your real estate salesman is as good of a cook as a pitchman, all he needs to do is to flip on the switch of a portable scent machine.

Nostalgic smells are the best bet when a company is looking to increase sales or customer perception. If we can introduce a Proustian Effect that will trigger a positive reflection or memory while a consumer is making a decision, we cannot go wrong. Some industry professionals believe that we respond to flower scents so positively because we first encountered them during a happy event or occasion in childhood. Leather scent is also categorized as a nostalgic scent, triggered from early experiences. Baby powder, Playdough, Crayola crayons, and the perfume from a first crush are all examples of nostalgic scents.

In the future, we can anticipate many memorabilia products, such as photographs, picture frames, and greeting cards, to be designed to take advantage of the nostalgia triggering capacity of scent. Aroma can communicate an emotional greeting and has the power to remind us of happier days. With fragrances we can tell people we love and miss them.

We also predict that important public events will be scented. Funerals not only will be themed with props and pictures of the deceased involved in favorite activities, but also will include a scent of that activity. The favorite scent of the loved one will be diffused in the air during the ceremony. Brides already have so much to think about when planning the details of their weddings, but they will surely be interested in deciding what their weddings will smell like from a menu of choices prepared by wedding professionals.

Mood

Mood arises within us like nostalgia, except that it is emotionally triggered in the present moment. In the last two decades, researchers around the world have conducted studies that focus on the influence of aromas on mood. We are now certifying what the ancient Egyptians knew: Aromas can assist and benefit us in maintaining a positive outlook on life, especially in times of stress and worry. Pharmaceutical companies have been interested in unlocking the secrets of plants for decades in search of cures for our endless lists of maladies. Today science is validating many of the benefits of scent as a catalyst for mental and emotional well-being that have long been touted by practitioners of aromatherapy.

A 1983 study conducted by Stephen Warrenburg, Ph.D., of International Flavors and Fragrances (IFF), and Gary E. Schwartz, Ph.D., of Yale University, showed that eight major factors of mood are affected by fragrance.[5] Fragrances can have a beneficial effect on irritation, stress, depression, and apathy, and can further enhance the positive factors like happiness, sensuality, relaxation, and stimulation. What were some of the aromas determining results? Muguet (lily of the valley), which makes people happy, increases both relaxation and stimulation, and also has the ability to lower depression, and Douglas fir, which distinctly relaxes people, is effective in alleviating negative moods. London's Heathrow Airport has been reported as getting good results from diffusing the scent of pine needles into the air in order to alleviate stress in air travelers.[6]

In a study conducted in a large shopping mall, Robert A. Baron, Ph.D., M.S., professor of management at Rensselaer Polytechnic Institute, found that individuals exposed to pleasant odors were more likely to help a stranger than those who were not exposed to such odors.[7] When asked to describe their current moods, those exposed to pleasant fragrances reportedly felt happier and more positive than the others.

Environment and location can play a big role in affecting our mood. Not surprisingly, how those environments are scented can be an additional factor. Scent strategies for environments such as waiting rooms, conference rooms, offices, public spaces, prisons, hospitals, and schools will factor heavily in our future chapters.

According to Alan Hirsch, M.D., founder and neurological director of the Smell & Taste Treatment and Research Foundation in Chicago, and other reliable sources, the following floral scents affect our moods.[8]

- *Lavender:* As the smell of lavender triggers alpha waves in the posterior part of the brain, the scent of lavender can stimulate relaxation.
- *Jasmine:* By triggering beta waves in the front of the head, jasmine stimulates alertness. It improves focus and hand-eye coordination. The scent also enhances athletic performance, and improves scores in sports that require concentration.
- *Rose:* There are over 100 varieties of roses, and not only is this flower a symbol of romance, but its scent also increases olfactory evoked nostalgia. Because it will bring happy moments

back from memory, Hirsch recommends placing roses in social areas of businesses, as well as your home.

- *Violet:* Violets enhance learning speed by 17 percent and are known to improve concentration when used during study.
- Other aromas, such as *cinnamon* and *pine*, may also bring happy moments back from memory, and may lift one's spirits.
- The aroma of night blooming *Mexican Tuberose* increases happiness, decreases depression, and enhances romance or intimacy.
- Essence made from the flowers of the *Osmanthus* shrub has stimulating qualities that help alleviate apathy and depression.
- *Hyacinth* is another fragrance known to increase happiness, sensuality, relaxation, and stimulation, while decreasing negative moods.

While many of these fragrances have been shown to produce a substantial effect on the moods of research subjects, if you have a favorite fragrance, definitely use it. If it is associated with a Proustian memory it could bring you joy.

Desire

In April 2007, a string of 100 California gas stations started pumping more than gas at their station pumps, according to Carmine Santandrea, founder of ScentAndrea Multisensory Communications.[9] They now reportedly infuse the air with the smell of freshly brewed coffee. With over $5 billion in coffee sales in the convenience store market, these gas stations clearly want to increase their sales. When customers are triggered to leave the pump for a cup of Joe, the stores could increase the opportunity even further, by wafting the smell of fresh baked cinnamon buns next to the coffee pot.

We consume items, anticipating that they will fulfill a need or desire. Desire is an impulse that seems to be hardwired into the human nervous system, and is the foundation of our consumer system. By nature, as human beings, we consume everything related to our survival needs (food, shelter, water) and more. The "more" depends on our personal motivations, which for different people might include desire for status, achievement, pleasure, joy, sexual gratification, and spiritual fulfillment. So having (buying) things that we desire entails elements of anticipation, expectation and fantasy. For obvious reasons, smell has long been a factor in the hawking of foods and sensuality, but now savvy companies are funding new areas of research into the impact of scent on our desires and perception of products before we purchase them.

Select companies across a broad spectrum of sectors have been testing aroma's ability to influence desire. While the results are in for many, there are scores more trials in the research and development phase. Meanwhile, here are some interesting facts to chew on. When a swanky London nightclub added the scent of coconut to the atmosphere of the club, it found that sales of the rum drink Malibu more than doubled.[10] Similarly, Alan Hirsch studied the effects of odors on product perception. One of his tests consisted of placing Nike sneakers in two different rooms, one with an unscented environment, the other with the atmosphere scented with a mixed floral smell.[11] Eighty-four percent of the people in the scented room said they were likely to buy the shoes, and many would pay about $10 more for the product in that environment.

In another study, Hirsch tested aromas in a Las Vegas Hotel.[12] Over a period of several weekends he infused the area in a casino containing slot machines with an undisclosed pleasant scent. Revenues were compared with several weekend periods when no scent was used. The results? Astounding! Total revenues for the slot machines during the scented time periods increased by over 45 percent. When the study was repeated using a higher concentration of odorant, revenues shot up by 53 percent. It is small wonder that most of the world's casinos now pipe scent into their spaces, even though many don't wish to admit their reasons.

Of course, in any area of scientific study, from global warming, to evolution, to stem cell research, you will find skeptics. In 1999, researchers P.F. Bone and P.S. Ellen, comparatively reviewed several published aroma studies, including the sneaker and slot machine studies, and offered the opinion that the results were not "statistically significant," concluding, "Evidence is stacked against the proposition that the simple presence of an odor affects consumer behavior." [13]

Please note that these researchers came to a different conclusion than Hirsch from studying his findings. They did not conduct any counter studies, only opinion. They also offered no reason why casino operators subsequently spent substantial sums to scent large gaming areas from Las Vegas to Macau.

Wholeheartedly, I agree with the skeptics in their statement that "the simple presence of an odor" will not do the trick. It is the specific, strategic scent that makes the difference. Not just any odor will do. But as any human knows from life experience, certain odors have effects on us, whereas other odors do not. In order to achieve significant results, you must introduce well-designed strategic scents into the mix of your sales environment and marketing activities.

Hirsch has seen sales of his large corporate clients' products increase by as much as 40 percent during his years as a retail consultant.[14] Upbeat about the relationship of products and aromas, he asserts, "If you're looking to increase sales, the best approach is an appeal based on the emotions. And the quickest way to reach the emotions is through smell." [15]

Further research substantiates Hirsch's claims, and offers even more startling results. A study published in 2006 by consumer psychologist Dr. Eric Spangenberg, dean of the college of business and economics at Washington State University, perfectly validates skeptics' views that the mere presence of any pleasant odor will not necessarily have the desired effect on the consumer—but that the right scent can deliver dramatic results.[16] He conducted a test at a local clothing store and found that when specific scents, chosen for their appeal to men or women were diffused in the environment, cash receipts almost doubled.

Scents containing vanilla were dispersed in the women's department and an aroma called rose maroc was diffused in the men's section of the store. Both sexes browsed for longer periods and spent more money when in the presence of these specifically gender-targeted scents. However, when researchers switched the scents in each department, customers spent less then average. He noted that the mere use of a pleasant scent will not work, but that it must be congruent with the demographic.

Thomas Pink, a British based retailer of high-end men's clothing with outlets in the northeastern U.S., has been putting the scent of freshly laundered linen into the air in its stores for several years. Insiders tell us that the fragrance is considered highly important to Thomas Pink's brand identity, and that sales of promotional products that carry the store's signature scent fly off of the shelves during the holiday season. In light of Dr. Spangenberg's research, Thomas Pink's scent is apparently pleasing to both men and women.

Quite a few companies have been using environmental scenting lately to boost sales. One company that sees scent making sense is the Hard Rock Hotel in Orlando, Florida. Hard Rock had an underper-forming ice cream shop called Emack and Bolio's, which was poorly situated in the basement. What to do? The enterprising company employed a "waffle cone" scent to attract customers down the stairs to the shop. Sales increase? Forty-five percent.[17] Another test was done on a Hershey's vending machine. After deploying the scent of chocolate in the environment around the machine, sales of candy bars shot through the roof to an increase of 66 percent.[18] Overall vending machine products in the test increased 12 percent.

An enterprising Canadian entrepreneur pumped discreet traces of citrus fragrance into a local mall's general areas for a weeklong period. Shoppers barely noticed the scent, however the merchants were pleasantly surprised for purchases were up over $55 per customer in the time period.[19] The experiment was conducted during a slow sales period in which merchants agreed to withhold any competing offer of sales or promotions, so we know these results are as accurate as can be under real-life mall conditions.

How and where else are we seeing businesses apply the nostalgia, mood-, and desire-triggering capacity of scent? What additional appli-cations can we anticipate in the future that forward-looking entrepre-neurs could immediately begin designing? From airlines and cruise ships, to hotels and casinos, to private homes, scent has a purpose.

On the Road, in the Air, and at Sea

Singapore Airlines has been using a signature scent, called Stefan Floridian Waters, as an integral part of their multisensory brand strategy since the late 1990s.[20] This scent was designed as a perfume for their iconic Singapore Girl flight attendants and for use in the hot towels provided during flight. The aroma permeates the aircraft and has become a significant part of their experiential branding strategy. Also in the world of air travel, in 1999, British Airways began permeating their Heathrow Airport business class lounge with the relaxing, nostalgic scent of fresh cut grass combined with a hint of an ocean breeze.[21]

Another cutting edge company that knows all about the nose, Kleenex and Huggies manufacturer Kimberly-Clark, was the former parent and impetus behind U.S. airline carrier Midwest Airlines. Shortly after take-off on every flight, attendants pop cookie trays into the oven so passengers can enjoy the comforting, pleasant, and "homey" smell of fresh-baked chocolate chip cookies wafting through the cabin. Cookies have become Midwest's signature gift and scent to flyers. Several other major airline companies are presently studying scent as a significant part of their new branding strategies. However, we think that their most important next step will be using scent to eradicate infectious airborne microbes in flight cabins (see Chapter 5, "Scentsual Healing").

The cruise industry is also swimming in the school of scent. In 2007, Royal Caribbean launched its new ship Liberty of the Seas with a signature scent. In 2008, the luxury liner Queen Mary 2 also rolled out its scent marketing program. What scent are they using? Oceana, the smell of an ocean breeze. And to entice customers to travel to exotic tropical destinations, British trip-booker Thomson Travel uses scent delivery systems to pump out an airborne coconut mix in their retail locations. In an interesting experiment, in the still chilly English month of February 2007, Thomson implemented a scratch and sniff campaign, "Holidays, Heaven Scent." Select travel shops throughout London had coconut scent applied upon their exterior windows to entice passing pedestrians to enter the shop to book a holiday trip to a warmer climate. Once inside, the aroma continued being seamlessly delivered from hidden machines, continually emitting its nostalgic triggers.

Fragrant Hotels and Casinos

Scented atmospheres have made the biggest impact in the field of scent related marketing thus far, as image- and profit-conscious, trend-watching retailers, hoteliers, and casino operators have embraced the new multisensory design paradigm. Many are quite secretive about these activities because so much is at stake.

Even when scent-savvy companies are reluctant to discuss their strategies, they cannot hide the obvious: A variety of welcome smells greet the traveler in their lobbies and parlors. Las Vegas hotels MGM Grand, Bellagio, Venetian, Mandalay Bay, and Wynn Las Vegas have been using aromas for quite some time. Besides the obvious Dr. Feelgood implications with scent and gambling, these properties have created signature scents that imprint a special brand experience into their guest's brain.

Starwood's Westin Hotels & Resorts chain clearly took multisensory marketing seriously, naming its 2006 advertising campaign "This Is How It Should Feel." There is no mistake in highlighting the word "feel," for they were targeting the emotions of the customer. As Starwood's CEO Steven J. Heyer explained, "Westin's campaign is illustrative of its new positioning centered on personal renewal, well being, and restoration of the body, mind, and spirit." [22] His pitch sounds a little bit like Oprah or Wayne Dyer, instead of a corporate "rock star," but multisensory branding is truly the way of the new age. As a cornerstone to their marketing campaign, Westin created a signature "White Tea" scent to greet their guests as they enter their hotels.

Three other Starwood chains (Sheraton, Four Points, and the chic W Hotel) have also entered the scent dimension. And not far behind them is a list of other competitors: Ritz-Carlton, Hard Rock, Hilton, Four Seasons, Intercontinental, and Hyatt. Uniquely, the Mandarin Oriental in Miami has rolled out a program called Meeting Sense, designed to "enhance the overall effectiveness of meetings." Yet most of these lodgings providers are using scent only for branding the lobbies of their properties, and could really increase their positioning through a more intensive application in the guest rooms, ballrooms, and other prime areas. Initially, scent delivery systems in the guest rooms were cost prohibitive, but emerging technologies will enable operators to offer a choice of multiple room scents for just pennies a day.

Aromatic Home Design

Like big hotel chains, the private home of the future will adapt current state-of-the-art technology so it can deliver a variety of specific scents to any designated room in the home. As fragrance advisers will do for people, environmental scent delivery companies will do in the home. First, they'll create a customized profile of a user's tastes and influences, including data such as childhood memory and nostalgic scents. Such smells will be combined with aromas intended to benefit the lifestyle and mood of the user. Once a delivery system is installed, a preset timer can be triggered to awaken the user to the ambience of a richly scented rainforest, a cottage garden, or a summer breeze. As multisensory design in lighting, scent, and sound become more widely used, users can look forward to enticing, mood enhancing, and multisensory experiences in the comfort of their homes. An individual might use a scent to call up a memory of his holiday in the bazaars of Morocco or his childhood days on the farm.

With the push of a button, homeowners will be able to summon up the scent of old books, chocolate chip cookies, cinnamon, jasmine, Grandma's kitchen, or the fragrance of a loved one. Consumers will be able to influence their own moods and the perceptions of those who visit their domains. They will be able to enhance their children's recall during study time, and calm them down when they become a bit rowdy. Like the kids, they can elevate their own alertness and concentration while busy with office work, and induce a calming atmosphere while dealing with the monthly bills.

No matter what homeowners' intentions are, because of the technological advancement in scent delivery systems in recent years, scent is bound to become a mainstay in the design and function of homes of the future. Furthermore, as the public becomes more knowledgeable about the influences that scent can have upon capabilities and perceptions, the demand for sophisticated aroma delivery systems for specific applications will surely increase.

Some of the most exciting possibilities of scent communication are related to its impact on the brain, specifically including cognitive functions like judgment, alertness, comprehension, and decision-making, as well as spatial perception. This is where communication scents are going to profoundly shift our lifestyle and improve our public spaces and safety. The application of scent-based tools will create breakthroughs in the fields of education and entertainment. And believe it or not, scent can even help us to find ourselves.

Chapter 3
Thinking and Perception

Every year for a decade, I've gone to the same mall in the same urban area to shop for Christmas gifts for my family and friends. Every year I get lost trying to find the same stores in the same wing. Under the threat of death I could not tell you where Victoria's Secret, Bed Bath & Beyond, and American Eagle are located in the mall. Nor do I ever remember where to park so that I can avoid traversing the length of three entire wings (including the food court) while in search of a specific storefront. Regular visitors probably keep track of the locations of their favorite shops by remembering to enter through the anchor store entrances. But generally, those of us who are infrequent visitors to any mega-shopping center like this find ourselves spending an inordinate amount of time needlessly retracing our steps.

A similar lost feeling overcomes me whenever I am in a massive hotel. The Opryland Hotel in Nashville is a good example of my predicament. You have to be there a day or two just to get your bearings! The experience is similar for temporary residents of hotels in Las Vegas, Nevada, and Orlando, Florida. Except in Las Vegas you usually can identify your location and get your bearings in relation to the casino. All directions lead through the casino (that's Las Vegas hotel design law!).

What if smell was used to solve navigational challenges and similar dilemmas of perception? Beyond memory, nostalgia, mood, and desire, a major attribute of scent, and one of its strongest merits, is its literal power to affect human perception. Perceptions of direction, size, shape, proportion, age, beauty, and the passage of time, and judgments about personal qualities, like honesty and intelligence, can all be influenced by smell.

Do These Pants Make My Butt Look Bigger?

Want to appear thinner to your date or a luncheon companion? Then you should douse yourself in a fragrance of floral spice before heading out the door. In a fat perception study, men's perception of women was tested while the men smelled certain scents. Remarkably, those men who found the floral and spice odor to be pleasant, on average perceived the women to be a full 12 pounds lighter than their actual weights. The researcher concluded, "Wearing a floral-spice fragrance can reduce a woman's perceived weight by as much as 7 percent." [1] That's not all that much for the petite Olsen twins, but it is an instant 21-pound weight loss for a 300-pound woman.

Age perception was another area of influence. A subsequent study found that scenting men with the aroma of grapefruit gave them the perception that the women around them looked six years younger on average than they actually were.[2] If an enterprising company were to come up with a pleasing grapefruit-floral-spice perfume, they could take a real bite out of the cosmetic surgery industry!

A distinct dislike of someone can be directly related to his or her body odor. Of course, it doesn't take a rocket scientist (or even a chemoreception scientist) to point this out. But the presence of an unpleasant odor leads research subjects not only to give lower ratings to photographed individuals, but also to judge paintings as less professional.[3]

Fashion designers should take note regarding their advertising, for aroma makes a difference to the consumer's perception of photographs. In experiments, subjects exposed to pleasant fragrances gave higher "attractiveness ratings" to people in photos, [4] although some studies have shown that these effects are only significant where there is some ambiguity or unfamiliarity in the pictures. If the person in the photograph is "exceptionally beautiful" or clearly "ugly," fragrance doesn't seem to make a difference. But if the person is qualified as having "average looks," a pleasant scent can improve how they are evaluated visually.

The conclusions of nearly all the studies based upon our perception of other humans while under the influence of scent are similar. When we smell, we feel—and we report that our perceptions are influenced by scent. Recent studies show that scent even has the power to shape our perceptions of past events.[5]

According to a Brown University research project led by Rachel Herz, Ph.D., author of *The Scent of Desire* (see Bibliography) smells can be judged as good or bad depending upon our emotional state when we first smell them.[6] After running two separate studies on subjects playing computer games while smelling specific odors, the group that played easy, fun, positive games later identified the scents as positive and the group that played frustrating games later identified them as negative. Clearly the difference was related to the nature of the memories associated with the smell.

The Personal Touch

Sophisticated consumers soon will be knowledgeable about how to use a wide variety of strategically designed fragrance blends to provoke specific effects. If a female wearer, for instance, wishes to attract a new mate, impress during an interview, look younger or thinner, stay alert on the job, or induce a mellowing effect on those she encounters, she will apply the designated fragrance blend for the occasion.

Soon being fashionable will include a new dimension. Individually, we will intentionally be able to create an impression and elicit desired responses by employing a specific scent blend. Success and status not only will be relayed through clothing with a logo or design, but also—and more efficiently—by a permeating smell. Affluent consumers will waft in the scent of prestigious brands. Whereas today consumers choose a designer perfume or cologne to communicate style, in the future their scent-branded Mercedes cars, Rolex watches, and American Express Platinum Cards will lend them an aura of distinction and stature. Scented products and the emotional imprints that they carry will command brand loyalty.

It is already possible to order a personal signature scent with certain characteristics. Although still somewhat limited, when scent technology becomes more affordable, the use of custom scented perfumes is going to be more widespread. After completing a personal profile, answering questions about culture, tastes, intentions of how they want to be perceived, and personal scent preferences, consumers will be provided with a series of samples and ultimately be able to take home a bottle of their personal fragrance. In this way, future consumers will have the ability to create a unique brand identity. This concept can even become scalable as the technology becomes more sophisticated and portable, as the industry breeds a new line of educated personal fragrance advisors.

Commingling of the Senses

Studies have shown that a particular smell is more influential when it is presented in combination with a color or a word.[7] If a scent is accompanied by a color, it is perceived as stronger and retained more strongly in memory. If a smell is accompanied by a word, there also is a better retention rate for both the word and the scent. The commingling of the senses can really amp up results for food and beverage marketers.

When familiar smells are mixed up with unusual colors, the smells are perceived to be stronger. Red lemons smell lemonier than yellow lemon, and green strawberries create the perception of a stronger scent. If a beverage containing a cherry flavor has an yellow/orange tint, the consumer is more likely to say that the drink tastes like orange.

Speaking of taste, what we are referring to is actually flavor. Flavor combines the sensory information of taste and smell. The buds in our mouths perceive five basic tastes: bitter, salty, sour, sweet, and umami (an Asian term for "savory," "meaty," or "brothy"). The remainder of flavor's composition is produced by smell. Experts believe that as much as 80 to 90 percent of what we generally refer to as taste is actually aroma.[8]

Perception is everything! It seems that Mama's great cooking was all about the smell of the sauce, and most of what we love about freshly baked cookies is their aroma.

In a final study about perception—a consumer test of shampoos—the shampoo that participants ranked last on general performance in an initial test was subsequently ranked first in a second test after its fragrance had been altered.[9] In the second test, participants said that the shampoo was easier to rinse out, foamed better, and left the hair with a glossier look. But only the fragrance had been changed!

Aroma can make all of the difference in any type of product, and many times can be linked to its success or failure. Proctor & Gamble, Unilever, and Kraft Foods have known this for decades. Now you know it, too.

Getting Our Aromatic Bearings

The commingling of sensory information can work beautifully in unusual ways to help us all. Unless we were born with an internal global positioning system (as some of us think we have, but few actually do), we often find ourselves lost in a maze of hallways, wings, sections, towers, concourses, districts, areas, and other similarly challenging environments. However, in the future we will be able to follow our noses, knowing just where we are and where we are going at all times.

Although the signage industry has flourished, as buildings and mega-complexes have grown to gargantuan sizes, it always seems that the space planners and sign makers of these facilities were smoking something special while they were considering the needs of the pedestrians who would be negotiating their tortuous hodgepodge of hallways and connector spaces. The scent-memory connection would make it much, much easier to find our way when navigating a convoluted space.

With a scent immersion guidance network (SIGN) system signifying each wing of a mall with a specific scent, the mall shopper's mind can be imprinted permanently. For example, if the three separate wings of the mall I visit each December were immersed with a light fragrance of orange, lemon, and green apple, and the separate exterior entrances to the mall were each branded with a picture of an orange, lemon, and green apple, from that moment forward we would equate direction with smell identification. While recalling the Abercrombie & Fitch storefront location, we would recall that it was located in the orange wing, and that the Radio Shack is located in the lemon wing. Scent along with logos and pictures create a very strong cognitive imprint, which translates to improved recall.

Theme parks are another navigational quandary. Sure they offer maps and signs. And someone is always around who can give directions. Nonetheless, at any given time of day, you can always spot at least one pasty white, sunburned couple, with three young impatient children, quizzically studying a map to try to find out where they are. Subtle use of a SIGN system in these spaces along with visual recognition would assist in imprinting the memory of a pathway.

If the Dallas/Ft. Worth International Airport, Chicago O'Hare Airport, and Heathrow Airport in London switched from designating their concourses alphabetically (A, B, C, and so on), to using apple, cherry, lemon, and banana scent identifiers, along with color coordinated signage, folks could navigate their way to the next gate easily—and they would know right where they were the next time they landed there.

Most major airports are constantly in the midst of construction. Consequently, passengers are routed through endless temporary halls. Many times we are frantically wondering whether we are going the right way and don't know how long it will take to get there. Some airports have signage indicating how many walking minutes can be expected to the next wing, but sadly, they don't tell you whether that is a fast paced walk or a leisurely stroll, which makes most of the passengers hurry even faster. This leads to heightened frustrations which can lead to the impatient, rude, and disruptive behaviors so prevalent in airports today. However, if maybe 100 yards before arriving at the concourse we were seeking, we began to smell its cherry scent, it would certainly help to lower our anxiety level. We would enter the crowded concourse in a more relaxed state.

I worked in a hospital many years ago that had many hallways and sectors—literally the after-effects of years of additions. On my first day of work in this confusing maze of offices and departments, my coworkers advised me that I would get a feel for the landscape after I had been there for a few weeks! So what does that say for the poor, bumbling, sick patient who is trying to make his way to radiology on the second floor in the Haughton-Miller Wing? Color coordination used in tandem with a SIGN identification system is a very simple and effective solution to spatial traffic planning.

Human beings can detect the direction from which an aroma is emanating. You will usually know whether that barbeque joint, steakhouse, or donut shop is ahead, behind, or to the left or the right of you. This is just another wonderful ability afforded us by our olfactory organ, designed to assist with the daily challenges of survival. Where there is smoke there is fire, and it is always a good thing to know exactly where fire is coming from. Understanding this capability is important to present-day marketers, for when they place scented ads, displays, and products in the retail aisle, they are meant to first catch your attention, and then to capture your emotion. What good would all of this effort be, if you couldn't sniff out the source of your distraction?

In enclosed spaces with air conditioning systems and air handlers, the flow pattern of scent being delivered from above will follow the airflow in the room, making it a bit more difficult to identify the source. Yet when consumers are passing within a few feet of a scent delivery system or a scented point of purchase (POP) display, they'll immediately identify the origination point. So when adding scent to a visual display or activity, such as a digital screen or even a theatrical play, be mindful that it is often important for the scent to appear to be originating from an identifiable source; otherwise viewers' might find it confusing.

You understand the confusion this can create if you've ever watched a movie, a band, or a play and heard the sound emanating from a set of speakers erroneously placed behind you. The primary intention of a movie or play is to first convince the viewer that the premise is plausible. But if an actor is saying a line in front of you and you hear his voice behind you, it is difficult to buy into the premise. Our brains are wired with a sort of multisensory depth perception, and in order to create the intended reaction, design and implementation are key factors.

Cognitive Aptitude Triggers (CAT Scents™)

Despite the sound of the acronym, CAT Scents™ have nothing to do with kitty litter-boxes or feline perfumes. Rather these are specific aroma mixtures that have been formally researched and are known to increase a person's capabilities and abilities (aptitude) of specific cognitive functions such as memory, problem solving, attention, alertness, perception, learning, and comprehension. In other words, one CAT Scent™ could sharpen your recall. Another could improve your efficiency. As scientific research continues to unveil more details about the relationship of aromas to improved mental activity, smart companies and institutions are seeking ways to apply these discoveries to the marketplace.

CAT Scents™ that enable us to learn more quickly and retain information over the long-term are one of the most intriguing applications of aroma. Japanese businesses have a long tradition of using aromas to boost brainpower, often much more adeptly than in other cultures. Important research in 1985 by Shizuo Torii, M.D., [10] showing the mind-altering effects of some aromas, has caught the attention of entrepreneurs. Interestingly, a large construction company was one of the pioneers of scent delivery in Japan. The Shimizu Corporation started to incorporate aroma systems into their buildings, diffusing lavender or rosemary into the lobby, and lemon or eucalyptus in general office areas to keep the workers alert.

A fragrance company, Takasago showed the results of a study relating the reduction of clerical error to the use of essential oils. Keyboard punching errors fell by 20 percent when the air was scented with lavender and 33 percent when jasmine then was substituted. There was an astonishing 54 percent reduction in clerical error when workers were exposed to lemon oils. And by intermittently changing aromas, efficiency levels were maintained.[11]

The Kajima Corporation, in the construction industry, infuses strategic blends of aromas into different areas of buildings at specific times of day according to the male-to-female ratio in specific departments. Scents include lemon in the mornings, soothing floral and wood fragrances at midday, lemon-jasmine to combat after lunch fatigue, and lemon again in the late afternoon to revive and refresh the workers.[12]

Smelly playthings also help young kids to learn. Toys can be enhanced with specific CAT Scents™ to increase speed and comprehension. While many adults fondly recall the smell of Playdough, Crayola crayons, and tiny plastic army soldiers, children today are being imprinted with pleasant memories of their favorite playthings. Fisher-Price, Hasbro, and Baby Boom have rolled out lines of scented playthings. Fisher-Price makes Sesame Street infant toys packaged as Scentsations. Playskool has a line called First Senses. One of the items is the Whiff 'Ems Lunch Bag, which contains fragrant faux apples and peanut butter and jelly sandwiches. Baby Boom manufactures Smart Scents, a set of products that enhance learning in the earliest developmental stages of life. Sue Phillips, founder of a company called Scenterprises, has developed scent-based board games that enhance children's memory and recall.

Just as ancient Egyptian mothers put a drop of lavender oil on their children's pillows before sleep, modern mothers can follow suit by using Johnson & Johnson's line of lavender scented natural baby products, which include baby shampoo, bath gel, and bedtime lotion. After a successful launch of these products several years ago, the major toy manufacturers took note. Now scented toys are on the way, designed to calm young children. However, some toy manufacturers admit that certain of their scents are purposefully geared toward mothers.

Action figures, dolls, trucks, airplanes, and stuffed animals can all be endowed with an added thematic scent that enhances the reality or other perceptions of these products.

Scentertainment

In the near future, marketers will trigger consumers' memories, perceptions, and comprehension with the use of CAT Scents™, which may soon become commonplace in the field of entertainment. As we reinvent a new and improved era of Smell-O-Vision (see Chapter 7,

"Market Reconnaissance"), scented films, television, and Internet games will be produced to take advantage of comprehensive knowledge, targeted responses, and state-of-the-art technology. When we watch a show, see a movie, or view a commercial from our Internet-based 5,000-channel television, a scent delivery system will offer us an aromatic texture designed to bring the scene or message fully to life—harnessing aroma, the emotional underscore of multisensory perception.

When a beautiful actress appears on the screen, she may be identified by a signature perfume. When she readies for a big onscreen kiss with her leading man, the scent will segue into a heady, steamy, aroma of a pleasant musky odor. As we watch her walk through the streets of the big city, we will be suffused with urban smells. When she stops into a café for a bowl of French onion soup, a hint of broth will waft from our screen. When the movie builds in a series of thrilling outdoor sequences, a metallic smell reminiscent of danger will add to our emotional investment in the outcome.

Product placements will undoubtedly replace commercials in the future, and knowing marketers will enhance the recall of the movie's product placement with strategically placed CAT Scents™. When a consumer's perception is at stake, of course marketers will want to implement specific CAT Scents™ when creating scented branding strategies. We will no doubt remember that cell phone, computer, or Toyota better after exposure to a subtly scripted scent.

Spatial perception, age perception, and aesthetic perception are all important elements in the marketing field. Nostalgic memory and mental picture recall are invaluable tools in designing the fragrance to be utilized on a given project.

While we surf our future computers, savvy marketers will trip the sensor systems attached to our monitors, adding CAT Scents™ to the video sales pitch for insurance, medical treatments, and trendy gadgets. While scrolling for watercraft, wouldn't you feel more excited if your memory centers were triggered with an added scent of an ocean breeze or a bikini-clad beauty scented with coconut oil? (We can only wonder what computer application for scent delivery systems will bring to the online pornography industry.) When visiting online travel brochures, the aromas of distant places can be an impetus to decision making. The spices of Asia, the fields of lavender in France, the tropical scents of Fiji will enhance the perception of the destination, and ultimately lead to increased sales.

As manufacturers, marketers, and advertisers become more familiar with the strategic use of CAT Scents™, we will see everyday products scented in an aromatic costume designed to elicit a specific response. High quality products will deliver premium aromas and responses, while low-end brands will smell just as they are: like cheap imitations. We will be able to discern and differentiate between products with our noses.

Read It, Perceive It

The book industry can also benefit from harnessing the power of CAT Scents™. Memory, recall, nostalgia, and perception all play a part in the business of instruction as well as storytelling. Romance novels may be sensually fragrant, while historic novels can be themed to correlate with the era in which they are set (or our modern perception of the era). Guides for "dummies" and "idiots," or any other kind of handbook, textbook, or training manual, can be laced with CAT Scents™ intended to increase learning and recall.

Religious books could be accompanied by frankincense and myrrh. Cookbooks would stick to their themes: a dessert book would be scented with chocolate and an Italian cookbook with tomato and spices. In fact, cookbooks should fly off the shelves more readily if the picture on the cover also emits an enticing aroma when touched.

Smelling the Way We Were

Museums are jumping into the scented fray, offering a sample of how things smelled in history, or at least how we imagine they would have smelled. The Lower East Side Tenement Museum in New York City uses the smell of a coal fire in its exhibit of an 1878 immigrant apartment dwelling. The Museum of Natural History in London uses a boggy, acrid, earthy scent in its *Tyrannosaurus rex* display. Curators took an earlier stab at concocting a "real" dinosaur smell, but it was too putrid and sickening. The National Museum in Prague, Czech Republic, delivers the scent of prehistoric beasts displayed in an exhibit called "Hunters of the Mammoths."

Other curators are tapping the scent dimension to bring life to their exhibits. Across the fruited plane of the U.S., children's museums and science centers hold an annual National Sense of Smell Day, sponsored by the Sense of Smell Institute, which is a division of the Fragrance Foundation (see Resources section). The museums offer hands-on exhibits and informational displays about scent and mood, fire-warning scents, scents of farm animals, and details about the olfactory systems of people and canines. These events are coordinated to teach children the basics about that thing sitting between their eyes, and how we interact with aromas in our everyday lives.

After learning how scent effects our perception and judgment, we can easily surmise that scent must have something to do with our perception and judgment when it comes to choosing Mr. Right or even Mr. Right Now. Let's dig further.

Chapter 4
The Scent of Sex

One of the most famous cases of sensual scent marketing occurred in 41 B.C. Marc Antony had ordered Cleopatra to sail to Tarsus to answer a charge that she was in cahoots with one of his adversaries. Cleopatra, fully equipped with in-depth knowledge of scent used by the ancient Egyptians, sailed into Tarsus upon a magnificent barge filled knee-deep with rose petals. Legend says that the fragrance of the ship could be identified long before it came into view. When she walked off the vessel dressed as Aphrodite, the Greek goddess of love, Antony was immediately smitten. He was so intoxicated upon meeting Cleo, in fact, that he ceased his warring campaigns, left his wife, and followed his new mistress back to Alexandria.

The Egyptians had been employing the use of aromas for many thousands of years before Cleopatra ever met Marc Antony. They would create perfumes and unguents to soften their skin and mask body odor. Myrrh, thyme, marjoram, chamomile, lavender, lily, peppermint, rosemary, cedar, rose, aloe, and various oils were the basic ingredients of most of their perfumes, and the intent was to alter perception and stimulate desire.

Servants with pitchers of sweetened rainwater would cleanse wealthy ancient Egyptians. At parties, servants would place a cone-like hairpiece of perfumed grease on the head of each guest. As the grease melted, it would serve a dual purpose of cooling the face while emitting a sweet fragrance. If someone ever worked for, or was a member of the Pharaoh's court, that individual would have been required to wear perfume and have pure smelling breath. Bad breath and bad body odor were a cause for shame and therefore to be avoided at all costs. The Egyptians believed that the aforementioned perfumes, or essential oils, contained the captured spirits of plants, so they looked upon fragrance as a spiritual element.

Ancient Egyptians believed that aroma and sex had a sacred connection. When Alexander the Great and his army invaded Egypt in 332 B.C., the Egyptians went to great lengths to conceal the spiritual nature of perfumes, for they viewed the Greeks' sexual appetites and debauchery as deplorable. Nonetheless word got out.

Demand for the perfected Egyptian science of perfumery increased as time passed. After the Romans invaded Egypt in 30 B.C., the cultured locals were introduced to an unabashed hedonism that they could never have imagined. Egyptian oils that were once used for sacred purposes became nothing more than highly sought after sexual tools in Rome. In fact, these fragrances were so in demand that many Romans went into debt to obtain them. By 1 A.D., Rome was going through more than 2,800 tons of imported frankincense and 550 tons of myrrh per year.[1]

In 54 A.D., Emperor Nero spent today's equivalent of $100,000 just to scent one party.[2] Carved ivory ceilings concealed hidden pipes that sprayed mists of fragrant essence upon the guests below. He also had sliding panels built into the room, which when opened, would release massive quantities of rose petals upon the guests. A tried and true hedonist, he was determined to create the party of the century with an unforgettable set of multisensory experiences. It was evidently quite an orgy—the talk of the town for several centuries—even though one guest purportedly died of asphyxiation from the perfume.

History books provide overwhelming evidence that fragrances were used by most ancient cultures and viewed as an obligatory accoutrement to a woman's allures. One 13th century Persian poet, Sheikh Muslih-uddin Sa'di Shirazi, offered us an interesting insight in strong, compelling, yet concise language that reveals the history and nature of scent and sex more than 800 years ago. This could just as well be true today.

> *Essences of roses, fragrant aloes, paint, perfume and lust:*
> *All these are ornaments of women.*
> *Take a man: and his testicles are a sufficient ornament.*[3]

Natural Body Odor and Pheromones

There can be no doubt that smell and sex are connected. As the world's population has grown, the demand for perfume has grown along with it, as evidenced by the many billions of dollars spent on fragrances. The products released by the apocrine glands of the armpits and genitals of both genders have long been associated with the smell of sex. Many of our ancestors delighted in these aromas, yet in Western culture we have become more and more inclined to wash away our natural smells for fear of offending or turning off our mates.

As little as 200 years ago, one historical figure left evidence of his desire in an urgent note to his wife. Napoleon writes his Josephine, "Je reviens en trois jours. Ne te lave pas! [I'll be home in three days. Don't wash.]"[4] Some people still delight in the heady scent of sweat, yet it has come to be viewed more as a fetish in modern times.

The role that human sweat may play as a sexual turn on is still a literal feast for debate among scientists. Is it related to our memory/nostalgic/desire scent triggers? Or is it, as some noted scientists claim, the result of human pheromones? The term pheromone, translated from Greek, means *phero* "I carry" *hormones* "to stimulate/excite," or literally, "I carry excitement." The term was first used in the 1950s to describe the essence that female moths release into the air to signal males for sex from over a mile away.[5] One whiff and the little male creatures transform into zombie-like mating devils. Scientists have understood for years that animals communicate their sexual readiness through biochemical cues. These chemicals are not only used in mating, but also relay danger, the presence of food, and territorial boundaries.

The debate over the role of pheromones in humans has a long history. Almost two centuries ago, while Napoleon was enjoying his unwashed pleasures, an observant Danish anatomist named Ludwig Jacobson discovered two tiny pits that lay on either side of the nasal septum, just above each human nostril. This find was dubbed the Jacobson's organ and remained an anatomical curiosity for over 100 years. Gradually, as scientists found similar organs in higher animals and related discoveries in reptiles and birds, a hypothesis over the reason for the organ's existence was formulated. But not much interest was generated by the discovery, and if the organ, later renamed the vomeronasal organ (VNO), was commented upon at all throughout the years, it was described as a leftover evolutionary relic—a non-functioning, unnecessary piece of anatomical equipment.

The story picks up again in the 1950s when a German chemist coined the term pheromone to describe the substance secreted by animals of the same species for communication. In the same period, an anatomist named David Berliner, M.D., was investigating the composition of the human skin.[6] He had an ample supply of dead skin to employ in his experiments, for his laboratory was conveniently located near a mountain ski resort. (A common occurrence at a ski resort was for unlucky guests to suffer a broken leg, so Berliner was able to harvest skin cells from many discarded casts.) As he worked in the lab with the extracts of dead skin cells, Berliner noticed an astounding phenomenon. Whenever he left open the sample Petri dishes for a period of time, he noticed that he and the other nearby researchers in the lab became warmer and friendlier. Conversely, whenever he closed the samples and put them away, the normally stiff and less amiable behavior of the staff resumed.

Although he was intrigued by these results, Berliner had no idea what to make of his discovery at the time. But by 1985, other researchers were sorting out the mysteries of the VNO in animals, and evidence that it was an important communication tool was becoming clearer than ever. In 1989, Dr. Berliner returned to his study of the VNO and with his associates, he conducted tests wherein he wired the subject's nasal cavities to an apparatus that read the electrical responses to various substances introduced to the VNO.[7] He tested responses to plain air, an inert pheromone-free solution, a clove mixture, and finally, a synthesized essence of human pheromones.

The results? The only reaction noted via the electrical impulses of the VNO came from the synthesized human pheromone substance. The other substances showed a flat line on the machine. It's also interesting to note that while conducting the tests, female subjects said they felt warm, comfortable, open, and at ease when exposed to the pheromones. Male subjects said they felt friendlier and more comfortable.

Okay, granted, this is not exactly the be-all and end-all answer in the search for an aphrodisiac. It would probably be more accurate to say that these results trigger some sort of desire to cuddle instead of to copulate. Yet, with these results and a lot of publicity, an industry was born, and Dr. Berliner blossomed into an entrepreneur. In 1989, he formed the Erox Company. In 1993, he launched two fragrances: Realm Women and Realm Men.

According to propaganda on the Company's website their products are "the only fragrances that contain human pheromones duplicated in the laboratory and have shown to stimulate the human vomeronasal organ." It goes on, "Those who wear them may find themselves and those around them responding not only with their sense of smell, but also with this relatively unexplored 'sixth sense' for a richer, fuller sensation of pleasure." [8]

These claims don't have the entire field of science drinking the Kool-Aid. So the debate wears on. Yet, Berliner has certainly offered evidence that these small cone-shaped nostril novelties are not merely unused remnants of evolutionary history.

Certainly, more solid data exists concerning the human pheromones released in sweat. A recent study led by Claire Wyart, a post-doctoral fellow at the University of California in Berkley, has demonstrated a change in women's hormone levels induced by sniffing an unidentified compound of male sweat.[9] Her study piggybacked on research by Noam Sobel, Ph.D., who found that the chemical androstadienone (a compound found in male sweat and an additive in perfumes and colognes) changed moods and caused sexual arousal, physiological arousal, and brain activation in women.[10] When sniffing this masculine molecule, women's heart rates, blood pressure, and breathing increased.

Studying the Secrets of Sweat

Sweat has been the main focus of research on human pheromones. In fact, male underarm sweat has been shown to improve women's moods and affect their secretion of a certain hormone that is involved in stimulating ovulation.[11] Other studies have shown that when female sweat is applied to the upper lip of other women, these women respond by synchronizing their menstruation with the woman whose sweat is used.[12] Of course, these types of results are not terribly surprising to women who have lived with other women in a college dorm or household, as this synchronization phenomenon is common.

In addition to his purported aphrodisiacs, Dr. Berliner has developed a pheromone-like substance that he claims will alleviate symptoms of premenstrual syndrome (PMS) suffered by an estimated two out of every five women.[13]

Here are a few more interesting tidbits on the power of sweat. Men can tell by smell when a woman is fertile. A University of Texas study reported that males sniffing the tee shirts of females could easily differentiate which women were in their peak fertile stage by determining that the fertile women's shirts were more pleasing or "sexy." [14]

When women are in their middle of their menstrual cycles, they are most attracted to masculine faces.[15] Just before and after the cycle, when they are least likely to conceive and their sense of smell is diminished, they are more attracted to men with "feminine" faces. Women on birth control pills are likely to show no particular preferences at all. Birth control pills are known to reduce a woman's sense of smell.

Scent and Sexual Orientation

Now a revelation for those who belong to the "homosexuality-is-a-choice crowd." Some crow-food for thought. A study by the Monell Chemical Senses center reveals that when a group of 82 heterosexual and homosexual men and women were asked to evaluate underarm sweat from 24 donors, the gay men and women had body odor preferences that were different from straight men and women.[16] Gay men preferred the odors from gay men and straight women, whereas the odors from gay men were least preferred by straight men and women, and by lesbians. From the reports we've read, the study did not reveal the preferences of homosexual women.

This startling information adds credence to the school of thought that believes sexual orientation is a biological imprint. Another question, however, is raised: Where do bisexuals fit into the matrix of sweat?

Aromatic Turn-ons

No matter your sexual preference, it is clear that specific scents can turn you on. The Smell & Taste Treatment and Research Foundation studied men's sexual arousal by monitoring their penile blood flow while introducing them to various scents. No pornography was used in the study. The overall results were a twisted confirmation of the adage, "The way to a man's heart is through his stomach." That is, if the way to his heart is routed through his penis. It seems that each of the 30 odors introduced increased blood flow to the penis to a degree, from a dismal 2 percent increase all the way up to 40 percent.

Scents used ranged from orange, black licorice, and buttered popcorn, to lily of the valley, doughnuts, cola, pumpkin, and lavender. What was the hands down winner? A mixture of pumpkin pie and lavender; this blend showed a raging 40 percent increase in a male's arousal. Next in effectiveness, at 31.5 percent, was the combo of black licorice and doughnut. (Beware of fat policemen eating licorice-flavored doughnuts.) The least effective smell for blood flow was cranberry, which registered only at 2 percent. Depending on the men's ages, they reacted differently, with vanilla creating the strongest effect for older men.[17]

Another study showed greatly increased penile blood flow while men smelled cinnamon buns.[18] Roasted meat, cheese pizza, and chocolate also made the list. One might get the idea to open a sex shop in conjunction with a bakery or steakhouse. It seems that men's appetites are pretty interchangeable. Guys, have you ever noticed how hungry you become after a round of healthy sex?

Regarding women's response to scents, according to Dr. Alan Hirsch, men's cologne usually causes a decrease in vaginal blood flow unless it's a natural scent.[19] What actually makes a man most appealing to women is a light deodorant or spray of scent, such as the aroma of an ocean breeze, kiwi, or a combo of baby powder and chocolate. The aroma of a man's clean skin combined with a little fresh sweat and any fresh fruity scent has proven to be the strongest stimulant of all for a female.

For the ladies who think that sexy, musky-smelling perfumes are attractive to men, think again. Women's sensitivity to musk is 1,000 times greater than men's. [20] In fact, these perfumes are more likely to arouse the woman wearing them. Of course, this is not such a bad thing if you want to please a woman. Men may wish to take note of it.

Arousal Inhibitors

We've already reported that women on the pill or in the course of menstruation have an inhibited sense of smell. Smell is also substantially decreased in men who are taking Viagra, especially in 100-milligram doses.[21] No studies have been conducted in relation to Viagra and a man's ability to resist eating cinnamon buns or pumpkin pie. Could there be a new diet product waiting to be discovered?

Sex and smells are forever interrelated, one enhanced by the other in myriad ways. The advertising industry may take note of the many ways it can enhance sensual imagery while hawking products. Should a photo of a bare-chested Calvin Klein model with rippled abs be accompanied by a scent of chocolate, baby powder, or maybe a hint of ocean breeze? Should ads that portray curvaceous, long-legged women emit a scent of pizza, roasting meat, or glazed doughnuts? These are questions to ponder while strategizing how scent may help stimulate sales.

One More Interesting Fact

Our sense of smell is renewed after we have sex.[22] In that moment, production of a hormone called prolactin surges. In turn, this causes stem cells in the brain to develop new neurons in the olfactory bulb, essentially bringing new life to our noses and enabling us to experience the world's ever-fragrant banquet. Pity the priests, eunuchs, and dedicated celibates—if they only knew what they were missing.

After learning how scent plays a role in our most basic biological functioning, you might be surprised at the significant impact scent has upon the other physiological processes of the human body. Actually, scent plays an integral role in most every part of our existence. Aromas can enhance our health and well-being, help to diagnose illness, and they can even be employed to save lives.

Chapter 5
Scentsual Healing

Therapeutic use of aromatics was noted in ancient Egyptian texts and frequently cited by the early Greeks in the centuries leading up to the Common Era. Plato had a particular disdain for perfumes because of their implications of effeminacy and physical pleasure. He felt that aromatics were the playground of prostitutes. Socrates held the more practical view that aromas differentiated one's social class.[1] Honorable men smelled pleasant, he reasoned, whereas peasants reeked of stench.

Socrates' contemporary, Hippocrates, who is known as the father of modern-day medicine, lit scented stakes and planted them throughout Athens to combat the plague. He was also a true believer that one may sniff out illness when examining a patient's body odor. Socrates' friend Crito exclusively used aromatics when treating maladies, as did Galen, another renowned Greek forefather of modern medicine, in a later century. In the early 11th century, the famous Persian physician Avicenna, author of some 450 books on medicine and philosophy, successfully used his sense of smell when diagnosing illnesses—by noting the subtle changes in the fragrance of his patients' urine.[2]

Beliefs and observations that body odors can indicate physical maladies have been made throughout history, yet many early physicians also erroneously believed that odors actually were the root cause of diseases. Such beliefs carried over into the 17th, 18th, and even the 19th centuries. Doctors thought that rotting corpses, urine, feces, swamps, and vapors that rose from the earth created the plague and malaria (literally translated as "bad air"). The belief of the day was that subterranean earth held within it a "stench" laboratory, permeating smells that, when allowed to seep through to the surface, would create sickness in man. These beliefs in the detrimental effects of bad smells were derived from the hands-on experience of successfully combating maladies and diseases with the essences of essential oils and good smells.

This line of thought led to a frenzy of empirical research to find anti-stench remedies that could eliminate both the malodors and the dangers of disease, and eventually led to a common practice of the lighting of aromatic fires to purify an area. Additionally, people were ordered to carry scented pouches and torches in order to ward off typhus and the plague. Aromatic therapeutic concoctions made up of essential oils and herbs were constantly formulated against all types of disease. These age-old remedies to fight disease and infections were improved upon by generations of healers. Yet in 1788, chlorine bleach was discovered to be a powerful antibacterial disease combatant, and many of the older remedies were slowly abandoned.

Upon the advent of modern medicine and more practical pharmaceuticals, therapeutic uses of aromas eventually gave way to skepticism from the medical brotherhood. Much of the knowledge carried forward from ancient cultures about uses of aromas to treat maladies was belittled and discredited. Slowly, these aromatic practitioners and their treatments went underground, and public acceptance waned dramatically. The new conventional wisdom was to develop a pill for every ailment, and we now know how well this "wisdom" pervades our culture.

Aromatherapy practitioners have been fighting an upward battle ever since. Not until recent decades have we returned to the study of aromas' effects on illness. Very compelling and startling information has surfaced from these efforts. Most notably, one British study has seemed able to affirm what Hippocrates knew so long ago.

The Superbug Solution

During the course of our research into scent's effects on disease prevention and healing, we came across one of the biggest discoveries ever noted on the effects of scent. To me it comes as no surprise that scent has been found to combat one of the biggest public health emergencies of our generation. But it's a pretty remarkable story. Here's some background.

Most of the public has heard media reports of a deadly infectious microbe dubbed the Superbug, which is also known as killer Staph. As this "bug" sweeps the globe, its given name, MRSA, is becoming more familiar.

MRSA, which is short for *Methicillin-resistant Staphylococcus aureus*, is a virulent mutating microbe that has become pervasive throughout the U.S. and around the world in recent years, as a result of the excessive use of antibiotics to treat infections. The MRSA problem has been making headlines internationally, with new strains appearing regularly and no true solution in sight.

It all began with the accidental discovery of penicillin in 1928 after mold had grown on a Petri dish and was shown to inhibit the growth of bacteria. By 1941, Pfizer Pharmaceuticals had developed a way to mass-produce this new drug and others like it, which were dubbed *antibiotics*, to combat infection. Consequently, by the mid-1950s, many infectious microbes had already mutated and become antibiotic-resistant. In 1961, following the advent of a new drug called Methicillin, a new, highly resistant microbe was discovered and named MRSA. Although it was one of many, it is considered one of the worst problems because it is so prevalent and tenacious.

By the mid 1980s, antibiotics were being used en masse as a panacea. Doctors would prescribe them for many ills, as a precautionary measure, and for non-urgent uses, such as to clear up acne and other rashes. MRSA had spread to hospitals all over the globe by this time. From 1995 through 2005, however, MRSA infections doubled in U.S. hospitals. The MRSA situation grew into a pandemic, spreading outward from hospital environments into the public arena.

In 2008, close to 2 million people will check into a U.S. hospital and contract an infection during their stay. Of these overall infections,

100,000 will be identified as cases of MRSA, and close to 20,000 (20 percent) will be fatal cases.

Hospitals have been called the most dangerous places to visit, for good reason. It is widely believed that MRSA infections are massively under-reported, and sometimes even misreported, due to the stigma of a hospital appearing to have poor hygiene practices. There is legislation presently being proposed to demand proper reporting procedures from hospitals.

Since 2003, a new strain of the Superbug called CA-MRSA (Community Associated MRSA) has migrated into the community appearing in schools, health clubs, nursing homes, and gymnasiums. MRSA was formerly known to kill only those with weakened immune systems, the very young, and the elderly. As it has migrated, however, it has continued to mutate—and it is now invading the bodies of healthy adults and teenagers with deadly results. Student deaths and school closures are now common occurrences. In 2007, deaths from MRSA outpaced deaths from AIDS and other well-known diseases. The nation's prisons are a hotbed of MRSA activity, with an explosion of cases resulting from drug use and the poor hygiene practices of the inmates.

As of 2007, 2.5 million Americans had been identified as "carriers" of MRSA – with colonies of the dangerous bug nesting within their nasal passages. In fact, it is estimated that over 53 million of the world's inhabitants are now carriers. [3]

Preventative measures, including hand washing, alcohol scrubbing, and patient screening, until now have been the less than satisfactory solution to this crisis. Toxic Hydrogen Peroxide gas and UV lighting are also being used to deep-clean hospital settings, however, evidence shows that within 24 hours of the treatment, colonies of MRSA microbes return.

Arriving just in the nick of time is a scent-based discovery, which offers an unorthodox solution for this pervasive problem. After a decade of cumulative international research into the effects of essential oils at inhibiting bacteria and other infectious microbes, researchers in England have made an amazing find. Most of the previous studies involving the successful use of essential oils to eradicate infectious microbes had tested only the physical application of essential oils. The following study was different because it utilized the vapors of essential oils to successfully and dramatically reduce airborne counts of infectious microbes.

A team led by Professor Valerie Edwards-Jones of Manchester Metropolitan University (MMU) conducted a ten-month study on the effects of certain essential oil vapors on airborne microbes, including MRSA.[4] During this 2006/2007 study conducted within a Manchester area hospital burn ward, a proprietary essential oil blend was dispersed through the air into two patient rooms and a third control room. Researchers found that the solution, BioScent, actually reduced the evidence of MRSA and other infectious microbes by 90 percent. The researchers believe that the maximum reduction of 90 percent is due to the fact that MRSA carrying healthcare workers and visitors were constantly re-contaminating the wards during the study. Regardless of the efficacy rate, the wards had no MRSA outbreaks during the period that the oils were used, even though new MRSA-infected patients were brought into the wards. MRSA outbreaks are usually a very common occurrence in burn wards.

It is significant to note that it took up to ten days initially to achieve the maximum 90 percent reduction, and several weeks for the MRSA to return to its original levels after the scent diffusion machines were turned off. This suggests that the scent molecules take time to completely saturate all of the surfaces within the rooms creating a sort of prophylactic shield. Once the machines were removed, the microbe counts slowly increased, as the scent molecules dissipated. More research is planned to gain more insight into the results.

Science once assumed that these infectious microbes were transferred only by touch. With 53 million humans carrying MRSA in their nasal passages, this assumption has proved erroneous. MRSA is an airborne microbe that settles on curtains, windowsills, doorknobs, bedding, and people. Air currents keep the microbe moving and migrating. You can be contaminated by shaking hands or by touching an open sore after touching your nose or another contaminated surface.

Upon learning of the discovery, I traveled to England to interview the researchers and their associates on several occasions. I felt that a discovery of this magnitude required a lot of attention. Lead researcher, Professor Valerie Edwards-Jones is a well-respected medical microbiologist and expert in MRSA research. Since 1994, she has published about 80 peer-reviewed papers and has lectured internationally on the subject. Her colleague, Dr. Anna-Louise Doran, is also a published researcher and esteemed lecturer.

This great discovery was conducted with the collaboration of a small scent delivery manufacturer located in Wigan, England. Scent Technologies provided the funding, support, and machines for the study. Its chief executive, Roy Jackson, retired from his successful electronics business in 2003 and became interested in the research that was taking place. After acquiring a major stake in Scent Technologies, he invested over one million dollars in the company's efforts to bring this product to market.

There have been a few roadblocks along the way, most notably in educating the medical community to view scent from a new perspective. These oils and most other fragrances can be dispersed legally into hospital environments and, in fact, Scent Technologies uses these machines to deodorize hospitals all over the U.K. Yet if the BioScent product is advertised as an antimicrobial solution, heavy regulations come into play. After developing a friendship with Jackson over a period of months, I have been working to help him introduce the product to the U.S.

As in the U.K., fragrances and essential oils can be dispersed legally in the U.S. But if any "antimicrobial" claim is made, the EPA regards the product as a pesticide. There are no exceptions. Although these safe, non-toxic, sweet smelling fragrances can be used to enhance the atmosphere, if they are designated for the alternative purpose of ridding the environment of microbes, they become a heavily regulated pesticide. Go figure. Efforts are now underway to register the product formally with the EPA.

It seems that modern medicine has yet to learn its lesson. Our antibiotic culture is creating an entirely new line of Superbugs—most notably Clostridium difficile (C. diff), a deadly diarrhea-inducing microbe, that experts predict will rage throughout the U.S. by 2009. What are the big pharma companies doing about these problems?

Over a dozen new antibiotics were introduced by drug makers in 2008, and big-box retailers like Publix and Meijer are offering "free antibiotic" promotions.

Implications of Scent for Public Health

Highly sensitive technology now exists that can ferret out the particular molecules that make up a scent. As the ability to interpret odors using technology grows, scent detection will become a more purposeful part of our public health landscape. NASA's Jet Propulsion Laboratory (JPL) and the California Institute of Technology jointly developed a three-pound, paperback book-sized E-Nose that was designed to "smell." [5] The device, an electronic nose that uses computers and special sensing film to work much like a human nose, has proved its value in identifying contaminants in the air on the Space Shuttle. In March 1997, JPL licensed the technology to Cyrano Sciences, which renamed the device the Cyranose 320 and put it to work in the food industry, testing for spoilage. This particular technology is also being tested to detect toxic materials, water pollutants, and chemical leaks.

A company called Smiths Detection acquired Cyrano Sciences in 2004. [6] Now several medical institutions are attempting to determine how well the Cyranose can be adapted to physical diagnostics. The big fragrance developers also have proprietary scent detection technologies used to sniff out molecular structures, as do bomb detection companies and government contractors. All of these technologies are advancing at a fast pace and will find future avenues for growth both inside and outside the healthcare industry.

The hope is that these devices may provide physicians with a quicker and more accurate way to diagnose various types of health conditions, perhaps catching an illness before it advances or eliminating the need for invasive testing and unpleasant procedures.

But perhaps we don't need to design a machine for this purpose. Another way to take advantage of smell to benefit our health involves our canine friends. Dogs could be part of the health screening process for cancer detection in the near future. Two separate studies in 2004 and 2006 revealed that canine detection of different cancers were

41 percent and 99 percent accurate, respectively.[7] The more that we understand about how some odors are an indication of disease, the better we can put these keen smelling dogs to use.

Health Applications of Aroma

Today the use of aromas in medical diagnosis and treatment is being scientifically studied more than ever before. We now know that certain aromas can reduce blood pressure, heart and breath rate, as well as settle nerves, inhibit appetite, lessen pain, and induce drowsiness. Despite a new understanding that aromas can stimulate significant physiological changes in the body, we have only just scratched the surface of aroma's effects.

Scent preferences play a role in its effectiveness as a therapy. As we mentioned in Chapter 1, the scent of green apple was found to alleviate migraine headaches in subjects who like the aroma of green apple.[8] But it is important to note that the aroma was not effective for those who do not like the scent of green apple. The much more definitive Australian study using vanillin did not entertain such caveats, but the smell of vanilla is more universally appreciated. These results need to be considered when trying to understand just how scent affects us. Could the emotional significance of a given smell be a major factor in its healing power? Must these healing scents first pass the test of how we feel about them before they can make a positive impact upon our physiology? As the research shows, when a person smells an aroma while in the midst of a negative experience, that specific smell will be linked to the experience.

Individuals working in the medical field should make special note of this fact, for medical and surgical treatments could unnecessarily induce negativity in a patient if that individual associates the ambient smell of the hospital, clinic, or medical office with a previous negative experience. As we have heard for decades, maintaining a positive attitude is extremely important when approaching surgery or any major medical procedure. Negative attitudes may adversely affect the outcome of procedures. Unfortunately, many people say that they don't like the sterile smell of hospital cleaning supplies or the distinct smell of medicines. This intense dislike may be related to a childhood memory formed while having been hospitalized for an illness, or possibly to the memory of visiting a loved one who lay dying in a hospital bed. Fortunately, many of the smells that hospitals have long produced can be eliminated, and new more pleasing aromas can be used to mask other lingering smells.

A positive scent memory could make a world of difference in attaining positive results to a procedure. Remember the automatic physiological response triggered by the glucose-smell study that we cited in Chapter 1? The study showed that we could possibly use scent as an alternative remedy to drugs by using it to trigger some sort of physiological memory-response in our bodies. Just as this particular study used scent to mimic an insulin dose, what if we could use it to treat heart palpitations, asthma attacks, and migraines? What if we could imprint physiological memory-responses to positively affect people's appetites, smoking, drinking, or other addictive cravings? Complementary aroma techniques like this could prove to be a substantial gain in a wide range of biofeedback and behavioral therapies in the years to come.

Saving Lives Through Scent Identification

The U.S.-based Center for Medicines in the Public Interest, predicts that counterfeit drug sales will reach $75 billion globally by the year 2010, an increase of more than 90 percent from 2005.[9] Crafty, heartless, crooked entrepreneurs have made a literal killing in the business of distributing a wide array of sham medicines to an unknowing public. The advent of the Internet, the promise of cheaper branded drugs, and the corruption of third world governments have all become sorrowful ingredients of a deadly cocktail in the prescription drug industry. The staggering amount of money in these bogus drugs is not even the real story, for people are dying preventable deaths while mistakenly ingesting spurious sugar pills and, sometimes, much worse.

Trade in bogus products is much more prevalent in developing nations, where regulation control, enforcement, and scarcity of supply create a demand. Yet, as counterfeiting methods become continually more sophisticated, these mock drugs are deluging the western markets. A 2000 World Health Organization report stated that

40 percent of these drugs were being sold in industrialized nations, while 60 percent of the counterfeit medicines were distributed in poor countries.[10] Even crooked U.S. physicians have been caught diluting chemotherapy drugs and injecting bogus Botox into patient's faces causing permanent disfigurement and death. The fact is, we simply cannot be sure what we are putting into our bodies anymore.

Scam drugs range from fake malaria pills, to antibiotics, HIV medications, pain pills, and Viagra. Any potential drug that is in demand—either expensive or in short supply—can be replicated in size and shape, shipped in convincing containers with official looking labels, and sold to eager distributors for healthy profits, with deadly consequences. Authorities have released a multitude of studies offering the sad news that many of these mock lifesaving drugs contained no active ingredients and therefore offered no therapeutic benefits. Some contain filler ingredients that can be deleterious to our health.

With the global proliferation of computerized industrial equipment for making pills, bottles, and labels, it is virtually impossible to target and reign in the perpetrators. After all, many of these mercenary pharmaceutical manufactures have no need for identifiable ingredients. Therefore to be a counterfeiter all that is needed is a suitable factory, cheap labor, and a shameless distributor with marketing savvy or good connections.

Fortunately, this staggering phenomenon can now be attacked head on, and possibly eradicated with the use of aroma as an authentication device. Fragrance is not as easily duplicated. The sophistication level involved in microencapsulating scent and integrating it into products is a far more difficult process than copying graphic images from a label or packaging. In fact, scientists can actually make scent molecules that are almost impossible to duplicate. If reputable pharmaceutical companies added an inexpensive branded scent into their medicines and packaging, it would make it much harder for the bad guys to sell their cheap imitations of popular drugs.

When the poor African villager (or poor Bostonian, for that matter) learns to sniff out the authenticity of a pill before he swallows it, he can be assured that he is in fact taking a legitimate medication for his illness. We can safely assume that the exponential growth in sourcing of products from the Internet is not about to decline, and therefore it behooves all parties (both consumers and manufacturers) to utilize aromas for authenticity verification.

Most humans can identify up to 10,000 different scents, making it possible for suppliers to create an almost unlimited combination of aromas for individual brands, or more simply, to produce a single signature scent for each of their products. Furthermore, if a pharmaceutical manufacturer were to integrate a scent into a sealed product, the consumer will come to expect a fresh waft of aroma as the seal is broken. Additionally, if the product itself was also scented, a subtle communication would be relayed to the user's emotional centers that all is safe and secure.

Even if only a handful of pharmaceutical companies were to adopt these measures, when the public begins to identify safety with branded scents the others will follow, for their products may suffer from a silent apprehension of a wary public.

One day we may see the consumer that first takes a whiff of the contents before absently-mindedly popping a pill from his overfilled medicine cabinet. The implications are astounding, for we are dealing with the emotional centers of the brain, training and imprinting the consumer to search for and satisfy his basic need for security. There is a possibility in the future that we may no longer rely on the label on the bottle, or on the shape and color of the pill, for we will be authenticating our medicines as we do our foods, with a quick sniff for safety and comfort, before we ingest them.

It is evident that not only can scent assist us in our actual physical healing processes, but when used as a communication tool, there are other ways it can protect our health and safety. With all we have covered so far, we could consider scent as nature's physician. Now let me show you how scent can play the role of nature's guardian angel as well, by safely guiding us through the course of our daily lives and sending us unmistakable warning signals when danger is present.

Chapter 6
Danger Will Robinson

"Fee! Fie! Foe! Fum! I smell the blood of an Englishman. Be he 'live, or be he dead, I'll grind his bones to make my bread." The old English fairytale *Jack and the Beanstalk* draws a perfectly clear picture of how scent acts as a warning signal. The giant had clearly experienced some prior encounter involving light-fingered Englishmen and golden goose eggs. That negative experience generated a dislike for the smell of Englishmen, imprinting a danger or warning response which would be triggered by their signature aroma (tea and crumpets, perhaps?). From that point on, the same odor served as a danger trigger and arousal mechanism. And as you will learn, this danger scent phenomenon in itself is a figurative goose that will lay endless golden eggs for enterprising entrepreneurs in the years to come—and make us all much safer.

Another old adage applies. "Fool me once, shame on you. Fool me twice . . . then it is clear that I must have nasal congestion, because I should have been able to smell the trouble after the first humiliating event." We know that smell is linked to positive and negative memories, and therefore someone who smells an aroma while experiencing fear or anxiety will later recall those emotions when the smell is reintroduced.

The human brain is hardwired to sense impending danger from fire, rancid materials, harsh chemicals, smelly people, and wild animals. When we detect these odors, they automatically signal the body's "fight or flight" system to respond with adrenaline, speeding heart rate, increased respiration, and other physiological changes. In the ensuing hyper aware state, we immediately seek safety or get ready to rumble. But we also have "software" that teaches us to recognize danger. As we mature from childhood to adulthood, we learn to associate certain smells, from spoiled rotten food to vaporous gases, with danger. What is dangerous is an integral part of our subconscious belief system.

In his classic book, *Smell* (see Bibliography), Piet Vroon offers an example of a panicky woman who is stuck in an elevator for two hours, all the while smelling a distinct perfume.[1] After this traumatic experience, it is likely that she would always associate any encounter with that specific perfume with negative feelings, because she would recall her anxiety and fear during the situation in the elevator.

Some danger scent responses are learned behaviors based on feeling-memory imprints. Other scents trigger our natural responses. The brain has a built-in warning system that has the reaction capability of a spring-loaded rattrap. Upon encountering a danger scent, we go on high alert, the pulse quickens, and our brain waves can increase.

Olfactory High-Alert Pathways

Since the olfactory system is a pathway to our emotions, it is a perfect warning system. Upon taking a whiff of a naturally occurring danger scent, the brain is alerted via the first cranial nerve (aka the olfactory nerve). As a result we immediately experience a feeling of fear or alertness. Simultaneously, the fifth cranial nerve in our face (the trigeminal nerve, which is the largest cranial nerve and the primary sensory nerve for the face, teeth, mouth, and much of the scalp, jaw muscles, and nasal cavity) is triggered, causing heat and irritation in the nasal lining and surrounding areas.[2]

Danger scents can be acrid, pungent, or spicy smelling. If you have ever caught a whiff of a noxious cleaning solution or battery acid, and subsequently lost your breath, felt your eyes water, and your nose burn, then you've already had an experience of your body reacting automatically to perceived danger. These were signs of the dual reaction of your first and fifth cranial nerves. Even though the trigeminal nerve is slightly activated by as many as 70 percent of the aromas that we inhale, it is especially reactive to tobacco smoke, pepper, mustard, ginger, horseradish, vinegar, and cocaine.[3] To a lesser degree, alcohol, turpentine, and carbon dioxide also trigger the trigeminal nerve.

Although trigeminal nerve irritation is a part of the body's built-in warning systems that alert us to possible danger, some of us become accustomed to its activation, actually enjoying the feeling when downing a half-dozen jalapeno peppers, for instance, or smelling strong substances. It appears to be a matter of personal taste. Little is known of the variability of sensitivity in this nerve between people. Some may have a reaction to certain smells while others do not. But most people react to truly dangerous odors in a similar fashion. The fifth cranial nerve also acts as a backup to the olfactory organ, and can still work sufficiently even as some people lose their sense of smell.

Fear and Scent Communication

Scent is a natural communication device utilized by numerous species on Earth for many purposes, including ensuring the survival of the herd, flock, pod, or pack. It is well documented that animals experiencing stress and fear produce chemical warning signals that can lead to behavioral and physiological responses in members of the same species. For instance, if a herd member were under attack, the animal would release a scented fear message to the others, warning the entire herd to flee as fast as dominoes may fall.

Animals are not alone when it comes to chemical warning release systems. Many plants have built-in communication systems that warn each other of impending danger. As Lyall Watson points out in his beautifully written book *Jacobson's Organ* (see Bibliography), researchers have found that when certain plants and trees come under stress due to encroachment by herbivores, insects, or being cut down by humans, they communicate with each other via airborne chemicals.[4] So when a hungry animal in the field is munching on a lone tree, within minutes hundreds of other trees triple the tannin concentration in their leaves, making them bitter to the taste and thus discouraging the predator herbivore.

Do we have the ability to communicate fear to one another through scent? Yes. Apparently human beings can distinguish between fear signals and other chemical signals based upon olfactory cues. One reason we have been able to determine this is because it alters our mental functions.

A Rice University study was conducted to understand how people respond when introduced to human fear chemicals.[5] Would these subtle signals affect the speed and accuracy of their cognitive performance? In a double-blind experiment, female participants performed a word-association task while smelling one of three types of olfactory stimuli: fear sweat, neutral sweat, or a control odor carrier. Results showed that the participants exposed to the fear sweat performed more accurately (without sacrificing speed) than the other two groups. This study demonstrated that when we smell fear, we are more alert and accurate in our thought processes.

In an even more startling study undertaken in Vienna in 2002, researcher Karl Grammer, Ph.D., demonstrated that women could detect the smell of fear in secretions from the armpits of people who had watched a terrifying film.[6] The implication is that a chemical signal is secreted in sweat that communicates the emotion of fear so that we may respond. As a culture, we've understood this anecdotally for ages, but contemporary science, engineering, and product design will help us to put it to good use. Fear-related aromas could be converted into marketable products and public safety systems.

Humans and animals respond alike to the smoke of a forest fire. Many poisonous objects are perceived as having an equally unpleasant odor. Rotting food and decaying flesh also emit highly unpleasant smells. Fortunately, we can usually trust our noses to evaluate most situations, for we are hardwired to sense what is good or bad for us.

If business innovators respond to market forces, they will soon harness fear-triggering aromas to create safety systems that communicate with both our built-in and our learned olfactory alarm mechanisms. One such innovator is Susan Schiffman, Ph.D., who is a professor of medical psychology at Duke University. Schiffman points out that hearing-impaired people are unable to respond to auditory signals usually used in warning devices, such as fire alarms.[7] But odors and sounds share several characteristics that make them equally good warning signals. Odor molecules, like sound waves, travel through darkness and can flow around corners, making both odors and sounds suitable to alert people of danger.

For many decades, companies have been adding the aroma of Ethyl Mercaptan to propane, so that people could detect the presence of the odorless gas in their immediate vicinity. Why this ingenious application for warning people of danger has never been applied intuitively to alternative uses is a mystery. The use of scent to alert the brain's naturally occurring alarm systems is virtually non-existent today.

Scented fire and burglar alarm systems may also be extremely beneficial to the deaf. Apartment buildings, private homes, and government and public buildings would all benefit from a specific branded danger scent not unlike the propane model. Branded as a Skunk-Warning System, it could be used internationally as a standardized, recognizable odor in order to alert every inhabitant of fire and theft. The authors are presently working with fragrance developers to formulate a Skunk-Warning scent.

Scent alarms and warning systems are an almost untouched business opportunity that will soon realize tremendous growth, as more sophisticated entrepreneurs begin to understand its implications. If we synthesize the information we have learned so far—that scent can serve as a communication device, as a memory imprint element, as an emotional recall stimulator, or as a trigger to alert us—and put all these elements to work in an entirely new paradigm of warning signal communication devices, the potential applications are unlimited.

Let's look at several other practical applications.

The Scent of Deception

If it walks like a crook, and acts like a crook, it's probably a crook. More importantly, if it also *smells like a crook*, our nose can increase the likelihood of apprehending the sly thief. When robbing a bank today, the thief may receive a bag full of loot implanted with an ink bomb, which once it detonates will identify the loot as stolen currency. Imagine now that the moneybag also includes a device that drenches the perpetrator with an overwhelming stench. Certain scents will linger for several days, despite repeated washings.

If the specific scent were standardized for universal use, every passerby and person the thief encountered would suddenly be able to "smell the thief." Since smells waft around corners and through alleyways, the perpetrator would have a much harder time eluding authorities. When everyone can identify the scent of deception, John Q. Public will be able to sniff out trouble and better assist the police.

The same technology could be implemented in ankle bracelets for monitoring non-violent offenders who are placed on house arrest. The same ankle bracelet that is tracked by a global positioning system can now contain a remotely activated Skunk-Warning that will saturate the offender who has wandered off. If the subject being monitored gets the bright idea to remove the bracelet, a release mechanism would be activated, and the authorities could track him down to the last reported coordinates, then just follow their noses in the direction of the offender's offensive odor. It's difficult to hide when you are wafting the smell of rotting fish.

Valuables, collectibles, and important documents are rarely kept in absolutely secure cases or cabinets. We can only put so many locks on these tightly sealed containers, but they are still subject to tampering by individuals who hold the key or combination. We are all too familiar with the sad news stories of children of unwary parents who, overcome by their curiosity, rifle through closets and cabinets to discover a parent's loaded revolver, only to end up as victims. The child may have taken the weapon out repeatedly before the tragedy, without the parent's knowledge. Yet a simple seal can be attached to a case, drawer, or cabinet, releasing a lasting waft to alarm the guardian that the area has been tampered with, giving them a chance to prevent a tragedy.

We are talking about a small device that could attach to any door, crevice, or container, so that when a breach occurs, a long lasting scent releases into the environs. This device would be similar to a security tag used by retailers to attach to expensive clothing and electronics. The device's latchkey can be kept on one's key ring.

One can imagine myriad uses for this sort of Skunk-Warning system. Whenever we want to know if someone has entered a forbidden area, we can merely survey the area with our nose. Should the cleaning lady, a houseguest, or a workman have a tendency to be a bit nosy, we can identify even a stealthy intrusion by concealing a Skunk-Warning seal on drawers, cabinets, or any portal in the house. If we have a sneaking suspicion that our teenage children might be prying open the liquor cabinet, sampling the elixirs with their friends and then replacing the contents with water while we are away, we will have the answer on arriving home. From lingerie drawers to the secret spaces that we keep our most important valuables, we can be notified of an unwanted intrusion as soon as the act has been committed.

These same devices could be used in every aspect of the business environment, from an office desk and file drawer, to inventory containers and product display cases. At the present time, many retailers utilize garment security tags that release an ink stain when tampered with, permanently ruining the item for resale and use by the shoplifter. A highly noticeable odor release system can do the same job, and only a few days after the tampering incident the product can be replaced to the shelf display and be sold.

Even though there is a new wave in the revolutionary use of radio frequency identification chips (RFIDs) in the loss prevention industry, there are still flaws in the system. The radio frequencies located on the security tags are only activated at certain geographic exit points within the retail environment. In other words if the security tag has not been deactivated by the shoplifter or the checkout clerk, management can only verify that a theft is taking place at certain checkpoints within the environment. Yet with the addition of a scent release device, if the security tag is tampered with, the nose of every attendant and fellow shopper can be used as roving security sensors throughout the store. Jewelry, expensive garments, electronics, and other valuable inventory can be further safeguarded with the use of a Skunk-Warning. Most buildings, from those housing retail businesses to public facilities, have prohibited areas that they wish to keep the general public from entering. Employee theft is a continual problem in many businesses, when an employee might slip a case of goods out the rear door during peak times, when the rest of the workers are too busy to notice. A sound alarm on the door would be disruptive, but the management could be made aware of security breaches with a subtle odor release every time the door opens. This could also prove useful in restricted areas of museums, airports, bank buildings, and other similar institutions. Scent release alarms make a good option for communicating security breaches, and when they become universal they could easily become a great deterrent for sneaky, if not illegal, activities.

Public Warning Signals

On a bright, balmy December 2004 morning, off of the coast of Sumatra in the Indian Ocean, deep below the water's surface, a shift occurred in the earth's crust that caused a massive quake measuring 9.0 on the Richter scale. The underwater earthquake created a tsunami wave that traveled quickly under the ocean, building a wall of water up to 30 feet high. In the ensuing minutes and hours, the massive wave rushed outward from its epicenter for more than 1,000 kilometers, reaching a multitude of shores without warning, resulting in over 120,000 needless deaths.

Imagine if a warning system to communicate the impending disaster had been in place, a warning system that could have alerted the senses of tourist, villager, and fisherman alike, whether deaf, blind, or simply unaware. Imagine how many lives could have been saved if the beaches and coastal areas were flooded with the smell of rotten eggs, for example, triggering and alerting the locals' built-in warning signals, and offering them life-giving time to reach higher ground.

Public emergency and warning systems are a logical place to relay specific information to the public. Whereas an emergency siren may alert us to some unknown danger, the application of a distinct scent is more efficient. Tsunamis, earthquakes, impending disastrous weather conditions, terrorist attacks, dam breaks, avalanches, oil spills, and a wide variety of possible emergencies would have their own aromas.

Thus, with the push of a button, an entire community can be fore-warned of the exact nature of an emergency. Once a practical public drill has been accomplished, an entire community's collective memory will react and respond to each individual scent that is communicated. Used in conjunction with a blaring siren, we can communicate first an emergency situation and, second, the details. And most importantly, the deaf community would not be lost in the shuffle.

The use of scent as an effective, ubiquitous warning device on a mass scale has already been made in the U.S. Although unintended, and still something of a mystery, a pervasive bad-smelling gas was reported throughout Midtown Manhattan in January 2007,[8] and similarly, a maple syrup odor was reported throughout the same area in October 2005.[9] Everyone took notice. The nasty smell frightened some people so much that they succumbed to anxiety and collapsed, even though the gas apparently wasn't poisonous. The earlier sweet smelling scent was a topic of wide discussion and interest that was appreciated by many people.

With the brain's natural warning system in place—directly linked to the olfactory system—the fundamentals exist to utilize odors in order to greatly benefit all humanity. Add to this proposition, our scent memory capability and precise ability to differentiate individual odors, and we have the basis for a tremendously powerful alarm system.

In Part Four, "Winning Strategies for a New Century," we'll explore many specific applications of warning scents, including on college campuses.

Embedded Warning Triggers

We now have the technology to manufacture plastic and rubber parts that can release scent when worn down, broken, or disrupted. Here's an example of how this could spare us from disaster. A specific odor can be used to warn of breached containers of hazardous materials. Should a package or container be accidentally opened in a warehouse, en route during shipping, or under any other circumstance, an odor would be emitted from the container alarming all within the vicinity.

Automobile safety warning systems are one of the most important areas in which to implement scent-based signals. Assessment of the wear and tear of automobile parts and decisions about their subsequent replacement has been left up to the consumer's educated guessing in the past, or involves a costly inspection and determination by the neighborhood mechanic. These limited options in order to diagnose replacements and repairs will be expanded by market forces. For example, today a consumer must make a subjective decision regarding the relative thickness of his car's tire treads (weighing his family's safety against the cost of new tires in the process). In the future, as the tread wears down to an unsafe thickness, a scent will be released from the rubber, signaling that it is time to get a replacement. The continual release of scent will keep the impending danger in mind until the consumer takes action. Now if the man chooses to ignore the scented warning signal, his wife and children will also know the smell of worn tires, and he will be doubly urged to take action each time they go near the car. This is good news for Goodyear, for it is probably the most efficient means possible to ensure a timely purchase of replacement tires.

Embedded warning triggers can also serve as embedded *marketing* triggers. They are a true win-win proposition, as they can ensure the safety of the consumer as well as trigger the timely sale of new products. This same concept can be applied to a host of products where safety and product replacement are necessary. Imagine embedding scent release systems in water and fluid hoses, or in "O" rings and gaskets. There would be much less need to disassemble an engine when one must only sniff out the diagnosis. Scent alarms can also accompany sensitivity gauges for overheating, pressure differential, and other limitless possibilities.

What's terrific is that the costs are negligible for both the manufacturer and consumer. A universal standardization and branding of specific warning scents would complete the process, for the consumer must be able to understand and differentiate between scent signals. Picture the handy mechanic with his scent registry in hand, who would quickly be able to diagnose a problem with his nose. One could also detect a slow leak in a tire wall or valve if scented air was used to inflate the tires. In another application for car safety, the car's scent-diagnostic system could also come equipped with aromas to arouse a sleepy driver and calm the fidgety kids.

Aircraft, water vessels, and other means of public transportation can benefit from these concepts. Aircraft warning gauges can be supplemented with a strategic warning scent that can also double as an alertness enhancer in times of stress. With our understanding of scent's capabilities of imprinting memory, training, and response while perceiving danger signals, the use of aromas could possibly minimize errors and response times in stressful situations. On long flights, a series of scents can be released in the cockpit to keep the crew refreshed and invigorated. The passenger areas can also deliver pleasant calming scents during long flights and unfortunate delays. Scent warning systems can be utilized to warn of cabin air pressure changes. Many of these concepts are applicable to other types of transportation and their individual dynamics.

Hull breaches and other impending disasters can be immediately communicated by scent, and located more quickly by strategically scenting each location with its own designated scent. Scent-related diagnostics can be used in a large array of industrial machinery and heavy equipment. Anywhere that wear and tear may be caused by friction, scent can be embedded. Presently scent is captured and encapsulated in a variety of products, but not yet in metals, due to the intensity of heat during casting, forging, molding, and other engineering processes. Yet a metal tool or component could contain within it a layer, or ring, of rubber- or plastic-encased scent release capsules. Upon perfecting this process, entire industries would be affected, for the cost savings in bypassing visual inspections would be massive.

Batteries and other naturally corrosive products can also benefit from embedded scent. From industrial-sized batteries to the D-batteries in flashlights, technicians and consumers could become automatically aware that the product is in need of replacement. Septic tanks, water heaters, piping, and many sorts of containers that suffer from corrosion can alert the user not only of the need for attention, but also the exact location of the damage. Wrapped with a thin layer of scent release material, as soon as an eruption takes place, a branded scent will be released from the product to its surroundings.

Warning signals can be used in any venue for any application. In the home, embedded scent can be used in underground pipes, plumbing, and conduits. The extensive process of tearing out drywall or pulling up sod can be minimized by narrowing down the location of the damage, as determined by smell. If there were a breach in unseen pipes, a high pressure gauge filled with scented air would signal the location of the damage easily. Water heaters, condensers, and compressor units can emit a scent-warning signal when they have reached a dangerous condition. A scent release system can be piggybacked onto a pressure valve or heat sensitive component, adding to the measure of safety in the home.

All these warning systems would naturally be suitable for hotels, government buildings, and commercial property. Even though regular maintenance is warranted in most of these situations, it is often neglected. The addition of scent warning signals only makes common sense, as it can significantly improve the safety quotient of many products.

The Smell of Victory

Pam Dalton of the Monell Institute located in Philadelphia, Pennsylvania, has created an alternative application for the negative effects of aroma. She has concocted what she calls "Stench Soup," an odor mixture that smells so bad it makes you feel like throwing up.[10] Where, you may ask, would one find a market in demand of Stench Soup? Well, the military, of course. The armed forces are interested in non-lethal weapons that can debilitate an enemy on the battlefield.

This brings us to another interesting concept. What if we could create an odor or substance that could instill fear in our adversaries, a chemical that would stop people in their tracks by instilling anxiety and unease in them, rather than wounding or killing them? Do you think that this sort of commodity would find its way to market?

We credit Lyall Watson for spotlighting a little known rodent-like creature that resides in the highlands of East Africa in his book

Jacobson's Organ.[11] What makes this creature special is neither its size (little more than an inch or so) nor its bristle-brush hollowed-out hair follicles that can each emit a substance. No, these characteristics are not what make this locally infamous animal, called a Lophiomys, so remarkable. Its existence is legendary among the indigenous people of the region, a product of the stories told by those who have suffered an attack from this unusual animal.

This "little merchant of fear," as Watson has dubbed it, emits a volatile odorless substance that makes the recipient feel dry-mouthed and distinctly uneasy or fearful. Anyone who's been the target of its venom (evidently aimed at the limbic system of the recipient) feels its effects instantly and wants absolutely nothing more to do with it. Perhaps this creature can serve as a model for industry?

The battlefield is a venue where scent delivery could both be lifesaving and cost efficient. A new-technology supplier for the U.S. military has devised a "scent collar" that would communicate with the individual soldier in the midst of battle. It serves as a default form of communication when vision and hearing become inhibited during highly stressful and rapid maneuvers.

Imagine the chaos in the midst of a battle. The ability of a commander to communicate to his troops, directly into their brains' emotional centers would be invaluable. If the commander wanted to communicate the simple directive "move forward," "move to the flanks," or "retreat," every soldier would receive the message instantly. An army could learn the specific movements of the enemy, its retreat, or the location of attack, through the commander releasing a predetermined scent directive to communicate with the soldier in the field.

Ordnance could also be scented. Furthermore, if missiles and explosives were branded by type with a universal custom scent, we'd be able to determine the make of the ordnance and the party who manufactured it—all without extensive delays and forensic investigations. International conflicts might be reduced, or correctly attributed, if world governments agreed to establish this type of recognition system.

We could also administer real life practical training exercises, simulating chemical and biological warfare, by mimicking the scent of assorted chemical weapons. With our understanding of memory, recall and emotional response with aromas, emergency standard operating procedures could be implanted more efficiently in the trainee's memory.

Even though mustard and nerve gas agents are odorless, many chemical agents have a distinct smell. The blistering agent, Lewisite, smells a bit like geraniums. Phosgene, which attacks the respiratory system, smells like moldy hay. Hydrogen Cyanide, used under the infamous brand of Zyklon B by the Nazis to exterminate the Jews during World War II, smells like almonds, as does Cyanogen Chloride, another cyanide-based chemical agent. White Phosphorus smells like garlic, and is a highly combustible chemical weapon.[12] During my own military training as a young man, we were made to memorize these identifiers, but never had the opportunity to experience them. This was a constant concern during major practical exercises, for during these complicated and stressful trials, memory failure would often be the cause of costly mistakes.

By using mimic scents during practical training, these chemical agents and the exact procedural response can be ingrained in the trainee's memory with a higher recall value than any other training method.

Scent communication can be utilized anywhere that specific warnings or commands need to be relayed instantly. The most beneficial aspect of this type of communication is that the desired response to any given situation can be imprinted into the psyche of the trainee during practical training exercises. Errors could be significantly reduced during highly stressful situations, because scent-triggered memory recall produces a simultaneous emotional response resulting in an immediate, instinctive reaction. This form of communication could be adapted for use in house-to-house searches, SWAT team procedures, and fire fighting exercises.

Another intriguing scent-based application lies in crowd and riot control. Military and police authorities have long-played loud rock music as a method to draw out hostage-takers that are holed up within buildings. In 1989, the fleeing Panamanian dictator, Manuel Noriega, took diplomatic refuge in the Vatican's Embassy as the U.S. military closed in. The military responded by blasting deafening rock music into the building 24 hours a day for several days. But it took a while before he finally surrendered.

What if they used a stench bomb instead? Do you think that he might have given up sooner? And what if we used stench bombs to diffuse and quell rioting mobs that threaten our American Embassies around the world? Smell may be annoying and even sickening, but it might be the most humanitarian solution to violence.

• • •

Yes, to date, the mysteries of scent and its beneficial uses for mankind are both vast and largely untapped. But as we continue to investigate the underlying language of this ubiquitous phenomenon, I believe you'll soon become fluent in employing its powers to convey your message and persuade the receiver. Of course, in order to gain fluency in any language, it takes more than just learning the vocabulary and grammar. One must become immersed in the culture, and attuned to its customs and idiosyncrasies. To advance your education and assure your fragrant fluency, get ready for the next step with a full baptismal in the Scent Dimension.

Part Two

Entering the Scent Dimension

*The first condition of understanding
a foreign country is to smell it.*

—Rudyard Kipling

Scent is the communication solution of the 21st century.
It overcomes the new dilemma of information-overload through a
return to the primal language of instinct and emotion. But if we are
going to use it in this manner, as a communication tool, how do we
make it work? What are the practical mechanisms of using it? Who
knows about this? And from where does this knowledge come? In this
next step we take a look at the origins of the contemporary fragrance
industry, and find out how it has already laid a foundation for the
future paradigm we're describing in this book.

Penetrating the mindset and culture of the exclusive fragrance
trade is a bit more difficult than in many other industries, especially
when it comes to fragrance marketing. Scent communication is a
relatively new field that relies entirely upon the good graces of the
longstanding, monolithic fragrance houses. Their conventional business has to do mostly with perfumes and the more mundane scents
used in cosmetics, soaps, detergents, kitty litter, and garbage bags.
Even though this new category of scent communication is making
strides, not all of the big fragrance houses are that interested in help-
ing our cause. You'll understand why when you realize that a good
perfume is worth millions, and that a very small client purchases a
single fragrance in the six-figure range. But there's no need to fret,
for we're going to introduce you to those that have embraced the new
field of scent communication.

Attending tradeshows and reading industry magazines won't begin
to help you comprehend the complexity of this industry. But we cover
enough here to help you navigate your way into and through the scent
dimension, and to break on through to the other side.

Chapter 7
Market Reconnaissance

Fragrances and perfumes have been used for thousands of years, and in general the fragrance industry classifies its products into three broad categories:

- *Fine fragrances or perfumes:* Inhabiting the world of haute couture fashion houses and high-end beauty salons, fragrances of this kind have adorned the bodies of both women and men throughout the centuries for the exclusive purpose of aesthetic enhancement.
- *Functional fragrances:* These types of scents are added to products, such as fabric softeners, shampoos, and cosmetics, to improve their appeal. Product developers and marketers have been making good use of functional fragrances for decades.
- *Communication scents*: The core ingredient in a new era of communication, this type of fragrance offers us the ability to trigger mental and physiological effects, and can convey information when built into the design of products, spaces and technology.

Just a decade before the dot-com boom occurred, most of us could not envision the day when we'd be carrying our laptops and Blackberries with us wherever we went, staying connected to others 24 hours a day. The Internet, wireless technology, cell phones, and iPods are examples of how cutting edge innovators created new social paradigms. As we have unlearned the communication habits of our youth—the stuff of land-line phones, "snail" mail, network television, and record albums—we have shed our old ways of thinking, never looking back, as entire industries have toppled and become obsolete. Scent marketing and signaling is one of the latest and most personable communication technologies to be introduced. And uniquely unlike other late-breaking technologies, the essential elements of this one have been in place all along, patiently waiting for our attention.

Until recently, scent communication has been a poorly disseminated concept. With the exception of strategic environmental scenting, people outside the fragrance industry often have regarded scent marketing with suspicion. Although people know about simple air fresheners, and some are also aware of more sophisticated environmental scent diffusion devices, most have never heard about embedding products with scent for a purpose other than generating a pleasurable response. Fortunately, well-informed fragrance mavens are on top of the matter.

This begs the question: How do the people working inside the fragrance industry think about scent's new role? If taking advantage of the innovative applications of scent described in this book involves learning to collaborate with specialists who are already researching, blending, and manufacturing scent, what motivates them? In this chapter, we'll touch briefly upon the history of the two traditional categories within the fragrance industry—perfumes and functional fragrances—and then delve deeper into the origin of the new, third, nontraditional category: scent communication. To move forward confidently and pursue new ventures in this interesting field of opportunity, we need to gain a clear picture of where scent technology stands right now, and the nature of the tools and resources at our disposal.

So let's begin by tracing the path of scent in the marketplace through history.

A Brief History of Scent in the Marketplace

The social use of aroma for pure pleasure and to enhance physical attraction takes its roots from the ancient Chinese and Egyptians.

Over the centuries, perfumery was elevated to a haughty science of creating sensual fragrances for the elite in Asia, the Middle East, and Europe. Bottled fragrances originally were used to cover foul body odor. Later they became known as a tool of ladies of the night (a carry-over from ancient Athens). Gradually perfumes and other pleasing fragrances shed their licentious reputation, and once again became socially acceptable. Merchants eventually made quality fragrances affordable to the masses by the mid-20th century. By 1979, fragrance worldwide was a booming four billion-dollar business.[1] The world's perfumers were making a killing—bringing notice that there was money to be made in the business of smelling.

The surge of interest in scent's effects took on momentum in the late 1970s and '80s with the establishment of research institutions and fragrance and flavor centers, founded and seeded financially by big business leaders. (Due to their inevitable, intertwining natures, fragrances and flavors are studied and developed mostly by the same organizations.) As money for research poured in during this time period, the scientific studies into the effects of aroma on humans began to generate results. Experts realized the important nature of scent in influencing emotions, perceptions, and decision-making in our everyday lives. At that time, industries were interested primarily in making their longstanding products, such as packaged foods, detergents, soaps, and toiletries, more appealing to consumers in order to generate increased revenue.

Slowly, a seemingly unquenchable thirst for scented home products took hold. Sales of scented candles and air fresheners began a meteoric climb, achieving a remarkable $2.7 billion in annual revenues by 2002.[2] Originally baited by "lemon fresh" dish soap and pine and citrus cleaning products, by the start of the decade, predominantly female consumers were scenting their homes by design with an ever-growing catalogue of rudimentary scent delivery mechanisms, such as sprays, potpourris, and plug-in devices. By 2004, the candle and home fragrance industry reached $8.4 billion in sales.[3]

Like a rising scented tide, consumer desire has continued to elevate all categories of the retail fragrance industry, achieving revenues of $12.9 billion in 1999, a whopping $16 billion in 2005, and close to

$20 billion at the time of this writing.[4] In a mere three decades, our collective worldwide craving for scent and fragrant products has almost quintupled, bringing expanding research, technology, and new products with it.

While this rise was taking place, hundreds of studies were being conducted all over the world. Scientists were interested in how scent works on the brain. As amazing results poured in over the last decade, entrepreneurs from every corner took notice. As we explored in Part One, "The Powerful Influences of Scent," the most significant discovery was that, unlike the other four human senses, smell travels an unencumbered pathway directly to our brain's emotional centers. Modern marketers learned that the olfactory system, which is hardwired to our emotional centers, produces an instant "feeling" in the receiver. By contrast, the perceptions of the other senses are routed through our interpretive brain centers before eventually arriving in our emotional centers. This explains why we easily see a picture, hear a song, taste a morsel, or touch a surface and can immediately identify it with a classification or name. Sensory data is received and interpreted first, before we can distinguish how we "feel" about it.

On the other hand, we have ambiguous language when it comes to describing odors. We tend to say that an aroma smells "like" something else, such as body odor, fruit, Chinese food, or motor oil. We primarily register aromas according to how we feel about them: positively, negatively, or somewhere in between. Most importantly, a smell imprints a feeling-memory within the brain, and this feeling is recalled immediately upon smelling the same scent on another occasion. Example: To a happily married man, the scent of his wife's shampoo may make him feel beloved. The scent of an ocean breeze could remind him of a sailing adventure from his youth, instantly flooding him with a sense of exhilaration, joy, and freedom. Responses to specific aromas are personal, and yet different people within the same culture often respond similarly.

The implications of these discoveries offer great potential for marketing and advertising. Every modern company seeks to establish a brand identity for its products and services. The intention is to "ink" a permanent tattoo of positive imagery and emotional experience upon consumers' minds, an evocative picture and story that attracts their initial attention and inspires their continued loyalty. Ever since food and beverage marketers began to grasp this concept, the public has been exposed to an ever-growing tide of applications.

These techniques seem commonplace nowadays, as the rise of scent-marketed products came onto the scene almost unnoticed. You probably didn't realize that most of the basic staples within your home are scientifically formulated for a positive response before they ever debut upon the market shelf. All of the foods, soft drinks, cleaning products, and toiletries in your home are the product of a multi-billion-dollar industry that thrives upon creating the perfect fragrance or flavor that you'll choose to call your own. Each brand has been meticulously researched and tested in accordance with your preferences and responses.

Unless you've spent time analyzing it, you may not realize exactly why you've been purchasing one shampoo, furniture polish, or toilet tissue over another. Why, for instance, do you prefer Star-Kist Tuna, Diet Coke, or Godiva Chocolates to its counterparts? Manufacturers of your favorite products understand the complex way humans map the world. If you believe that you choose foods solely by their taste, think again. For your taste buds can only differentiate between sweet, salty, sour, savory, and bitter flavors. Food preferences are more complicated. A taste mixed with an aroma defines the specific flavor of a food that you like. Just try holding your nose while eating a slice of your favorite pizza, and you'll quickly see how much difference the aroma makes. An exact science is now deployed in the creation of products. Marketers have designed many clever ways to use aroma to please you and gain your loyalty.

Think of Pavlov's dog that drooled on cue. Obvious siren scents have been used in a variety of tactics for years. Remember when fruit flavors and scents were added to bottled waters and sodas? Or the fruit flavored explosion in the liquor industry? Think citrus vodka and the obligatory Corona lime. Savvy supermarket operators have been successfully deploying innocent looking, motherly ladies in the grocery aisle with appetite-triggering food samples for years. So much for our waistlines!

The general appeal of functional fragrances is unquestionable. As mainstream home and food product companies experienced success after success with scent marketing, it was only a matter of time before others took note and went further.

While science and research rode the aromatic wave of the past several decades, innovative engineers and entrepreneurs were busy creating new technologies that could capture and deliver scent more efficiently on a massive scale. Essential oils and natural substances gave way to synthesized, laboratory-created aromas. Soon, 80 percent of all aromas were created in the lab. Scratch 'n' Sniff technology started out as a novelty in the 1970s, and became a leading means to offer scent samples to magazine readers by the turn of the century. Advances made upon this technology through a process called micro-encapsulation offer many improvements over the original Scratch 'n' Sniff, and have laid the foundation for what promises to be an astounding number of new products and purposes.

By the mid-'90s scent-related marketing was becoming more mainstream, while various groups from around the world were working on mechanical systems that would diffuse scent into large-scale environments. Eventually that technology advanced and today scent delivery systems of different types are being manufactured each month by the thousands. These systems and the media employed run the gamut in terms of quality, efficiency, and costs. In Chapter 12, "Fragrance Media," we offer you a basic understanding of these technologies and their implementation.

As excitement has grown, so has the buzz about scent in different industries. The mainstream media has devoted numerous articles to the various forms of scent research now being conducted. Research focuses on a variety of subjects from pheromones and sexuality, to learning, alertness, nostalgia, memory, and the emotional triggers of scent—all topics we covered in Part One. A newly scented path of progress was being paved toward the end of the century, but few have known where it was headed.

Over the past few years, leading edge companies, educated and determined to integrate scent into their marketing strategies, have jumped into the game. While at the turn of the millennium only a small portion of big business was aware of the implications of scent marketing, by 2006 the tidal wave of scent-related marketing had hit boardrooms across America. Fortune 500 marketing executives are now paying serious attention to the momentum of this new industry. In late 2006, *Advertising Age* magazine listed scent marketing as one of the top trends to watch in 2007.[5] In his opening speech at GlobalShop 2007 (an annual conference of 15,000-plus retailers and merchandisers), Doug Hope, Group Vice President and Founder, named scent marketing #1 on a list of the top five retail trends of the year—and for good reason. Those in the know are already in the game.

Communication Scents

If we look around, where might we see scent communication strategies being employed strategically in the present-day world? We see it most predominantly in the retail, hospitality and entertainment industries, with the advertising and marketing community following close behind. Several synergistic factors had to reach new levels of sophistication and innovation, and then slowly come together for these possibilities to emerge. Namely, we had to improve our current understanding of fragrance, our knowledge of human physiology, our technological scent-delivery systems, and our contemporary marketing concepts. The serendipitous integration of these elements has culminated into a kismet for the marketing industry.

While scent is changing the face of advertising, it's only because these scent-savvy advertisers understand the importance of storytelling and entertainment to the consumer experience. This style of experiential marketing uses the added element of scent to set the mood of the message. The entertainment industry has long understood the necessity of multisensory storytelling, and advertisers have now adopted this modality when designing their campaigns.

Now scent delivery is becoming available for every entertainment format, from MP3s and DVDs, to televisions, movies, and the Internet. Some of the technology has been in the making for a decade, but due to its complexity, has taken time to develop. The idea of linking scent to motion pictures has been around for nearly a century, almost as long as commercials. The entertainment field has long-awaited this missing link in the sensory experience being delivered, but technology lagged far behind.

That's Scentertainment!

The idea of scented entertainment is an old one. It all got started in the middle of World War I, when wind-up Victrolas were spinning tunes of famous vaudevillians and Dixieland jazz bands, and silent films were in their heyday. Charlie Chaplin was a star on the Silver Screen and sports were a popular distraction presented on the muted newsreels of the day. One day in 1916, in Forest City, Pennsylvania, the enterprising owner of the Family Theater got the keen idea to place a wad of cotton soaked in rose oil in front of an electric fan while showing a newsreel about the Rose Bowl Game. The idea of "Smell-O-Vision" was born, although it wasn't officially named that until 23 years later.[6]

Scent and movies had an ambivalent relationship for years afterward. In 1929, during a showing of *The Broadway Melody*, a New York City movie theater sprayed the audience with perfume from the ceiling.[7] The results must have been less than spectacular, for it took another decade before someone tried it again. In 1943, other attempts were made by a Detroit, Michigan, theater, using a time-released process of scents for the movie *The Sea Hawk*, and for the 1940 movie *Boom Town*.[8] The enterprising theater owners (not the films' producers) encountered some challenges. The biggest problems were that it took a large amount of "perfume" to scent the audience, and that it lingered in the air, unpleasantly mixing with the next cue of perfume.

Around the same time, the idea caught fire with an inventor named Hans Laube, who created a complicated system of time-released scents that were piped through the seats of a theater for the 1939 New York World's Fair.[9] This visionary first dubbed his invention "Scentovision" and later changed the name to "Smell-O-Vision." By 1960, an improved version of Smell-O-Vision was finally ready to be tested on a mass scale for a major film release called *Scent of Mystery*. The reviews were less than kind and called the essence of the film a gimmick. Because the aromas used were inconsistent in concentration and their release was accompanied by a loud hissing noise in the theater, the idea was dubbed a flop and dropped again for another two decades.

Then, in 1981, the quirky rebel filmmaker John Waters released an enhanced "Odorama" version of his film *Polyester,* [10] which incorporated Scratch 'n' Sniff cards for the audience. Still the idea never took off. MTV later tried the promotion in the mid-1980s with a convenience store Scratch 'n' Sniff promotion, as did the marketers of the 2003 release of the movie *Rugrats Go Wild.* [11] These attempts were viewed as novelties, charming and retro. In 2007, just as the scent marketing revolution entered a new generational phase, the TV show "My Name Is Earl" adopted a similar approach in conjunction with *TV Guide.* [12] Different scenes were coordinated with numbered aromas.

Having TV audiences use interactive Scratch 'n' Sniff technology as a way to build emotional loyalty to a show is promising. But the process of forcing viewers to work for the result is a distraction from the emotional value and continuity of the film. The idea of cued scent cards seems kitschy to a technologically savvy generation of viewers. In essence, in order to create a full-blown emotional, immersive experience for viewers, scents really need to be delivered to them in a synchronized, yet subtle manner.

Finally, another market innovator achieved the answer to the Scratch 'n' Sniff dilemma. NTT Communications, a Japanese Telecom conglomerate, devised a machine that emits a series of scents by downloading a code from the Internet. The system made its debut in theaters in Japan in 2006, where viewers in premium seats were awarded with the scented version of Colin Farrell's movie *The New World.* [13] Right on cue, selected scenes released accompanying scents. A love scene emitted a floral scent and nature scenes were infused with complimentary scents. A sad scene was accompanied by a scent-mix of peppermint and rosemary. Finally, after decades of trying, the technology was deemed successful.

Other companies have been working on this technology for a decade or more, and at least one failed with the dot-com bust. Calling their product a breakthrough success, NTT Communications now offers the technology for home use. They are actively working on breaking into the U.S. market with their technology. There are also some exciting new and more advanced technologies coming out of Europe.

We must acknowledge that this scent enterprise achieved a giant leap in their ability to bring scent, the biggest driver of emotion, to the field of entertainment. But while the Asians were working on the big screen, others were thinking much smaller.

Since 1999, an assortment of companies have developed a series of digitally enabled scent devices. This means that through the means of a PC, laptop, cell phone, or digital television, an array of scents can be released into your living room or office, in sync with a movie, sitcom, website, or commercial advertisement. Companies have been racing to the finish line to bring this form of scenting to the masses. We'll talk more about these possibilities in Chapter 12, "Fragrance Media."

Why should we care about adding scent to televisions and computer screens? Let's just take a minute to think about the big picture. Personal home scenting has risen to over $8 billion in the last decade. This means that consumers are already paying billions to bring their favorite aromas into their home. However, most of these products like the massive market in candles require complete replacement after use, and may also be hazardous to health and the environment (See Chapter 9, "Stewardship and Social Responsibility"). What if we could realize the same benefits without the hassles?

For about the cost of a computer printer, products are now available that can emit multiple scents from any room in the home, triggered through a wireless or broadband system. Now the consumer can use his cell phone to scent his house in advance of his arrival, while on the drive home, letting his honey know that he's on his way. Conversely, he can turn it off from the office computer. As the public is continually educated on scent's benefits, demand will continue to rise for scents that can calm us, help us with learning, clean the environment, and put us into any particular mood. We once lit candles to read by, but Thomas Edison's discovery literally decimated that business. In modern industrialized nations, scent alone was the savior of the candle industry. Another savvy set of inventors has now emerged, to help simplify our lives once again with the flip of a switch.

Once the new Bluetooth-enabled scent devices are in the home, viewers will be able to watch scented television programming. Popular shows, sitcoms, and movies can be coded to emit specific scents in sync with important scenes. Coding and syncing scent with program cues is made possible with software compatible with any PC. Literally anybody can learn to program this simple technology in minutes.

This brings us full-circle to business. With new technology in place, advertisers will be able to reach into the consumer's home with a deeper, more emotional message. Think of smelling new leather, classic perfume, lawn products, swimwear, and most of all, foods and beverages. Surely Dominos and Pizza Hut would want to add a little aroma to Friday night programming. Wouldn't Betty Crocker and the Pillsbury Doughboy love to be able to offer you a sample of their wares in your living room? All of these strategies and more are on the horizon, and advertising will forever be indebted to the entertainment industry.

This is all in the making. Millions of dollars have been spent on research into the powers of scent, developing products, and establishing a vision of future technology. But that's not all. Music and video can now be scent-enabled, and technologies are now being hawked to add scent to MP3, CD, and DVD players. Some artists have already created their own signature scents that go with their CDs. And you can expect this phenomenon to continue. Think also of relaxation tapes, New Age music, aromatherapy programs, workout tapes, and other niches where scent could play a complementary role.

My goal here is to inform you of what is happening so that you can take it further in any direction you would like. The important thing is to realize that advertising means communication, and scent is its most powerful form. If entertainment is a key strategy of advertising, then adding the communication-booster of scent should be a part of that goal.

Thinking outside the old, worn-out box is needed to create strategies that work. There are endless ideas for promotions that incorporate scent. Combining a message with a bit of enigma and a dash of interactivity, all in the name of art, can create a strong buzz about your brand. Take the following as an example.

In 2006, nine male models were the subjects of an extremely funky art exhibit at MIT's List Visual Art Center in Cambridge, Massachusetts that could be classified as art-communication. It's unfortunate that their modeling careers were unlikely to be enhanced by this traveling exhibit, for the panel-sized canvases that displayed their profiles, were—shall we say—impressionistic at best. Offbeat creator of the art show, Norwegian-born Sissel Tolaas had an otherworldly inspiration for creating the paintings. Titled "Fear of Smell-Smell of Fear," her exposition was the laborious result of collecting the perspiration of nine anonymous men while they were in various states of fear. One subject, whom she calls the "S&M guy," evidently collected samples while he was frequenting sex clubs.

Easily characterized as "severe minimalist art," the exhibition displayed large monochromatic, but differently hued panels, depicting only a number as the focal point of each display. Upon collecting the sweat with what can only be described as an absorbent maxi pad-type of specimen collector, Tolaas embedded the sweat into the paint mixture she used as her medium.

As art admirers touched the paneled walls they smelled hints of cilantro, vinyl, and aged cheese. Tolaas, a highly educated linguist/chemist/artist, maintains a laboratory filled with years of collections of over 6,700 off-the-wall smells, like dirt, toys, and rotten bananas. A unique and visionary artist, she also has a second career designing branded signature scents for corporate mavericks Ikea and Volvo.

The lesson here for advertisers is that the avenues available for promotion are only limited by our imagination. There's plenty happening in the scent world of today, and as you can see, there's an army of inventors and entrepreneurs making every effort to bring this stew to a boil. While most advertisers have been following the herd with unrealistic expectations of leading the pack, others have seized the opportunity to effectively convey their creative message, using groundbreaking science and the persuasive, silent, language of scent.

Advertising Just Ain't What It Used to Be

We have come to a fork in the road when it comes to advertising. The familiar path that we have been traveling for so long no longer leads us to where the action is. The well-known advertising vehicles that we've been riding have grown cumbersome, costly, and ineffective. They've gone the way of the horse-drawn buggy and the choo-choo train. Are advertisers going to continue to beat this dead horse, hoping for a miracle? Or will they accept that there are innovations on the horizon that can get results faster, cheaper, and more effectively? Just ask the CEO of any major company what he thinks of the outdated advertising methods of yesteryear. He'll tell it to you straight.

Yes, advertising and marketing certainly aren't what they used to be. We are inundated with an overkill of ads, logos, slogans, gimmicks, and slick messages. Competition is everywhere in print and on radio and TV, the classic visual and auditory media. The average adult sees over 86,500 television commercials each year.[14] Newspaper circulation is down as Internet surfing rises.[15] Magazine circulation is on a downward slope, too. And radio-advertising revenues are decreasing. Competitors are scanning the horizon in search of the next best way to reach the consumer, even posting ads in public restroom stalls. Consumers simply tune out when it comes to the blitzkrieg of ads that wash over them each day.

Over $450 billion is spent on advertising each year with less and less effect. The news for advertisers is ominous at best, as they compete with DVDs, VCRs, TiVo®, cable TV, YouTube and other Internet destinations, and over 500 entertainment channels on satellite television.

Although research has shown that the aromas that waft to our brains generate 75 percent of our emotions, relatively few companies have yet to incorporate scent into their marketing and advertising strategies.[16] But one by one, they are finally starting to come around, albeit in some cases kicking and screaming.

Advertisers weren't attracted to the scent marketing business by its sweet allure. They were pushed into this new field as their long-trusted communication tools became less and less effective. And as we've discussed, it took the drastic paradigm shift in the way we obtain and offer information to bring marketers to the realization that just putting a message in front of the customer no longer suffices. The idea of visual "impressions" has become tantamount to approaching a blind man with promises of a peep show. Our eyes are blinded by the barrage of visual propaganda that deluges us every day. In order to reach anyone in these changing times, selling has had to undergo a metamorphosis.

As newspapers, magazines, network TV, and radio have begun to take a back seat to the Internet, cellular phones, digital signage, and branding events, consumers have become accustomed to interactivity and greater personal engagement. Experiential marketing has opened the door to diverse methods of captivating and communicating with the customer. Now that the research results on the influences of aromas have begun to roll in, astute advertisers have taken note, and have begun creating new fragrant lanes of communication on the information highway. Kraft, Proctor & Gamble, and Pepsi are just a few of the bold, forward-looking companies that have tried this new shortcut through the convoluted maze of messaging that leads directly into the consumer's brain. Perhaps a good role model for advertisers to follow, however, is the scented candle doyen, Yankee Candle.

Yankee Candle started scenting its promotional catalogues as early as 2004 with Rub 'n' Smell technology by a company called Scentisphere. By the fourth quarter of 2005, sales had increased by more than 20 percent. President and COO Harlan Kent admitted that "aromasizing" his catalogue had much to do with the increase. Avon has been silently doing the same for a decade with comparable results. As both companies already were in the scent business (candles and cosmetics) it is natural for them to mail scented materials. You might be thinking, "Hold on a minute, these companies were in the scent business, so naturally their sales would increase." But as you read on, you will find that all scented ads fare better than their "naked" brethren.

Coupons, direct mail, and other forms of printed communication are already being scented, with high expectations for the future. Soon we will see more of this phenomenon when a fragrant invitation will waft up from the mailbox, promising discounts that smell like a new car, a pizza, or a travel destination (coconuts and ocean breeze might be the brand scent for an island resort). Companies that embrace this tactic will see their coupon redemption rates multiply. One of our own high profile resort chain clients claimed a doubling in response to scented direct mail.

Scented magazine ads are no longer the sole realm of perfumers, as a wide range of companies have begun advertising their brands and products using scent. Smart companies are already leading the way by publishing scented food ads that emanate a variety of smells to trigger cravings for their large line of products.

In October of 2006, Pepsi went all out by placing a full multisensory ad of their new product Jazz diet Pepsi in *People*.[17] This print ad spectacular displayed a pop-up pop bottle, a jazz sound-bite audio chip, and a Rub 'n' Smell scent of Black Cherry and French Vanilla. Not to be outdone, in December 2006, Kraft scented an array of ads in the Kraft sponsored holiday issue of *People*.[18] Kraft's ads were enhanced with the holiday smells of gingerbread, sugar cookies, white fudge chocolate and even strawberry cheesecake. These aromas smell good and also stir up nostalgic childhood memories. The marketers decided against adding scent to their macaroni and cheese advertisements, and completely avoided a fresh-cooked bacon scent in an Oscar Meyer ad. These companies remained hush-hush about the results, but something was up.

According to Scentisphere's President Bob Bernstein, during the last quarter of 2007 and the first quarter of 2008, many major magazine publications joined the scented ad campaign bandwagon. We're talking tens of millions of pages of scented ads. And it is not just magazines. By early 2007, newspapers were getting into the game. In February 2007, the freebie newspaper *Metro New York* made news history with a dragon fruit-scented ad for Glaceau's Vitamin Water. At the same time *The Wall Street Journal* and *USA Today* were already in the beta test phase of adding scent marketing to their publications. After being scooped on the news of scented newspapers, both publications went public with their intentions to jump into the game by mid-2007.

February of 2007 saw a lot of excitement in the print category, but none more than the results of a Roper Starch study that was commissioned by Time Inc. The Pepsi Jazz ad, which was a part of the study, scored a record 100 percent in reader recall and engagement, measured by readers remembering at least a part of the ad. Starch Communications Research senior vice-president Philip W. Sawyer predicted that a future of "spectacular" ads is coming soon, with an impact similar to the ads during the Super Bowl, where readers will pick up a magazine just to see the ads.[19]

Sawyer also relayed that less spectacular ads (scented ads) still do very well, revealing that readership of ad copy increases 136 percent when scent is included. Now that's proof that you can reach out and touch someone.

Other scent-savvy advertising we've seen recently includes Domino's Pizza using touch release technology for a promotional game piece as a part of the Fudgem's brownie bite product launch. Verizon created chocolate-scented POP signage as a part of the company's Chocolate Phone rollout. McDonald's used a coffee-scented free-standing insert promotion. Kellogg's scented Froot Loops packages for a promotion. And Calvin Klein stuck scent strips on the back of Ticketmaster concert envelopes.

In 2005, for Warner Home Video's release of the DVD of the movie "Charlie and the Chocolate Factory," they added scent to the package insert. During the original movie premiere event, they pumped the rich smell of Wonka Bars outside the theater and inside the lobby. In 2007, Sony Style Stores promoted the release of "Spider Man 3" by showing video trailers of the movie and a 14-foot villain breaking out of Sony's window onto Madison Avenue—complete with a "Big Apple" smell.

DVDs are not only used for movies—they are fast becoming the mainstay for use in collateral brochures. In 2003, a Swedish company rolled out the first ever "3-D" media platform—merging print, video, scent, and Internet formats into one combined product. The product, aptly named the "Expericard," can be used as an insert for magazines and mailers, or merely as a multimedia experiential marketing handout. The original company initially found success in the snowboarding publication *Method Mag*, and then teamed up with Sony DADC to introduce the next generation as the Expericard. This product is multisensory marketing in the flesh. It can be used for high-resolution film, Internet links, instructional videos, as well as limited scent marketing, and other applications. The company's website includes the Vatican as one of its Expericard customers.

The Multiple Media of Advertising

As we all know, advertisers have found their way into every imaginable form of media. Word of mouth and product trials have been around for millennia. Since the onset of the printing press, words and images have become available in every conceivable format. We were urged to "See Rock City" on rooftop billboards decades ago, and have since become a society of billboard-littered highways.[20] Radio and television brought the advertising medium to new levels, but now the abundance of these ads are considered as litter on the airwave and cable channels. To improve lagging consumer response, these ads began to take a more artistic storytelling turn. Graphics, animation, special effects, music and humor eventually became an art form, hopefully to be anticipated by the viewer.

Nowadays, we have ads that are made not to look like ads. They entertain us on YouTube and through viral emails, in hopes of gaining attention. As new technologies unfold, we will continue to see advertisers nimbly try to make their mark and make an impression on the public.

Recent lessons learned in the advertising field, are challenging conventional wisdom. Primarily, we have learned that merely getting our product in front of the customer is simply not good enough. The new generation of consumer needs to be engaged, interested, and most of all, entertained.

With this important element of entertainment in mind, new avenues have opened up. Advertisers realize that they don't always have to create the content, but they can partner in other venues where the consumer is entertained. Over a few short years, advertisers have tapped into branding sporting events, public venues, rock concerts, theme parks, museums, art exhibits, aquariums, charity events, publications, movies, and the celebrities themselves.

These various elements certainly get the job done when it comes to entertaining the consumer, but many of these avenues limit the advertiser to a mere logo image presence. We may be able to see the

IBM logo at a Rolling Stones concert, but what if we smelled IBM in the air? Don't you think that this strategy would substantially impact the impressions gained at such a memorable and exciting IBM event? You bet. And don't forget the Endorphin Branding™ concept (see Chapter 1, "The Nose Knows").

But there's no need to stop there. Once we have a branded corporate signature scent, we should be using it in all of the advertising media. With this new form of communication, we can make a much grander statement in virtually all of our media planning. With scent, not only can you see and hear a brand, you can now sniff the air and "feel" its presence.

Getting the Lay of the Land

When people are first introduced to unfamiliar concepts, they usually come to a fork in the road and have to make some clear-cut choices as to which way they will turn. This is similar to being introduced to a religion. After encountering a proselytizer and hearing the message, one can decide that it is all poppycock and move on down the road, or choose to listen a bit more. A third and final choice: Jump in with both feet, drink the wine, eat the wafers, join the choir, and sing hallelujah!

The knowledge of the amazing powers of scent that you gained in reading the preceding chapters of this book has little to do with religion, for they relay a story backed up by science and research. All the same, you've been introduced to some unique and out-of-the-box concepts. You now can choose to say, "That's cool," and merely use some of the material for water cooler conversations, or you can decide to learn more about scent communication and how it can enhance the success of your future endeavors. For my part, I am hoping you'll have a full conversion, complete with an aromatic baptism in the waters of the scent dimension, because I am sure that once you see the light, you will take the high road, and find your way to the Promised Land—complete with milk and honey, and the scent of fragrant money. Yes, I admit that I have swallowed the pill, bitten the apple, and taken the vow. I am a fully registered, card-carrying member of the International Scent Solution Society and parts beyond.

If you ever ultimately join our cause, you'll need to know a bit about the movers and shakers in the field, and a bit more about where their mojo comes from. So let's take a look at the big mojo machine we call the olfactory factory.

Chapter 8
A Visit to the Olfactory Factory

The field of fragrance is a broad and complex one with many layers, players, experts, supporters, and promoters. Attempting to paint the entire field with simple brush strokes does an injustice to those who have devoted their lives to fragrance, and yet limited space only allows me to offer you an abbreviated version, so you may understand how it works.

The more time I spend in the world of fragrance, the more it reminds me of Hollywood, not just because of its glitz and glamour, but also because of the scent design and development process. The creation of a unique fragrance can take as much effort and coordination as the production of a movie. Both industries start out with a concept or a story they plan to tell, and, when given a green light, professionals of different types roll into gear, spending time, passion, and good old-fashioned sweat to develop a product to entertain the masses. Also like Hollywood, there are the stars, the dealmakers, the production professionals, the editors, the groupies, and those who merely delight in conversation about fragrance. There are those in the know and those who circulate rumors, and others who will find a chance to name-drop to anyone who will listen. The traditional field of fragrance incorporates glamour and sensuality, along with a sprinkle of stardust.

Visiting the world of fragrance is also like traveling to a foreign country. So, if you will permit me to combine similes, it is like making a movie in a foreign country. Which is why it would be best to gain an understanding of the social strata and lifestyle of the natives if you plan to encounter the culture. By offering you a bird's eye view of this mega-billion dollar fragrant society, my purpose is to put a guidebook and compass into your hands, and teach you a few words of the local lingo so you can get around.

The Scented Cognoscenti

No matter where we turn in the world of fragrance, we find it peppered with France's culture and its citizens. Although the world's two biggest fragrance houses are based in the U.S. and Switzerland,[1] they are stocked with French men and women. The world's only accredited school of perfumery, Institut Supérieur International du Parfum de la Cosmétique et de l'Aromatique Alimentaire (ISIPCAA), is situated near the former palace of French kings in the city of Versailles. While ancient Romans and Egyptians originated and refined perfumery (the word comes from the Latin term *"per fumum,"* meaning "through smoke"), the French laid claim to the art and perfected it. They have dominated the fragrance industry ever since. The romance, the language, and the glitterati associated with the fragrance industry conjure a portrait of Parisian fashion and flair.

Try to envision a lazy afternoon in Paris, where chicly dressed locals sip espressos and smoke thin, unfiltered cigarettes from perches at outdoor café tables—backs to the wall, facing the bustle of the street—watching, viewing, and peering. Theirs is a see-and-be-seen social order of image, style, and compulsory commentary, with a dash of rude waiters to keep things in perspective. This is not to say that the scene is a superficial one, for passion fills the air. It holds purpose and meaning for players and spectators alike.

The fiercely curious, image conscious demeanor of the preceding scene is ingrained upon the global fragrance trade and artfully blended into the world of big business. The industry is a society of passionate individuals, from the leaders to the perfumers, to the chemists and the marketers. It is an abstract world of notions, perceptions, and affections—an outpouring of the heart and soul of its inhabitants— enchanting, sensual, and star struck. Most everyone loves what he or she does, and wouldn't be caught doing anything else. And while the passionate search for the next great perfume is contagious, people are similarly ardent when speaking about functional fragrances, such as the aromas for body lotion, bath bubbles, or dishwasher detergent. Fragrance is fragrance in whatever form it comes.

Why shouldn't the world of fragrance be filled with emotive people in pursuit of their passion? Aromas, after all, are fleeting substances that touch our emotions, our feelings, and our instincts. Most in the industry that I interviewed for this book speak with a fire in the eye and excitement about the subject. One of the most articulate enthusiasts of fragrance is Chandler Burr, author of *The Emperor of Scent* (see Bibliography) and first-ever perfume critic for *The New York Times*. Burr speaks of fragrance in utterly rhapsodic prose. I first met him several years ago at a seminar. We both spoke from the audience when the lecturer had difficulty explaining certain elements of scent. After the lecture, he approached me and asked if I was a scientist. I replied, "No, I just read a lot." Likeminded in our passion for scent, we went to lunch the next time I was in town.

Over a bit of Thai food, I listened to this man emote about his favorite subject. I must admit that while I admired Burr's absolute fervor about all things scent, it was as if I was lost in the dream of a foreign language with no translator. His parlance is one of symbols and metaphors, astutely and entertainingly delivered to paint a picture onto the fragrant canvas of the mind. Added to this otherworldly conversation, this self-professed New Yorker would add a bit of French, Japanese, and Italian into the mix, so I was eventually lost and a little intimidated. I soon came to realize that I could only play the appreciative glazed-eye listener and hope that there wouldn't be a pop quiz at the end.

In describing a perfume called Dzing! in a *New York Times* article, Burr explains that it "smells of the circus: the smell of great cats, the sawdust in the ring and the leather whip." [2] In another animated description about a Christian Dior perfume called Diorella, he writes,

"It smells like a new fur coat that has been rubbed with a very creamy mint toothpaste. Not gel. Paste. It is a great, great, fragrance." [3] All of this talk about leather whips, fur coats, and toothpaste can be a bit confusing, nonetheless he is large and in charge in his descriptions. The man knows how to tell a story and describe the experience of the whiff of a new scent. Storytelling is an extremely important element of scent communication—as it is in brand creation.

Burr is also no shrinking violet when it comes to opinion. In his critique of the name of my organization Whiff Solutions, he admitted that it was certainly quirky and memorable, but with a crinkle in his nose, he expressed an unprintable description. After a few subsequent meetings and dinners, we have each followed our separate drummers, he into his world of descriptive perfumes and me into the fragrant world of commerce.

Burr may be unique in his critiques, but never alone in his ardor for fragrance. The aromatic aristocracy permeates the globe, and once every three years, comes together in what can only be described as a Perfumery Olympics of sorts. The World Perfumery Congress is a major international event organized by the American Society of Perfumers with the help of its French counterpart. Originally held in major American cities, since 1998 it has made its home on the French Riviera in Cannes. To add to the swagger and vibe of the event, it is held immediately following the world-famous Cannes Film Festival. It is fair to note that Cannes is the neighboring city to Grasse, which is considered by many to be the original perfume capital of the world.

The Congress is open to all those who maintain an interest in perfumery: creators, marketers, researchers, management, sales, retailers, suppliers, advertisers, and public relations firms. And of course, it also is open to affluent admirers that wish to waft in the radiant vapors of the scented cognoscenti.

New York is the home of the much-acclaimed FiFi Awards put on by the Manhattan-based Fragrance Foundation, the non-profit educational arm of the fragrance industry (see Resources). This annual who's who event of the *beau monde* brings together the beautiful people and the movers and shakers for a grand evening of hobnobbing in the world of fragrance. Regional FiFi Awards are also handed out in select European countries.

Awards are granted for the most popular fragrances along with the avant-garde and the most appreciated. Writers, retailers, packagers, and advertisers also receive coveted awards and recognition. In 2007, the glitterati included Sean Combs (award winner), Paula Abdul, Jane Seymour, and Donna Karan, to name a few. The event is covered in no less fashion than the Oscars, and reported with similar zeal and press.

The industry has yet to award non-traditional fragrances, such as signature branded scents and non-traditional scented products. But their time will come. They do honor technological breakthroughs and home interior products, like candles and air fresheners, but the big perfumes are the stars of the evening.

The glamorous side of the fragrance business is for those who swim in that particular stream. If you intend to work even a little bit with this industry, it helps you to understand the players, their world, and their motivations. Not everyone is star struck by the Hollywood-esque hype, and most keep their noses to the aromatic grindstone for much of the year. The real drivers of the industry must stand on the sidelines and watch from afar, celebrating vicariously through the celebrity of their clients.

The real world of fragrance is one of anonymity. Chemists, researchers, and perfumers work on famous brand name household products and many do not have proprietary ownership of the products' ingredients. Famous perfumes are created by fragrance houses that never receive public credit. Similar to the ghostwriter of a book, they put their time and effort into coming up with winning fragrances—and when a hit occurs, they receive a monetary reward, while their client, the brand for which they work, basks in the glory.

Because of the big financial stakes involved, confidentiality is a survival mechanism. If breached, it can send a company's walls tumbling down. Big brands often act like happy plastic-surgery recipients, refusing to acknowledge a talented doctor and his knife, yet everyone in the game knows that they had "some work done." In a discrete way, word gets around about who is talented and who has botched a few jobs. A botched job does not result in anyone being scarred for life, just a product that sits on the shelf untouched. Too many of these unfavorable results can mean the ultimate death of a company.

The Differences Among Aromas

The art of perfumery has been around for a couple of millennia, going back to an original practice of distilling the essences of plants and flowers used by ancient hunter-gatherer cultures. Even though plants and flowers are cultivated today for the same purpose of delighting us, most of the fragrances that make it to the market (and ultimately reach your nose) are created in the laboratory. The field is broader than perfume alone.

Natural fragrances, also called essential oils, are derived directly from botanical or animal sources through an extraction process, such as distillation, expression (pressing), enfleurage (absorption into fats or oils), with solvents, with carbon dioxide, and other methods.[4] They are concentrated forms of the original material. Common botanical sources include leaves, blossoms, seeds, bark, fruit rinds, woods, roots, resins, lichens, and seaweed. Animal sources include the musk of civets and Asian deer, and a derivative of honeycombs. Although all of these other aromas are deemed "natural," they often contain hundreds of different chemicals, and are not a particularly exact distillation of the original source.

The essences of classic fruits like apples, strawberries, and cherries are almost impossible to extract, therefore such fragrances must be created in the laboratory. They are deemed "synthetic," rather than natural.

Synthetic fragrances, also called aroma oils, are derived from chemical reactions. These are the smells you are most likely to encounter in products on the shelves today. Source materials include petroleum distillates and the resins of pine and fir trees. Resin is a valuable source of terpenes, which are building blocks for the process of fragrance synthesis. Some aromas are created solely through synthesis. Approximately 80 percent of contemporary fragrances are aroma oils created at least partly through synthesis.

Even though lower cost is often a driving factor behind a business' choice to use a laboratory created aroma, synthesis is also an important measure to preserve scarce natural aroma materials. Modern technology provides us with the ability to clone a high percentage of our natural materials, reproducing the molecular structures of the major components of a given aroma—modern science has afforded the tools to virtually duplicate the originals.

There are notable considerations when choosing aroma oils for any purpose. Since creating aroma oils is a scientific procedure involving chemical reactions, impurities can occur during the process that affect the quality of the odor. The purity of the aroma oil is one of the most important qualities in its evaluation, and it is a determining factor in the cost of the oil. This factor, along with how the oil is subsequently blended and delivered, can determine the difference between a good smelling fragrance and a less stellar copy. That's why it is highly recommended to seek expert advice both on fragrance and on its delivery.

On the "Hollywood" Back Lot

Bearing the analogy of film production in mind, I decided to visit one of the biggest fragrance production houses in the world, Manhattan-based International Flavors and Fragrances (IFF), a studio of sorts that is perpetually cranking out numerous "stories" in various phases of production on multiple stages at any given time. IFF is a 2.1 billion dollar fragrance behemoth with 62 facilities in 30 countries, and one of the world's most successful producers of blockbuster aromas. First drawn to IFF due to its skill at invoking the emotions of the consumer, I requested access to key players in the company in order to gain an understanding of what it takes to bring aromas for different types of products to the market. With the understanding of client confidentiality, I was granted interviews with some interesting characters with equally interesting stories.

Far ahead of anyone else in the pack, IFF was a trailblazer in the research tying psychology to aromas. Back in 1983, in collaboration with Yale University's Society for Psychophysiological Research, and under the leadership of former Chairman and CEO Henry G. Walter,

Jr. (1910–2000), IFF pioneered the concept of aroma science. After researching the effects of fragrance on human emotions for more than 20 years through the Global Consumer Science Program, this database of information is one of IFF's biggest assets today.

Earlier on, Walter helped to found the Monell Chemical Senses Center, one of the earliest organizations formed to study the relationship between humans and aromas. And as Walter was a key figure in the creation of the Sense of Smell Institute (SOSI), a division of the fragrance industry's non-profit Fragrance Foundation, SOSI named its annual award after him in 2001 as a tribute to his efforts in the field. A lawyer and businessman by trade, he had two attributes of a great scientist: an intensely curious nature and a willingness to ask, "What if?" That mindset pervades IFF even now.

The background of the company that Walter headed parallels the history of modern consumer goods. In 1833, in an era when sawdust was a regular ingredient on the pharmacy shelf, a druggist named Charles May and a miller named Stafford Allen joined forces to produce pure quality products. The original focus of their company was on the production of essential oils. After several decades, they branched out to Africa, a country rich with ingredients they needed to increase their ever-growing product line.

Over the ensuing years, the company naturally grew to encompass the broader field of flavors and fragrances (two heavily intertwined industries), and became a major player in the field through a series of acquisitions and mergers. Called IFF since 1958, the company went public in the early 1960s and rode the wave of fragrance and flavors to its present heights, by being an innovator and leader in the industry.

With more than 5,000 employees, at the time of this writing IFF maintains an 11.7 percent share of the global market. In nose-to-nose competition, the Swiss company Givaudan dethroned IFF as number one when it bought its way to the top through the acquisition of the fifth ranked competitor in 2007.[5] There are relatively few big players in the field of fragrance, with just a handful of major "studios" and the rest smaller "indie houses." It takes a lot of resources to compete: perfumers, production facilities, technology, and massive amounts of money for research and development (R&D).

IFF maintains its vanguard status through innovation and technology, spending approximately $185 million annually on R&D.[6] Along with myriad patents and inventions they have been innovators in capturing aromas from more than just flowers and foods. They have created technology that captures the scent of a flower or an environment, much the way a movie camera captures a performance through the lens on film. This technology can capture the fragrance at every stage of change in a living flower's lifecycle, and can even collect the molecular signature scent of a scene on the slopes of Mount Kilimanjaro. They even worked with NASA on a mission to collect scent molecules from a rose called "Overnight Scentsation" in zero gravity, resulting in the heavenly scent of Zen Perfume by Shiseido.[7]

Overseeing this considerable operation is Chairman and CEO Robert M. Amen, who joined IFF in 2006 upon retirement from the International Paper Company after 26 years. In Amen's previous position, he was responsible for running a company whose annual gross revenues exceeded the revenues of the entire flavors and fragrances industry. With former responsibilities of managing 54,000 employees and $22 billion in annual sales, Mr. Amen brings the needed acumen to position IFF for much bigger things.

Individual presidents run the company's two divisions of flavors and fragrances. The flavors division, services food and beverage companies, while the fragrance division services perfumers, product manufacturers, and non-traditional fragrance industries like scent marketing and communication scents.

The fragrance division is run by a charismatic French native named Nicolas Mirzayantz, who is lauded for his leadership and vision by subordinates in an almost devotional manner. He speaks in somewhat metaphysical terms about empowerment and energy, and the unified nature of the team. One gets a sense of his more sensitive nature and appreciation for the bigger picture of fragrance from the following snapshot of an address delivered to the 2007 World Perfumery Conference in Cannes.

"Scent can even heal. IFF partners with CEW at Raimond Poin Care in Garches Hospital in Paris to work with patients that have suffered serious trauma and accidents. Many have lost their memories, and some even lost their ability to speak. Our partnership with this program allows us to use fragrance to help patients recover. One patient lost all abilities to speak after a motorcycle accident and began to verbalize only after being presented with the smell of tar. After nine months of not speaking, he finally said three words: 'tar, motorcycle, and death.' That moment was critical in his recovery—a major breakthrough.

"Another 19-year-old patient had just woken up from a coma after 12 months and still had not recovered his speech ability. Staff at Garches gave him a spice bread note to smell—something very popular in France. The patient said his first word in a year, 'Prosper,' which confused many of the hospital staff at first. But then someone realized that Prosper was a popular character from a spice bread commercial from 20 years ago."

For Mirzayantz to focus on the healing benefits of scent at a gathering of the perfumery elite in the French Riviera shows not only an empathetic nature, but also a visionary quality that foreshadows where fragrance is going in the years ahead.

In our first meeting, I relayed to him the details of some of the late-breaking health-related discoveries that we had uncovered while researching for this book. He was visibly excited about the potential power of essential oils to prevent disease and treat illness, and in "green" farming and agriculture. He replied, "I always knew that we would find fragrance to have many benefits to the health and wellness of mankind."

He's a man who loves what he does and he does it with the zeal of a globetrotting proselytizer. While we were communicating, he was hard to pin down, with a perpetual itinerary that included Asia, India, and repeated European tours. I was also duly impressed to receive an email response from him at 11:00 pm one Sunday night. Now that's commitment!

As the *de facto* "studio head" of global fragrance operations, Mirzayantz has a lot on his plate, yet since he and his boss have been in their respective positions, there has been nothing but a successive string of positive growth quarters for the company. IFF's global fragrance arm is divided into six regions with Europe and North

America leading the charge. In Mirzayantz's former position as the regional manager for North America is another former Paris native transplanted to the Big Apple: Christophe de Villeplee.

De Villeplee is delightfully direct and to the point in his view about the fragrance industry and life in general. When I asked him how his wife and three children have acclimated from laid-back Paris to life in New York, he chuckled. "This is a busy place," he said, "with activities and noise around you 24 hours a day. It is not Paris. But we like it." He got his start in the industry right out of school, selling fragrance in the Middle East and Turkey. This is a fortunate region to be in the fragrance business, for a weekly dousing of perfume is compulsory for every male Muslim who has attained the age of puberty, according to the teachings of Muhammad recorded in the *Sahih Bukhari*.

After cutting his teeth in more exotic destinations, de Villeplee rose through the ranks at IFF with moves from Geneva to Milan, Paris, and New York.

When asked what he thought made IFF shine in the industry, he quickly answered that it was in the quality of the people. He has worked for other companies, and seen the extreme when it comes to the competitive nature between employees. The field is full of artistic people with an equally artistic nature—not always conducive to working in groups. He claimed that the longevity of employment and the cohesiveness of the team atmosphere are what make the organization click. Egos are left at the door for the betterment of servicing the clients.

In speaking about the future applications of scent in the non-traditional fields discussed in this book, de Villeplee showed his enthusiasm in his twinkling eyes. He admitted that the world of traditional perfume is approaching a near-saturation level, but that there are many new growth categories yet untouched. Even though scent marketing, health, security, and other fields are in their infancy, he sees the possibilities: entire worlds that are yet to be conquered. It didn't take long to figure out why his favorite hobbies are sitting with a glass of wine and reading biographies of famous leaders from history. Who are some of his favorites? Why Caesar and Napoleon, of course.

Creative Development

When a client comes to IFF with an idea for a product, the wheels start to turn in this massive machinery to determine the right fragrance. Staying with the analogy of the movie business, if IFF is the studio with the know-how and expertise, the client is a director with a concept, but not yet with a script or studio. Most seasoned clients approach IFF with a concept, yet some might not—for example, celebrities or a Fortune 500 company in search of a signature scent. As more and more celebrities jump into the signature fragrance game, IFF has seen the need to start the process with a little education. They've created a course they call "Cosmetic Chemistry 101." This little course is for the novice and uninitiated, and discusses the process of creating a scent through delivery in whatever medium is required.

Creative development at IFF involves doing market research for the purpose of brand development, and drawing upon the massive aroma database that IFF has been collecting for the past 25 years. Their process was developed as the first of its kind in the industry, with the formulation of IFF's Brand Emotions™ unit that works in tandem with the psychological research from the Global Consumer Science Program.

Brand Emotions™ is another industry innovation, created with the sole purpose of assisting clients in brand and product development in relation to fragrances and flavors and targeted strategies. Director and vice-president of Brand Emotions™, Alex Moskvin, founded the in-house agency in 2000 and works with IFF's clients by analyzing their brand's qualities, which he calls their *brand DNA,* and using proprietary methods to come up with targeted branding strategies.

Moskvin is a native Australian with degrees in sociology, psychology, and scientific research methods. He has an interesting background with previous stints as an academic head at universities in Australia and Wales, has owned his own advertising development research firm, and even worked for a time for the Gallup Organization.

An opera and animal lover, he is stylish, knowing, easily excited, and speaks in tangential concepts with rapid-fire delivery. When Moskvin gets excited about a concept, he can't seem to be able to stay seated. It's as if his thought processes work better while standing or walking. His frenetic energy is contagious, and his delivery is that of an academic with an entrepreneurial zeal.

Moskvin is proud of the innovative work that IFF is doing. "We use the right-brain approach," he told me. "This reveals the consumer's deep seated emotional connections for brands and fragrances. This is new and compelling emotional territory."

He spoke of a proprietary approach to his research that integrates visualization, Ericksonian hypnosis, and neuro-linguistic programming (NLP). Milton H. Erickson, famous in the '50s and '60s for his innovative therapy techniques, conceived of the subconscious mind as being separate from the conscious mind, with its own awareness, interests, responses, and learning. For Erickson, the subconscious mind was creative, solution generating, and often positive. NLP, his system, is based on the idea that our view of the world is filtered by our beliefs, experience, values, and assumptions, and that we act and feel based on our perception of the world rather than the real world.

The purpose of Moskvin's approach is to discover the deep down truth of how consumers feel and what they want by studying their reactions. He speaks of traditional research, where the consumer responds to black and white questions, such as, "Do you like it or not?" and gradient scales, "Grade it on a basis of one through seven," as left-brain research. Although he does not dismiss it, he feels a lot of information is missing as the result of using only traditional methods.

Moskvin's method uncovers how consumers feel by bringing them to a comfortable level, allowing them to create nonjudgmental stories, to unlock their creativity, and to involve them in developing the idea. He believes this helps to get past the cognitive left-brain, a conscious gatekeeper that pre-judges before making decisions.

Using the metaphor of an iceberg to describe awareness, Moskvin stated that 90 percent of the stimuli introduced into the human brain are unconsciously processed and registered below the surface of cognition. Of the other consciously registered stimuli, he said: "This 10 percent tip of the iceberg is what traditional researchers use to gather information. But they are only speaking to the iceberg above the waterline. What a lot of people know, they can't say, or won't say, depending upon the circumstances."

As an example, he offered, "For instance, the polls say that a majority of American women don't like Hillary Clinton. But are they responding in the negative because it's just not P.C. or because it is not popular to like Hillary?" He feels that the traditional approach does not get to the bottom of the truth. And remember, he once worked for Gallup, the well-known polling organization.

"In my studies, we facilitate right brain responses," he stated, "bypassing the 'Judge' to let the subject respond without fear of criticism. We explore people's psyches, to reveal emotions: public, private, hidden, socially acceptable, dark desires, or superficial. All of these elements influence perception."

His aim is to get honest answers. He speaks of a Baylor University study using magnetic resonance imaging (MRI) to study the brain activity during a Coke/Pepsi taste test.[8] When the subjects were offered unidentified sips of both Coke and Pepsi, their preferences registered identically in terms of brain activity. In other words, there was no difference in taste according to the MRI results. Conversely, when subjects were told that one of the two sips was Coke, even when they were deliberately misled, their brain activity was much higher with whichever substance was labeled Coke. "This is just proof of how much the cognitive window shades our perceptions," he conveys.

You may wonder why a fragrance house is so deeply involved in consumer research, but it is quite evident that the creator of the essences of many of the world's most valuable brands must have a deep understanding of the consumer. No matter what company or product comes through their door, they must be able to analyze the brand and the product, and boil it down to find out what really matters to the consumer in relation to the brand. Every modern business must learn to do the same for its own products.

Moskvin excitedly relays the concept of "the edge," which was formulated by Saatchi & Saatchi CEO Kevin Roberts in his book, *Lovemarks* (see Bibliography). In this book about branding, Roberts relates that growing a brand is comparable to how a swarm of locusts have managed to expand their geographical territory exponentially into the U.S. in recent years. It is the genetic predisposition of the beast to acquire new territories, so the swarm of locusts will send out scouts to the edge of their territory, where many die without returning, due to climate, predators, and other factors. But eventually they re-engineer themselves and conquer these new territories, in essence growing the swarm by going to the edge. Moskvin characterizes scent marketing as a great example of how companies go to the edge to conquer new territories and expand their brands.

Companies that are considering scent marketing and other unorthodox scent-signaling concepts can compare the move to expanding to the edge—taking risks in order to grow their brand and expand their market. If you plan on using fragrance to communicate your brand identity, doing research to evaluate consumers' reactions to the fragrance and your brand will be an invaluable step in your marketing efforts.

Brand Emotions™ has created a powerful treasure chest of information by forming brand strategies with IFF's clients. The Global Consumer Science Program has been a calling card for Brand Emotions™ since its inception. Both of these programs are overseen by the marketing division at IFF, for, of course, they are the quintessential secret weapon in marketing the company's products and services to businesses, as well as a vital asset in supporting IFF's clients.

Psychophysiologist Stephen Warrenburg, Ph.D., has run the Global Consumer Science Program since 1986. At Yale University, he studied directly under Gary E. Schwartz, Ph.D., one of the fathers of biofeedback and the field of behavioral medicine. Active since then, Warrenburg has led and co-led many studies on mood and aromas, publishing frequently and becoming a legend in his field. His most famous finding came in 1993 through collaboration with another aroma scientist Craig Warren, Ph.D. Together they developed a way to map mood associations that are spontaneously evoked by different fragrances. They call this proprietary technique *mood mapping*.

The results of this research into the emotional link to smells was a list of feelings boiled down from 44 to eight—four positive feelings and four negative feelings. The four positive feelings are: stimulated, happy, relaxed, and sensuous.[9]

Warrenburg admits that he had to think long and hard about taking the job with IFF, for he was a skeptic. Even after joining the program, he told me, it took him a couple of years to become absolutely convinced of what he describes as the power of aromas on human emotions. His most notable finding involves the striking similarity between fragrance's effects on the psyche, and the more conventional understanding of psychology and emotions.

In our interview, he matter-of-factly stated that the power of fragrance has now been proven. Yet he was cautious to say just how far beyond the realm of mood enhancement fragrances take us. When questioned about aroma's power in relation to warning signals, health, and directional enhancement, he had little to comment. His perfunctory, cautious, scientific answer: "That is not my field of study." His caution was not to "over promise," adding, "Aromas are not specifically a panacea."

When measuring mood changes in relation to the products in his research, he uses a clinical mood scale test called the Derogatis Affects Balance Scale (DABS). This psychological test measures both positive and negative emotional experiences against stimuli. The testing involves using this scale both before and after using a product, to understand its effect upon the consumer. The end result of these studies is what Warrenburg calls the "halo effect" of the products. This term has been traditionally used to describe how a person's perceptions and expectations of another person are preconceived and categorized, and therefore affect their ensuing perceptions.

Warrenburg is a family man with two teenage daughters. Therefore, he was aptly prepared when Samsung came to IFF to create a signature scent for use in their electronics stores. Teenagers are the gadget mavens of the future. In reporting on the results of Samsung's scent program, Warrenburg was enthusiastic. With nearly a 100 percent positive reaction from customers, he stated, "Two-thirds wanted to stay longer in the store," and, "Customers visited three times more sections of the store." Overall the project was considered a success because it had clear-cut results and improved the customer's perceptions. The most notable improvements were perceptions of Samsung's image in terms of "innovation," "imagination," and "premium."

As you can see, significant effort frequently goes into the creation of a strategically targeted and effective fragrance for mass-market products. Once IFF's clients are confident about the response they wish to trigger in consumers, they move on to the most talked about part of the fragrance business: interacting with the "nose." But before we meet the creative talent, we should learn a little about the melodic language in which he speaks.

The Lyrical Language of Fragrance

As any wine connoisseur can attest, aromas are often described in melodic terms, as three distinct notes. In making perfume, top notes, middle notes, and base notes are orchestrated like a symphony to tell a specific story in three movements. Top notes are the ingredients that create the first impression of the fragrance on the nose. They are the lightest and briefest in duration, like high notes on a musical scale. In a well-designed fragrance, as top notes evaporate they harmoniously segue into the middle notes that comprise the main body, or second movement, of the fragrance. The middle notes evaporate at an even slower rate than top notes, and also soften the usually stronger base notes. As the middle notes dissipate, the base notes linger like the final strains of a cello concerto.

The key to an appealing fragrance is telling a story with the unraveling aromas, not unlike playing a harmonious chord of resolution. Top notes, also called head notes, which are commonly described as fresh, assertive, or sharp, include aromas like citrus or ginger. These compounds are strongly scented, highly volatile, and evaporate quickly. Middle notes, also known as heart notes, are usually mellower, softer, less demanding aromas. Common middle note scents are rose and lavender. The main theme of the fragrance is a combination of the middle and base notes. Base notes are chosen to become more pleasing over time. They support the top and middle notes, and contribute depth and strength to a fragrance. Some typical base notes are clove, jasmine, and sandalwood.

The art of perfumery has been utilizing musical metaphors for centuries. Even though originally intended for perfumes, the symphonic structure is also used to design most custom non-traditional fragrances. With a basic understanding of the lyrical language of fragrance, you will be able to relate to fragrance professionals while working to create your brand's own storyline. You will learn to differentiate between well-composed and poorly blended fragrances as you consider their unfolding notes.

Furthermore, as in all artistic endeavors, the beauty of the fragrance ultimately rests in the eye (or nose) of the beholder. Just as no musical composition is considered pleasing to the ears of all listeners, no fragrance is pleasing to every consumer who smells it. The key to a standing ovation is to know your audience and give them what they like.

Scripting the Storyline

Perfumers are the "creative talent" part of fragrance production, many famous for their ability to identify the most prominent three notes in any product with a simple whiff. Often these "noses" can tell who a fragrance's designer is, for many leave a stylistic signature trail. These well-paid professionals spend more than a decade of schooling, apprenticeship, and whiffing up thousands of compounds before actually being awarded the official title "perfumer."

IFF employs over 80 perfumers and runs its own private perfumery school and apprenticeship program—one of only three such schools in existence, and the only one in the U.S. The company regards its noses as a major asset in its war chest, and therefore dictates that no more than two perfumers can fly on any one airplane at a time.

Pascal Gaurin is everything that one would envision a perfumer to be. First, he is French. (Of course, there are plenty of perfumers who aren't.) Next, he is a good-looking 30-something with a fondness for expensive watches and chic, masculine designer duds. Most notably, immediately upon encountering him I observed that he effortlessly exudes passion from every pore. His eyes light up when discussing any subject, and his interests are broad and varied. During our interview, he sat behind a desk that was filled with small amber bottles labeled with an army of well-known household product names. By viewing those labels I learned more about the identities of IFF's clients than I had in more than a dozen previous visits and countless interviews at the company. But I shall maintain my vow of confidentiality. I noticed how Gaurin had created an artistic set of origami-like sculptures made from paper scent strips branching upward from the myriad bottles all over his desk. They looked somewhat like a paper flower garden.

After commenting on his paper sculptures, I started by asking him what it takes to get a "nose job." He smiled patiently at my joke and offered his story. Not knowing what he wanted to do after high school (his parents were pushing for economics or business school) he came across an article in *Vogue* about the original perfumer for Chanel. This ignited a fire in him, and from that moment on he knew what he wanted to do. He attended ISIPCAA, the renowned perfumery school in Versailles. He started with IFF in the mid '90s, interning in Hong Kong and eventually winding up in the global headquarters in Manhattan. Born on February 21, he proudly admits his Chinese and Western zodiac signs. "I am a Rooster-Pisces," he stated, continuing, "Some other great perfumers are also Rooster-Pisces. It is a good sign for a nose."

"The first function of a perfumer is to listen," Gaurin revealed, "for our efforts must be relevant to the market." His conjecture was convincing and non-condescending, and I imagined the dynamic that he has with clients. He pontificated on the elements that make up an extraordinary perfume—the all-important first impression of the top notes and the intricacies of blending fragrances. His passion was contagious. I felt as though he could be as animated in talking about lotions or detergents as in discussing fine perfumes.

He doesn't smoke, although I mentioned hearing about perfumers that do. He knows who I am referring to, and suggests that it is not a detriment. The nose's sensitivity may only be affected if a perfumer quits. We talked about the art of perfumery. He looked me in the eye. "I am not specifically an artist, for an artist works without restrictions—without rules," he divulged. "Here, I am a designer—with a plan and parameters that surround the project." After I pressed the subject, he admitted that yes he is an artist at heart, but in his role as a perfumer he is more of a designer—with a blueprint and an objective to reach. He explained the process of perfume creation, and the teamwork and client expectations. He agreed that creating a fragrance is about telling a story and that he is a playwright of sorts. We didn't discuss particular projects, only style.

Asked how he feels about the project managers called evaluators—the designated in-house critics tasked with rating his work—he replied that he feels it is a necessary function and that he takes criticism well, even though these can be intense discussions. He told me that his wife is his best barometer in judging his concoctions. She has no emotional investment in his various projects, and most times doesn't even know what she is sniffing. She just honestly tells him how she feels.

Gaurin surprised me when I ask him how sex smells. "Sex is clean and fresh," he replied. And, yes, there are particular molecules that make up the scent of "clean and fresh." He spoke about perfumes that you smell once and never forget: Polo and Chanel No. 5. We spent a good portion of the interview talking about his admiration for craftsmanship in cinema, photography, and, most of all, watches. He is an avid fan of the Tourbillon style of watch, invented in the late 18th century in France. Where else? The price of these babies ranges from tens to hundreds of thousands of dollars. Although I know that perfumers make top-grade money, I decided not to ask him if he owns one.

In the production of a movie, the director, concept, and script are integral to the success of the film. In the creation of a fragrance, the client, in the role of "director," collaborates with the perfumer, who delivers the initial "script," and then the real work begins.

Quiet on the Set

The next job is to take a diverse cast of "performers" and to meld them seamlessly into a wonderful story that will have audiences returning again and again. In this case, the cast is made up of performers (ingredients) with names like Rose, Lilac, Violet and Jasmine, and even though they are seasoned actors in the theater of fragrance, they need quality direction and a great production crew to pull off a grand performance.

Leading the production crew in the IFF studio is Steve Semoff, vice president and director for technical services at the global headquarters. With a boyish grin and quick-witted delivery, Semoff effortlessly translated the language of chemistry into layman's terms for me. The son of a senior executive in the fragrance industry, his father pulled a few strings while he was high school—got him to leave his job as a lifeguard, and get his feet wet with a summer stint at a flavors company. He found his niche, and continued part time while earning degrees in chemistry and pharmacology. He trained under a man he calls the Zen Master in the field, who basically wrote the book on cosmetic chemistry, Sabbat J. Strianse. After cutting his chops as a bench chemist (a hands-on specialist), Semoff rose through the ranks to become one of the leaders in his field.

Semoff's department is a maze of offices and laboratories filled with bottles and machines. The air only offers a hint of fragrance, despite the nature of the work being performed. Offering me the nickel-tour, he led the charge through the labyrinth, zipping past a slew of bench chemists in various stages of their work. After quite a speedy jaunt, we halted at a massive stainless steel machine, sprouting bundles of thin, opaque hoses, connecting various orifices, girdled by buttons and gauges. "We call this the Monster," he revealed. "We used to call him Elvis, while we were anxiously waiting in anticipation before the thing was delivered. Everyone kept asking, 'Is Elvis in the building yet?' Well, Elvis finally arrived several years ago, and has been a major part of the team ever since.

The Elvis Monster is a finely tuned, automated dosing system that does the work of ten people. Its cloned siblings are housed in IFF's facilities in Holland, France, and New Jersey, where Semoff's counterparts are also based. "The perfumer creates an electronic binary code of the compounds of fragrances and we feed them to Elvis," Semoff quipped. "It is a lot like writing music. But where a piano has 88 keys, we have 2,000 notes to work with." He looked fondly on the machine as he added, "The Monster helps us to do it right the first time." And the machine can play just about any "tune," from the simple fragrance equivalent of Chopsticks to the equivalent of Rachmaninoff's Piano Concerto No. 3 in D-minor. They use it to create samples of new compositions for a variety of trials and tests.

The in-house acronym for Semoff's technical applications group is TAG. Leader of the TAG team is a fitting handle for this 49-year-old who tears up the basketball court two to three times every week. TAG examines the stability of a fragrance under the anticipated conditions of its intended applications. "We ensure that the fragrance scales-up in terms of its odor, color, aspect, and shelf life," he explained.

When I divulged my movie production analogy for scent creation, he asserted, "Yes, we maintain the integrity of the script." He offered his concept that he sees the chemistry beaker as the "center stage" for the "performance" of the fragrance.

Fragrances have to be modified in their various applications, such as soap, detergent, plastic, sprays, and liquids. The job of Semoff's team is to test the fragrances and their performance in their intended applications. For example, the highly popular fragrance of vanilla is difficult in some applications, for it can make a bar of soap turn brown. How the fragrance interacts with the final product, as well as the packaging, are all factors for consideration. When a fragrance's performance doesn't hold up, it goes back to the creative department for "editing" of the "original script," the specific blend of fragrance ingredients that were customized for the project.

Semoff meets every morning with other members of management in what he refers to as the "Breakfast Club." In that meeting of the minds, projects are discussed and resources are assigned. There are three sources from which scents are pulled. First, aromas can be sourced from IFF's massive library of proprietary scents (produced over the years). Second, they may choose to modify an existing aroma. Third, a customized fragrance may be designed. Many of Whiff Solutions' clients use fragrances that come from IFF's library in original or slightly modified form. Others use custom creations.

When Whiff Solutions asked IFF to create samples for Harley Davidson, they included half a dozen fragrances from all three categories, with the smell of gas, chrome, leather, exhaust, and the perfumer's representation of the smell of speed (the rush of the wind on a cool, breezy day). For a large farm equipment manufacturer, we requested samples of fresh cut hay, grass, and pine.

IFF spares no expense or effort to obtain fragrance samples for their massive library. In New Jersey they house over 2,000 fruits, vegetables, and flowers, including more than 750 varieties of orchids. In a state-of-the-art botanical research center, they use modern technology to absorb and record the particles that make up nature's fragrances. They also send their researchers through forests and fields around the globe to hunt and gather new natural aromas for their collection. IFF scientists have created a special pen-like device that can record the molecules emanating from anything with a smell.

When it comes to evaluating the performance of the fragrances and their delivery, Semoff works hand-in-hand with Michael Popplewell, Ph.D., vice president of research and development for IFF. This father of twins is a chemical engineer with a degree in food engineering. He works directly for Chairman Robert M. Amen, and supports both the flavors and the fragrances divisions of the company. R&D, which is heavily funded, constantly delivers new technologies for IFF. They create tools to support the perfumers, as well as the chemists.

The most exciting part of R&D is cooking up new ideas for the delivery of scent. Speaking of cooking, Popplewell admitted that one of his hobbies is performing experiments at home in his kitchen. This becomes perfectly understandable when I find that before landing at IFF, he worked for McCormick & Company, the famous spice manufacturers.

IFF has been working on technological advances in scent delivery media for decades. The list of patents from the last decade alone goes on and on, and includes concepts for diverse subjects like kitty litter, insect repellant, and scented plastic for garbage bags.

Popplewell told me about promising new scent-delivery systems for plastics, textiles, and multi-media. The company has even patented a personal device intended for the home-entertainment and gaming industries. This prototype has personal controls to adjust intensity and volume, which he feels is important in scent delivery—for your neighbor or housemate may not share your preferences.

Back to the TAG team, I talked to Semoff about the glamour involved in his business, and asked if he has worked with many celebrities. "Sure," he said, giving an example of working with Sarah Jessica Parker on her product line "Lovely," which rolled out in 2005. Upon deciding to work with IFF, they first enrolled her in their "Cosmetic Chemistry 101" instruction, and then worked with her daily to create her successful line of perfume, body lotion, and shower gels. The project's success was highlighted when Oprah chose it officially as "One of Oprah's Favorite Things" in 2005, alongside a Burberry purse and Williams-Sonoma croissants.

A Dedicated Storyteller

After spending countless hours examining IFF's well-oiled creative machine, the comparison to moviemaking became more and more natural. Missing, however, are the hype, bravado, and publicity that come with the territory in Hollywood. During the entire interview process in the course of writing this book, the staff I met was more concerned about client confidentiality than the company's notoriety. My handler and gatekeeper, Melissa Sachs in corporate communications, did her best to assist me while maintaining the veil of client identities. Hers is not an easy job, being charged with spreading the word to the world, with a constant caveat of "can't talk about that."

IFF is a heavy player among only a few in the field, positioned with a global presence and a vision of the future of fragrance in the marketplace. We have spoken with other firms prior to writing this book, and have come to realize that their understanding of the big-picture of scent marketing and other non-traditional applications is still in the early stages, yet advancing. Surely other fragrance houses such as Firmenich, Symrise, and the Swiss firm Givaudan are formulating aromas for new fields of endeavor, yet mostly in alliance with fragrance technology suppliers.

We expect the industry to awaken to its full potential, as the explosion of scent communication unfolds and the dollars being invested in it grow. In the meantime, IFF's Brand Emotions™ division, consumer science research, and technological innovations lend it credence and make it well positioned to take the lead in scent communication.

Now that we've equipped you with a better understanding of how this age-old industry plays the game, you might think that you know enough to jump in and play a round or two. But like many others who have come and gone, you might know just enough to be dangerous. With this in mind, we felt that it was our responsibility to offer you the next chapter on what can happen if you, or even the government, take the wrong path on this scented journey.

Chapter 9
Stewardship and Social Responsibility

For all the wonderful feelings and fond memories we conjure up while inhaling aromas each day, we certainly look down on the very thing that gives us access to these subtle pleasures, that amazing instrument that sits squarely in the middle of our faces: the nose.

We speak of the nose as a nuisance, a subject of ridicule and shame. Using derogatory slang, we call it a beak, honker, hooter, nozzle, schnozzle, and snout. We worry that it doesn't fit into society's norms. We feel it's too large, too small, too round, or too red. More and more of us are going under the knife to "fix" it. We make jokes about how it runs in the family: "You can't pick your family . . . but you can always pick your nose!"

We may turn the nose up in pride, look down it in disgust, and stick it into other people's business. We comment about cutting it off to spite the face or threaten to punch it. We can pay through it, lead others by it, and thumb it at authority. We regard others as nosy. We say one person's got a nose for business. We comment that another can't see what's in front of his nose. Whatever the adage, it is clear that we have little respect for this God-given apparatus. That's as plain as the nose on your face.

We are also prone to describe its function in less than positive terms. When we say something smells, we usually don't mean it smells *good*, unless we tag that adjective onto our statement. We can smell trouble and we can smell a rat. When we sniff or take a whiff, it can be in apprehension. When we say something smells, it can mean that it stinks, reeks, or has a malodorous funky redolence. We have positive words for odors, like fragrance or essence, but usually smells are considered guilty until proven innocent.

With all of the bad press the nose and odors have received over time, it is only natural that some may see the glass half-full when it comes to marketing with scent or using scent more prevalently in other ways throughout our culture. What about scent pollution, you may ask? Or what about the people who are super sensitive to smells? These are relevant questions, and here we answer them as best we can.

Scent Abuse

Will the increasing use of scent as a marketing, branding, and signaling tool prove a reason for concern? Will we end up with an environmental cacophony of aromas, much like the noise pollution that we have today? The answer is that it is up to those of us in the industry to use these products responsibly. Certainly, the use of low quality, high concentrations of fragrances could make for a less-than-desirable malodorous way of life. But there is a reason this outcome is highly unlikely to come to pass. If scents were being strategically formulated to create *positive* images of the companies that employ them, it would prove deleterious for these organizations to abuse us with aromas and displease us. Emitting only pleasing scents in very low concentrations is the only viable solution that will prevent a discordant mix of scents from wafting through the air.

With new technologies, despite the best intentions, sometimes you just can't win. The following is an example of a good idea in the wrong place. In December 2006, California's state milk board incorporated Arcade Marketing's MagniScent technology into its "Got Milk?" ad campaign in San Francisco bus shelters.[1] The smell of fresh baked cookies wafted a few inches from the poster-sized billboards. In literally no time at all, there was a public outcry that the homeless were being taunted with intangible cookies. After just one day, city authorities ordered the ads removed, stating officially, allergy concerns. When was the last time you heard of someone being allergic to the smell of cookies? Arcade executives told me that the public outcry ended up being the best advertising they had ever received. Whether or not it was good publicity for milk is unclear. Arcade has no immediate plans to return to San Francisco. The fear of public outrage doesn't stop M&M World from pumping the smell of chocolate into their store in Times Square.[2] Marketing is all about location, location, location.

Cookies and chocolate aside, when marketing with scent, it is recommended to only use small concentrations of universally accepted fragrances, with the goal of enhancing people's moods and triggering pleasant remembrances of things past. It is foolish to employ scents that you suspect might antagonize the receiver. This is why it is imperative to consult with an expert and to commit to using quality aromas in the marketplace.

The truth is that we are already awash daily in aromas, and for the most part we ignore them while subconsciously registering them as good or bad.

As I have consistently asserted, everything smells, from your local convenience store, to the hotel room you stayed in on your last business trip, to your mother-in-law. Nothing is devoid of scent. Therefore the goal of marketing professionals from this point forward should be to take control of this communication instrument in order to present their brands and products in a more strategic manner—without offense. We need to emulate the role that perfumes have always played in our lives: to substantiate our personal image and to produce a strategic impact on those we encounter.

The goal of a brand or service in displaying its scented image should be like a beautiful woman who uses fragrance to speak to her admirers. A little dab here, a little there, not too much, just enough to make the point. There will always be those who abuse the medium, overestimating the dosage and resulting in an image more like an under-dressed harlot strolling the shadows of rue St. Denis. Scent marketers must avoid this mistake at all costs. Less is more. Choose quality over quantity. Conservatism is the rule.

A scented credit card should not permeate the purse, just as aromatic lingerie should not drench the dresser drawer. This is why the technology of microencapsulation is pure genius. It can release scent upon touch and otherwise holds the fragrance in bondage until the user inquires. Just as we do not smell a person until we enter his personal space (unless his hygiene is in question) scented products should not waft their aromas into our personal space unless, by lifting them to our noses, we offer them a gracious invitation. They should not confront or attack us. This is an intimate form of communication. And in intimacy, an aroma must persuade the user, and infuse the senses only when bid.

The same concept should be used for scented spaces. A retail store is a company's personalized space. It is the body on which the company dabs its seductive perfume. The essence should be inviting and alluring, enticing the customer to become the pursuer. It should beckon the visitor into its space without being an affront to the senses. The scent can create its impression at or even below the detection threshold of the customer.

These are the subtle nuances in the art of delivering scent. It is no less complicated than the art of seduction, and neither endeavor should be taken lightly—for obvious reasons. If these measures are ignored, then the process can backfire. Due to scent's capabilities to make an imprint upon the consumer's emotions, a poorly executed scent campaign can result in a negative emotional response, and an ultimate distaste for the product or service that the scent was advertising.

Should we tiptoe around and not use scent for fear of offending? If we can grasp the bigger picture, it behooves us to take our destiny into our own hands, employing a strategic scent in lieu of some enigmatic odor or the lingering smell of stale, manufactured air. As our customers undoubtedly will be judging us on first impressions, we should go to great lengths to make those impressions positive.

Many smells that we encounter throughout the day are undesirable, yet unavoidable: bodily smells from flatulence, sweat, and poor hygiene; the odors of dogs, cats, discarded trash, un-mopped floors, spoiled food, and a host of other redolent items greet us continuously during each waking hour. What do we do when we encounter these smells? We hold our breath and move on when we can, or wait for the air to clear when we can't.

This is the way man has dealt with aromas since the beginning of time. If a smell offends him, he moves along. However, if he cannot escape a smell, the olfactory system adapts so that the odor is no longer registered. This is why a feline-loving homeowner cannot smell the strong odor of cat urine, while a new visitor gags at the stench. The person with smell sensitivities may have an extremely sensitive olfactory system or decreased ability to adapt.

There have been numerous studies on the relationship between personality and olfactory sensitivities. These studies show that an individual's personality-type predisposes the way they process emotional and sensory information. For example, emotionally labile (neurotic and anxious) people are more sensitive and reactive to loud noise, unpleasant visual stimuli, bitter taste, and pain, than calm and stable people.

Research shows that anxious and neurotic people have greater sensitivities to some smells and lowered sensitivities to others. Emotionally labile people can also process smells more rapidly and their attention to that smell is heightened. Odor sensitivity can also be affected by the emotional state of the activity experienced while a person in subjected to a smell.

According to the *Merck Manual of Diagnosis and Treatment* (used by physicians) "Hyperosmia (increased sensitivity to odors) usually reflects a neurotic or histrionic personality, but can also occur intermittently with seizure disorders." This may not be the most tactful reply to someone who complains that he has a heightened sensitivity to smells.

For instance, we recently encountered an email inquiry from a woman who wrote, "As someone with severe chemical sensitivities and…stays often in hotels, I am curious how you advise your clients in the hospitality industry – where scenting lobbies is all the rage…There are very few scents that I can tolerate without getting ill." We responded to this woman in a tactful and respectful manner, explaining that in actuality, she was bombarded by smells throughout each day, and that it only seemed that there were very few scents that she could tolerate without getting ill.

Given the fact that we humans can identify around 10,000 smells, and that we would be at a loss without our ability to smell them, it only seems like we have a low tolerance. We cited the extremely low ratio of complaints in the scent marketing industry. And we explained to her that we felt that it was the duty of hoteliers to effectively manage the smell of their environments in lieu of allowing less pleasant smells to permeate their lobbies as well as their guestrooms.

There are indeed some people who react negatively to certain scents, usually the by-product of a prior emotional experience. It is our duty to know the science and potential emotional reactions to the scents that we employ, and to commit to the use of only high quality, universally accepted, emotionally pleasing scents.

Whatever the reason, there are those who are sensitive, and we must be respectful in how we approach them. From my perspective, that is a social and ethical obligation.

Safety in Numbers

Luckily for us, the fragrance industry has been dealing with issues of chemical sensitivity for many years. A host of ongoing checks and balances have been established in order to minimize and, whenever possible, eradicate the use of any fragrant substances that may be considered unsafe. The International Fragrance Association (IFRA) establishes stringent standards for the industry, collected through scientific data in the field. They publish a Code of Practice manual that is considered by over 2,000 companies worldwide to be the fragrance bible. These standards for product safety are based upon recommendations of another organization called the Research Institute for Fragrance Materials (RIFM). RIFM's research and recommendations are made from evaluations by a distinguished panel of toxicologists, pharmacologists, and dermatologists who have no biased commercial ties to the fragrance industry. The Code of Practice Manual is continually being updated and distributed by IFRA as research unfolds.

One man who follows this Code of Practice to a tee is Paul Pieschl,

Director of Global Product Integrity and Research Perfumery for IFF. Pieschl started his career as a perfumer, but after earning a chemistry degree, it was clear he was bound for more than just a creative job. Both left-brained and right-brained (a rare combination), his job is to integrate the large amount of evolving data and IFRA's recommendations into IFF's products. He speaks easily in terms of chemicals, substrates, and similar jargon, and describes how his team responds in real-time to safety product data.

Immediately upon learning of an ingredient as a possible allergen, his team goes to work to find a substitute that can be used. When I interviewed him, he spoke with pride of his team's expertise and ability to adapt to any new information. He takes his work seriously, even though he calls himself a "Jersey guy" with a bent for muscle cars and big game hunting.

In our conversation I asked Pieschl his opinion on the safety of airborne scents. He replied that there are myriad fragrances that are completely safe for use, but you must have the expertise to know which are safe and which are unsafe. He says that he has many more issues with products that are spread on the skin than sprayed into the air.

I also asked how smaller fragrance houses, without the resources of a global scent creator such as IFF can keep up with the barrage of information and standards put out by IFRA. He shied away from commenting, but the tone of his voice spoke volumes to me. I inferred that he believes the smaller competition has it tough.

As far as overall safety measures, IFRA and RIFM are only part of the fragrance industry's compliance protocols. In the U.S., manufacture and sale of some scented products may be subject to regulation by the Food and Drug Administration (FDA), the Department of Agriculture, the Bureau of Alcohol, Tobacco and Firearms (ATF), the Environmental Protection Agency (EPA), the Occupational Safety and Health Administration (OSHA), and the Drug Enforcement Administration (DEA). According to IFF's annual report, the company's projected expenditures for compliance to these regulations in 2006 were over $20 million.

We discussed how too much of anything can be harmful, and he commented that a lot of the standards and practices in use today are the result of testing done years ago at higher than average concentrations. So he considers that this testing resulted in some ingredients being pulled from the market that most likely would be quite safe at lower concentrations. Critics of the cosmetics industry contend that after years of use, the toxic load from chemicals builds up in the human body. We discussed how just about any product can be abused, commenting on one recent death from the overuse of methyl salicylate, an ingredient used in pain alleviating muscle creams that is also found in Wint-O-Green Life Savers. In theory, Life Savers could kill you if you ate enough of them. The key to using any product and fragrance ingredient wisely is moderation.

Complaints about fragrances are not as common as you might think. There have been relatively few lawsuits over environmental fragrance use, and more pertaining to the overuse of perfume by employees in the workplace. According to the Fragrance Materials Association, the data from an FDA reporting program that was in operation for about five years showed that complaints about fragrance ingredients ran at less than one in a million, which is considerably lower than many other FDA regulated ingredients.[3]

Where There's Smoke There's Fire

Not all scent research and technology has been used for the ultimate good of the public. Eight billion-dollar R.J. Reynolds Tobacco Company, maker of a third of cigarettes sold in the U.S., has at least tested emerging scent technologies in the past, according to a 1986 in-house report entitled "Technology Development and Cigarette Design Product Test Information." This innocuous-sounding document spotlights the testing of microencapsulated scent in order to "develop cigarettes which addressed identified social acceptability of smokers," according to the stated objective on the report. This is proof that, yes, over two decades ago, big tobacco was battling the "social-acceptability" question raised by the campaigns of anti-smoking activists.

Understanding the positive consumer reactions to vanilla, R.J. Reynolds was experimenting with encapsulating the popular essence in the glue of the cigarette paper seam, in order to enhance the smell of the smoke lingering in the room, so as to alleviate its offensiveness to others. In the ensuing years, most of the tobacco companies were accused of marketing to under-aged consumers, describing their smokes with candy-sounding names and flavors.

This controversy prompted R.J. Reynolds to place a statement on its website, articulating their official policy regarding teenage smokers. The company asserted its rights to free speech and the ability to compete by communicating its products' differences to adult smokers, while "preventing unintended perceptions surrounding 'flavored' cigarettes." With this disclaimer, the company then offered a voluntary promise to restrict their advertising language, not to target children, and to ban the use of graphic depictions of candy, as well as the words chocolate, cocoa, mocha, vanilla, honey, cinnamon, licorice, and many more. Score one for the public.

Another public health tragedy has resulted from a boom of scented plug-in air fresheners and fragrant candles. Tragic deaths by fire have been on the upsurge. Fire deaths caused by candles saw a 750 percent increase over the same two-decade period as the scented candle boom. Candle fires have tripled since 1990 and were responsible for 18,000 home fires in 2002, causing at least 130 deaths, 1,350 civilian fire injuries, and a third of a trillion dollars in damages. Actual numbers of fires caused by plug-ins could not be obtained, as these have been melded in with other products designated as appliances.

The lesson from this epidemic of accidents and horrific loss of life is that open flames and humans (and cheap electrical appliances) are a recipe for disaster. This is evidence enough to advocate for the use of an alternative to candles as a means of scent delivery both in the home and elsewhere. For every hour of every day in the U.S. alone, candles start two home-fires. By the time you complete your work day, 16 home candle fires will have injured at least two or three people, and have caused one third of a million dollars in damage. And these statistics are only for 5 percent of the world's population. Imagine how many thousands of deaths this candle craze has caused. Scented candles may make us feel good (and we may be drawn to their flame), but perhaps we can convert our consumer desires to safer and more sophisticated scent diffusion technologies, and save countless lives in the process.

Science Fact or Science Fiction?

By spring 2007, the U.S. military had placed over 5,000 robots in Iraq and Afghanistan to search caves and buildings for insurgents, detect mines, and ferret out roadside bombs.[4] Most of these robots were used to defuse or to detonate bombs, some with video camera eyes, fitted to explore dark and hard to access spaces. But the amazing thing was that, these high-tech gizmos were not actually equipped to sniff out the bombs. We certainly had the technology, having used it in U.S. airports for several years, but where it really counted, on the front, we were impotent when it came to bomb-sensing technology. Then the military scarecrow finally found his brain, and the government ordered up a new army of what are called Fido robots. Someone must have picked up Isaac Asimov's book *I, Robot*, and then called on iRobot Corp, a big government supplier, to send over some robotic scent-sniffing hounds—four years and thousands of lives lost into the war.

Fido is a 52-pound bomb-sniffing robot with rubber treads, lights, zooming video cameras, flippers, and seven-foot long, jointed manipulator arms designed to disable and destroy bombs under cars and in hard to reach places. The mechanical dog costs $165,000, and the military has budgeted $1.7 billion over the next five-years for a legion-sized pack of the metal mongrels.[5]

Author-screenwriter Michael Crichton created "sniffer robots" for his 1984 movie *Runaway*.[6] These four-legged sniffing machines assisted police detectives in solving crimes. In reality, some governments have already started collecting the scent of criminals and would-be troublemakers, and are amassing a database of signature scents. Soon we may see a perpetrator being identified by the unique scent he left at the scene of the crime, much like DNA is used today. Each of us leaves a scented dead-skin-cell trail wherever we go, and it is only a matter of time before our smell can be used against us.

With *Star Trek*-like sensor devices (also see Chapter 1, "The Nose Knows"), government authorities will soon have the ability to collect personal scents just by zapping the headspace or environment around a person. As technology becomes more advanced, it is just a matter of time before we will be able to identify a person's unique signature scent and place it into the public record or a sealed medical record.

Does this ability foreshadow a potentially ominous future in scent detection? In 2007, during the Group of Eight (G8) Summit of industrialized nations in Germany, police collected the personalized scent samples of suspected troublemakers.[7] As a Reuters article pointed out, it was a move reminiscent of how back in the Cold War days of divided Germany, the East German secret police, the Stasi, would collect scent samples of various people on yellow cloths and store them in pickle jars to be used as needed for scent sniffing hounds.

A Central Intelligence Agency (CIA) document declassified in 1993 offers a whiff of where this technology is headed. In a paper by Spencer Tebrich, entitled "Human Scent and its Detection," the author details the various qualities of human scent and how dogs detect these unique signatures. An excerpt from the document reads:

"Once we have identified the medium of human scent . . . it seems reasonable to suppose that we shall also find the mechanical means to improve on animal olfactory capabilities, and not only detect but to record the otherwise unknown presence of an individual. Our mechanical dog, when he is born, should be much more unobtrusive than his ancestor, should be able to tell us just whom he has smelled, and should maintain a reliable permanent record of his visitors."[8]

This CIA paper is not dated, but it was written between 1955 and 1992. Since that time period, technology has made leaps and bounds into the business of detection. Equipment can capture the volatile chemicals of a human being, and can also capture and sequence our amino acid signatures. Organizations are now working on further advances, and no doubt will soon have the ability to collect and store a person's scent signature.

One such organization is the Defense Advanced Research Projects Agency (DARPA), the U.S. Department of Defense's primary agency for research and development. The "Unique Signature Detection Project," formerly known as the "Odortype Detection Program," is designed to help identify terrorists based upon the scents they secrete. According to *Seed* magazine, one DARPA spokesperson stated that it could be used "to identify and distinguish specific 'high-level-of-interest individuals' within groups of enemy troops or combatants." Gary Beauchamp, director of the Monell Chemical Senses Center and a researcher on the DARPA-funded project told *Seed*, "Even after leaving the scene of a crime, a terrorist's scent could spread over a large distance and linger for a considerable time."[9]

The program was funded to the tune of $15 million in 2007, and with its staff working on the development of a technology, military scent detection certainly seems imminent. And as these types of technologies are developed, the implications could be astounding. With the growing marvel of aroma sensor technology, like bomb and drug detection equipment, we will eventually be able to authenticate and certify the scent identity of a person with the mere whiff of a machine. This technology has no bounds in what can only be a dramatic shift in forensic science and eventually identity recognition. As with all of our government's high-minded programs and stated good intentions, they could also lead down an Orwellian road to where ice water and cool air are at a premium.

Think about it. If a mass database registry were to be organized, and the scent collected from every one of the over two million incarcerated convicts in the U.S. alone, the authorities could pick up the trail even after it has run cold, much like a keenly sensitive hound. The average human sheds at least 40,000 dead skins cells per minute,[10] leaving an invisible trail of miniature breadcrumbs for the future scent-sensing robotic hounds.

DNA evidence could end up a thing of the past if police were equipped with scent collection sensors to zap the scene of a crime, and slyly pick up someone's scent signature without evasive measures—just a zap in the air of their personal space.

Some security companies are taking this concept even further, realizing that thumbprints, eye scans, and other methods may be made obsolete with a scent scan—an organic signature that cannot be duplicated. If these aromas are collected for means of employee identification, an additional massive non-criminal database could be created, and eventually scent could become the standard ID for everyone.

If a children's scent registry were made available, parents could register their children on a national database, making for an interesting means of identifying missing or runaway children. The key would be to place scent detectors in public spaces, like schools and children's hangouts, verifying the children's status, and updating their whereabouts on the database. When a child is reported absent, the database computers would identify their last reported location, and be on the lookout for the missing child. The trouble is that children grow up. As adults, how many of us want Big Brother picking up our scent wherever we go? We will need to tackle significant privacy issues as this new technology emerges.

We could become a society that readily grasps the scent identity concept, as millions of us now become victims of identity theft every year. It might be welcome news that instead of passwords or documents, in the near future we may just have to hold out our hand for a scent scan. Scent ID may be ordered to accompany driver's licenses and passports. Scent detectors could end up being placed everywhere, in restrooms, stadiums, malls, at the checkout stand, and anywhere that verification of ID is necessary.

This amazing new technology has its definite upside, but it can also be a bit scary to contemplate what might happen if it were taken to an extreme by a totalitarian regime. Think of a world where you are constantly being identified, with no alternative available, a world where your unique organic scent is continually being fed into a giant database of personal information. You would have no way to ever alter this information and you would also have no idea exactly what information was being accumulated. This scenario, with its legal and ethical repercussions, adds to questions about our private information being maintained by credit card, utility, and healthcare companies, with possibilities of it being bought, sold, traded, or stolen: Who has access to our health and financial records? How secure are they? And, of course, if the use of scent identification became widespread, the challenges to our privacy would be vastly magnified.

Scent detectors can reveal much more about you than you might wish to divulge. Already your scent can betray some ethnic characteristics, indicate whether you are menstruating, whether you have been drinking, or if you have some forms of cancer. In the future, we will certainly keep adding to our scent diagnostic capabilities. Would you care if your employer had this sort of information? How about your government?

Now consider another recent technology, RFIDs. RFIDs are being embedded into most of the products that you buy, storing information and zapping it back to whomever has an RFID sensor gun. They are widely used to track retail products, everything from your shoes to your purse and your cell phone may have an RFID implanted in it. These microchip-based, RFIDs can hold all sorts of personal information about you, such as health records, purchasing records, credit history, criminal records, and just about any other pertinent information. They can track and hold your behaviors and history.

In the future, any RFID-embedded product might be accessed to obtain your personal records, while a scent detector authenticates your identity. As these methods become mainstream, they could ultimately be used against ordinary, law-abiding civilians.

With just a little imagination, if we look to the future we can see how these technologies could be used to limit our liberties and God-given rights. Do we really want to live in a society where we are tracked everywhere we go? Are we prepared to become citizens of a Big Brother society that no longer affords us the ability to maintain our anonymity? Are our children prepared for a future with no semblance of privacy, where every behavior is recorded and tracked by hidden sensors without our knowledge?

In this post 9/11 era, our personal privacy is not as it once was. The constitutional rights that were forged on the battlefields and in the courtrooms by our forefathers are being eroded. While advances in technology can facilitate rapid changes, unfortunately, in the hands of a cavalier, power-obsessed, fanatical bureaucrat with misguided intentions, these changes can have damaging results. Consider the current law allowing our emails to be monitored and our phones to be tapped at the whim of a suspicious official.

But we live in a world of constantly emerging and evolving technologies, and are subject to the potential abuse of its powers. We should be cautious about how we employ these new technologies, and do everything we can to insure that they are not used to shackle, control, or abuse us.

We Are the Stewards of the Earth

The ancient Egyptians felt that they were collecting the soul of a plant when they extracted its essence. It is my belief that they felt that their own personal scent was also the embodiment of their soul, their Ka, also called the life force. Why would they think any differently when comparing the plant's life force with their own?

They believed that the Ka was sustained through food and drink. And we all know that our scent is innately related to what we put into our bodies. They also thought that the Ka was passed on through the father's semen. Was that a result of their observations of the obvious smell of the semen? Did they equate that the noticeable, pungent, fragrance that pervades an adult male, his seed, and the new human offspring—was actually an invisible beacon of the Ka life force or human soul? Possibly.

Regardless of the reasons why all living things have their own signature scents, it is a fact to be recognized and addressed as we enter into this next stage of the information age. The enigmatic wonders of scent have much yet to reveal. We give them so little thought in our lives. As little thought as we give to the unseen marvels that assure the breaths that we take, the beat of our hearts, and the miraculous healing that we expect and demand when we cut ourselves. There are so many miracles that happen in our lives, and we ignore their magnificence. Yet, as science slowly peels away these perplexities, and brings them to light for inspection, it is up to us to use the information wisely—to breathe in a whiff of the wonders and secrets of this ancient language of scent as it transforms the world in which we live.

You might think that all of this Egyptian Ka talk might be a little bit corny, but I am merely stressing the point of how important it is to take your role in this scented journey seriously. Now that you know about scent's powers and its players, and the possible pitfalls, I think that it's about time that you learn how to play the game.

Part Three

How to Play the Game

If you don't mind smelling like peanut butter for two or three days, peanut butter is darn good shaving cream.

—Barry Goldwater

By this point you may be wondering how to incorporate scent into your marketing plans to boost the emotional impact of your brand or product. Well, why not learn it from the big guys? There are many organizations that have already designed signature scents to match the preferences and perceptions of their target customers, and they are now expanding their scent strategies to include marketing collateral, scent-embedded products, packaging, and various advertising mediums. And in this section, we're going to show you how you can do the same.

Imagine the effects of a Starbucks gift card enhanced with the aroma of a rich coffee blend. Think of a Godiva gift certificate, laden with the constant provocation of a dark chocolate scent. Envision a Home Depot credit card laced with the fragrance of cedar, or an Outback Steakhouse gift certificate wafting up the spicy aroma of its famous blooming onion. These marketing items are no longer *mere* transactional tools. Now they also serve as marketing triggers, by tripping emotional wires in the brain, inducing fond memories, and activating and eliciting desired responses in the mind and body. Stirring up an emotional response with scent can strengthen the bonds of brand loyalty.

Most people are creatures of tradition. I drank Maxwell House coffee for most of my life, as my parents did. It took a long stay in Europe to realize that I actually had a choice over quality coffee beans. Sales of cars, detergents, retail stores, lawnmowers, and power tools benefit from loyalty and tradition. When I opened a regional branch of Wizard Studios in Puerto Rico, I learned a lot about the strength and importance of tradition.

In our event business we always used Makita or Bosch power tools. My U.S. crews overwhelmingly voted these to be the most durable on the market. Yes, we could burn them out with exhaustive use, so we bought them by the case, but they were the "best product," according to our experience. Yet, while equipping my new crews in Puerto Rico, I discovered that they absolutely refused to use Makitas and insisted on Black & Decker. In our industry, Black & Decker was better known for consumer use. But I couldn't argue with the brand loyalty that my crews had with Black & Decker—or with Sears branded products. These island roadie natives had a long-standing tradition with these two brands, and these were the brands of their friends and their fathers.

Big brands come with longstanding traditions. If we have been using a Nokia phone, we are likely to buy another. If we are used to one operating system, we want to stay with it despite the computer. If we think that we look good in a certain designer's duds, we continue to buy them because we believe she understands our body type and taste. However, this is the multisensory century. This is not our parents' world where all it took to market a product was face-time, impressions and mind-share. There are too many products and too many choices for the consumer of today.

We no longer have to know a lot about our customer, we actually must know him. He has to look at our brand not as a choice amongst others, but as a personality and a possible friend, one with whom there is a possibility of having an enduring relationship. The idea is to intrigue your customer with your character and story, and to do this, you need to view your branding strategies as a performance. You are in the business of entertainment. Are you looking for a long-running series of command performances or a one-night stand?

Chapter 10
What's Your Whiff Factor?

You could have the most amazing product that the world has ever seen—even better than sliced bread or the little blue pill—yet if you fail to tell others about it, or fail to communicate its features and benefits, you most likely will be the proud owner of a fantastic idea that never made it in the marketplace. Accept that you need to have a marketing strategy.

Every person and every business has a brand—an appearance or identity in the world. If you wouldn't think about going around half-dressed, why would you fail to "dress" your brand? Your logo, style, and corporate culture denote who you are to your customers and employees. The elements that display your brand image are evident at every turn in your business. Once you have added the emotional element of a branded signature scent to the mixture, you'll view it as an integral part of the whole package. Where and how you incorporate scenting denotes your Whiff Factor.

Incorporating Your Brand New Scent

The simple fact is that every business has a brand and must advertise its brand, otherwise the brand will be poorly perceived. In the past, when hearing small business owners boast, "I don't advertise," I must admit that I've wondered if this might be the reason that these exclusive entrepreneurs' enterprises have remained small and never realized their full potential. Perhaps they defined advertising differently than I do. So let's clear this matter up. Anyone who stays in business for a reasonable length of time does advertise—we all do—whether it's through word of mouth, promotions, discounts, and product or service trials, or through the more conventional means of print, television, radio, and online ads, brochures, coupons, POP displays, or other avenues.

Marketing is integral to every type of business venture and individual. We market ourselves every day through appearance, demeanor, style, presentation, and responses—and we market our businesses in much the same way. No matter what your profession (doctor, lawyer, furniture manufacturer, real estate agent, or computer repairman) you are marketing your services—for if you aren't, you will soon be among the unemployed. In that case you'll *still* be forced to market, only with a paper cup and a cardboard sign!

With this concept in mind, let's briefly examine several of the many applications where *scent* marketing can make an impact on your efforts. As we work our way outward from the corporate office to the consumer, we'll be identifying strategic areas where your scented brand can make an indelible emotional mark.

The Lobby and the Boardroom

Once you have established your own unique branded signature scent for your business, products or services, it is only logical that you create a complete scent script for the entire brand experience. Just as you script your receptionist's phone responses for initial verbal contact with your customers, and put no small effort into designing the visual aesthetics of your waiting room or lobby—assuring a good first impression from visitors—it is equally important that the first impression of your brand be simultaneously imprinted with a scented communiqué.

Let's assume that after a short tour of the various offices and divisions in your business, you accompany your clients into the boardroom for your presentation and ultimate pitch. Wouldn't it make sense to touch the emotions of your clients with the pleasing waft of your scent while appealing to their judgment and decision making process?

Furthermore, clients aren't the only benefactors of your company's scent, for brand loyalty can be imprinted upon employees, suppliers, and partners during the run of ordinary business, or during strategic negotiations while seated in the boardroom.

In the Field

In most organizations, only the biggest clients visit the home office. Remaining business is done in the field. Sales representatives are equipped with collateral: business cards, brochures, product sheets, catalogues, and sample kits. Although it is up to the human resources department and designated trainers to select the quality of personnel that represent your brand, you can enhance your sales reps' presentations by equipping them with a signature-scented collection of marketing media. The technology exists to scent all kinds of printed materials, including plastics.

The business card is the ultimate statement of credibility for a salesperson. Usually it is the first symbol of a company that a potential client encounters after a hello and a handshake, thus making it an important medium through which you can communicate your brand. Scented business cards are a natural opportunity to mold the perception you intend your customer to develop. It is an unequivocal ally for your troops in the field.

Scent marketing will be distributed through all series of marketing paraphernalia. Accoutrements of business like sales brochures, letterhead, catalogues, product data sheets, white papers, and other printed information should also be branded with your organization's signature scent.

Why would you go to the trouble of scenting marketing collateral? Because, as it sits submerged within endless stacks of other paper and brochures, the scent's strategic nimble legs and wafting tendrils will be much more difficult to ignore.

This strategic style of branding covers every category of promotional item. Pens, key chains, calendars, bookmarks, cigar cutters, hats, tee shirts, and golf balls, and the entire promotional product inventory can be scented. Through them, a symbol of the emotional bond now sits upon the customer's desk, as well as in his pocket; a subtle scented reminder that returns his focus to your brand. As these items lay in your client's cluttered office, they will be calling out for attention, and speaking to the client's emotions and perceptions. These same items may make it into your client's pocket, home, or even onto the golf course.

Wouldn't it be nice to know that your clients think about you on their days off?

In the Consumer's Home

Today most consumers learn of products and services from the comfort of their La-Z-Boys or while surfing the Web on a home computer. Although televisions, computers, and musical devices are only slowly catching on to the power of delivering scented messages, there are many other avenues through which you can deliver your scented brand to their doorsteps: magazines, newspapers, and coupons, for instance. Perfumers have long been using scented advertising in magazines to offer potential customers a whiff of their products. Now other businesses are also taking the plunge by incorporating microencapsulated scents into their magazine ads. These ads release scent when touched. More and more printers and publishers are embracing this trend.

Newspapers have been primed for scent marketing. Advertisements that morning readers once may have overlooked, can now call out from the page—demanding attention wherever they may be placed. Scented "advertorials" and vanity articles can now move up the ladder to the ranks of the examined. They have 136 percent more chance of being read, instead of only being afforded a passing glance.

As print circulation has stumbled and declined, newspaper publishers may find their own reasons to add aromas to their marketing efforts. Wouldn't it be interesting if readers looked forward to the Wednesday food section, not just to search out the latest recipes, but also to take a little whiff of the week's selected dish? The travel section could be complemented with a scent from any chosen destination. And any pleasant smelling aroma should be able to offer a lift to the ever dismal and shrinking classified section. Here's a question to ponder in the editorial room: What should your op-ed page smell like? In fact, what do politics smell like . . . really?

Just a few more ideas on collaborative print advertising: *Sports Illustrated* swimsuit edition—tanning oil; *Car and Driver*—leather, rubber, and race car oil, *Condé Nast Traveler*—aromas reminiscent of specific destinations, like Greece, Bermuda, and the Yucatan Peninsula. Any publication could increase its presence on the news-stand by making a collaborative effort with its advertisers. This spectacular form of advertising can have consumers picking up your latest issue just to check out the scent.

The local yellow pages could offer more than block ads, red print, and tenured placement, for the owner of a corner pizzeria might be willing to increase his odds of attracting customers by taking out a scented ad. Other types of local businesses that could benefit from scented ads are lawn services, auto dealerships, dry cleaners, swim-ming pool companies, and plumbing services, which could all get a boost while their customers' fingers are doing the walking.

The final goldmine of in-home advertising lies a few feet outside the door, at the mailbox. Direct mail is big business and it doesn't seem to be going away any time soon. One of the leading American suppliers in this business, Valpak Direct Marketing Systems, which is headquartered in Largo, Florida, mails out more than 20 billion offers in 528 million familiar blue envelopes on behalf of 66,000 advertisers each year.[1] That represents a lot of trees and a lot of business owners. If the calculated rate of redemption could be increased 10, 20, or even 50 percent by the placement of scented ads, it would easily prove to be a great marketing strategy.

Public Spaces

You can undoubtedly attract more attention to your billboards, posters, banners, and outdoor signage if you add aroma to them. Of course, roadside billboards are neither a cost effective, nor efficient way to deliver scent messages to drivers. But you should not ignore areas where pedestrian traffic flows, where smaller billboards, street signs, and banners meet high traffic patterns. Fashion and food advertisements employing a seductive scent strategy can literally stop people in their tracks.

It is important to choose the right method of delivery, perhaps from an embedded scent release system or a machine delivery—you may need expert help to decide—but take note of this application, for it will soon make the grade.

Posters, banners, and outdoor company signage can all become more noticeable by adding an aromatic element. The recent deluge of digital signage in public spaces can expect to engage more consumers with a scented message.

On Premises

Once you have lured consumers to your home turf—the place where they buy your product or experience your service—you can implement your scent strategy through any number of mediums. Aromas can be diffused from POP displays, end cap booths, stand-alone kiosks, aisle displays, digital and conventional signage, and the shelves (from a device placed next to the price sticker or straight out of a coupon dispenser).

Once customers select an item in that particular setting, they can bring it up to your register, present a signature-scented affinity card to receive your club discount, then use your signature-scented credit card to pay for their purchase—and maybe even pick up an equally fragranced gift card for a loved one back home. They could receive a scented receipt—or not. It depends on how emotional you believe they'll become over the bill.

The relative importance of scenting your affinity cards, credit cards, gift cards, and gift certificates lies in the fact that consumers now carry brand messages with them wherever they go. These types of branded items are valued by the customer, carried on his person, or brought into his home. When strategically scented, an affinity card is no longer just a tool for transactions, but carries a subtle message reaching directly into the consumers' brain. It creates a stronger emotional bond between the customer and all of the products that the brand offers.

A card like this is not just a branded piece of plastic planted deep inside someone's purse, but a subtly scented marketing trigger that holds its nose to the grindstone, perpetually working to increase loyalty to your brand and possibly trigger an increase in your sales.

Full Coverage vs. Point of Purchase

No matter what study you read, if an aroma proved to influence consumers in a specific manner, most likely the scenting was seamless. Seamlessness means that there are no gaps in coverage. To brand your environment with a special scent, it makes sense to completely immerse the environment, instead of merely offering a whiff at the front door. You'll need to cover the entire public space.

Be respectful of your patrons. Full immersion does not necessarily mean using a highly noticeable or overbearing fragrance. It merely implies the complete coverage of an area. Your concentration levels need to be adjusted in accordance with the environment in which they are being diffused, otherwise you may cause displeasure. You can deliver a concentration just above or even below the customer's awareness level.

I point out the full coverage factor because many scent delivery systems offer only minimal coverage. For retailers truly wishing to scent their store environments, such technology is insufficient. If you are excited at the potential of increasing the duration of your customers' in-store visits with the appeal of a scented atmosphere, logic dictates that you deliver the essence throughout the store. This is common sense. Would you even think of branding your environment with partial lighting or partial flooring, or by playing music in only select portions of the environment? One would hope not. Full coverage is important when delivering a signature scent intended to represent the store's brand.

For regional or localized scenting to trigger specific effects, you need only create a seamless atmosphere within that locality. If you seek to scent a POP display, or one specific department, or an enclosed environment, a lower coverage delivery system would be adequate for your needs.

Scented Packaging

The next element of branding lies in product packaging and in the products themselves. The brand can be offered in a seamless fashion throughout all aspects of a company's messaging. The packaging and print may be laced with a branded scent, or an aroma may be released as the package is opened. The product itself will then continue the branding script, with microcapsules of scent embedded on the surface.

Large food companies are jumping into the olfactory-packaging field. Soon you will be able to scratch and sniff the outside of a bottle of barbeque sauce to get a whiff of the contents. From cookies and sweets to sauces and soups, scented packaging is in its infancy. It's truly amazing that the results of millions of dollars of research spent in perfecting flavors and fragrances for food products over the years remains bottled up inside the package upon the store shelf—and only realized once the product is finally purchased and taken home. The new paradigm in marketing is to offer a little teaser of the product, enticing the buyer with fragrant packaging.

Scented packaging is not merely the territory of food and beverage products. Consumers have been opening shampoo bottles and dish detergent containers in the aisles of stores for many years to take a whiff. This new marketing paradigm will extend to toothpaste, personal care products, dog food, and virtually every corner of the supermarket. The manufacturer now has an opportunity to show its wares and tell its story—relating directly to the consumer's emotions—right from the shelf.

An entire spectrum of product packaging is in its infancy. One day we may open up our new computer, DVD player, video game, lawnmower, barbecue grill, or linens, and receive a pleasant scent of the brand that lies inside. It's easy to imagine smells that could be used effectively to brand a barbecue grill, lawnmower or linens, but it will take a bit more brand strategizing for Apple, Dell, and other electronics suppliers to develop a scent.

On the Road—Tradeshows, Freestanding Exhibits, and Product Launches

The final frontier of your scent marketing strategy lies wherever your brand travels, in the community and at industry events. Traveling road shows, trade shows, product reveals and launches, and even shareholder meetings should be taken into consideration as a part of your full multisensory brand strategy. Whenever your logo appears, the environment should look, sound, and *smell* like your brand. Once you have entered the scent dimension, it is imperative to continue reinforcing the brand experience at every level and through every possible medium.

Conventions are ripe opportunities for scent branding. There is no better way of capturing the attention of a multitude of distracted attendees, than to waft a pleasant scent into the air, beckoning individual brains to pay attention to the product before they ever actually encounter it. At one trade show event, Whiff Solutions displayed its services to a group of over 15,000 attendees.[2] We released a rich, flavorful aroma called "Chocolate Addiction" into the environment that radiated outward more than 100 yards. You can imagine the attention generated as the attendees followed their noses to the booth. For three days, we experienced hordes of inquisitors, two and three deep, first attracted by scent, then captivated by the idea. Of course we expected this response, and therefore we rewarded our guests with a rich array of foil wrapped chocolates. Our purpose was simply to demonstrate how well scent marketing works, even though we used a desire trigger as a simple solution.

The idea is not new. Trade show marketers have been using less effective desire triggers for years: promotional giveaways, pretty models, magicians, and entertainers. The difference in this case is that we were communicating with our potential clients' emotions long before they ever spotted us, knew who we were, or what we had to offer. And when we followed up on the event the following week by telephone, we soon found out that our potential clients now called us the "chocolate guys."

Branded signature scents, thematic aromas, or any pleasant fragrance can be used to grab attention. Desire triggers are appropriate in some circumstances, but you can immediately see how it might get tricky at the National Restaurant Show or anywhere else that you're competing with a multitude of aromas. The evidence shows that scenting your exhibit will be more effective at capturing attention than many other methods, and can really boost visits if your booth is positioned in a low traffic area.

Sponsored sporting events, industry trade shows, and promotional events should be scented with your brand aroma. A popular promotional technique that's prevalent in the liquor industry may also work for you. Promotional companies are hired to send attractive young women to nightclubs in order to promote new liquors. Many of the trendiest spirits are concocted with an essence of fruity flavors, such as raspberry, lime, lemon, and even pepper. Since the essence of vodka or gin is not an attractive scent for many people, it makes perfect sense to diffuse a fruity aroma into the air. Emotionally the consumer learns to equate the signature scent and attractive women with the product.

Think back to the concept of endorphin branding that was proposed in Chapter 2, "Nostalgia, Mood, and Desire." By presenting your brand scent in combination with the adrenaline rush of a sporting event, thrill ride, or adventure, consumers will be imprinted with a full-blown memory of surprise, excitement, and joy, which will be recalled every single time they smell your brand's signature aroma.

The key to all promotions is actually to "promote" your product: to get it noticed, to get it sampled. And the trick to being noticed in a hustling-bustling atmosphere is to take an approach that will appeal directly to the consumer's brain.

Identifying Your Whiff Factor

Most of the branding, marketing, and advertising scent applications I have just described could be adapted easily to many business models. Whether your business has a hundred thousand employees or three dedicated workers, you most likely use several of the basic elements already in your marketing strategy. The integration of scent into your already successful marketing plan is relatively simple and one of the most cost effective marketing tools. And as industry leaders increase their appetite for results-oriented scent marketing, the costs of entering the scent dimension will become even more affordable.

The first step in creating an integrated marketing plan for your scent strategy is to identify your present Whiff Factor, the quantifiable percentage of your organization's marketing activities in which scent is *presently* being employed. Take the following brief quiz to determine your company's Whiff Factor.

What's Your Whiff Factor? —A Quiz

Instructions: Consider the ten factors below. Check the box to the left of any item that you currently employ in your business.

- ☐ Marketing collateral (business cards/stationary/brochures)
- ☐ Promotional items
- ☐ Promotional events
- ☐ Affinity cards/credit cards
- ☐ Gift certificates/redemption programs
- ☐ Print advertising/banners/signage
- ☐ Point of Purchase displays/in-store displays/digital signage
- ☐ Product manufacturing
- ☐ Product packaging
- ☐ Environments (retail space/offices/waiting rooms/exteriors)

Scoring: Each element in the Whiff Factor checklist has a value of 10 percent. Therefore if you are employing scent marketing only in the environment and in product manufacturing (think Starbucks), then you are literally only utilizing 20 percent of your full scent branding potential. That 20 percent may very well be the impetus for a good amount of revenue, but imagine the increase in sales if you raised the bar to 50 percent.

If yours is like a majority of companies, you may have checked off only one or two boxes, or even more likely, none at all. Yet, as the tremendous benefits of scent marketing are realized in the business environment, we will see these individual strategic marketing elements begin to take hold and eventually become a standard in industry.

Return to the checklist and identify the elements that could most easily be implemented into your present marketing strategies—with a goal of reaching a Whiff Factor of at least 50 percent. These are the areas you should discuss with a scent marketing professional.

Realize that the quality of scent and the efficiency of a delivery system can highly affect the outcomes. Therefore your initial efforts in laying the foundation for scent marketing must be diligent and well conceived. As you begin to employ scent tactics, it is highly recommended to run trials where you can measure their individual impact on business. We'll talk about these and other important considerations in the next chapter, "Four Keys to Creating Your Scent Script."

Chapter 11
Four Keys to Creating Your Scent Script

Many small business owners don't understand the basics of branding, with or without mixing in the scent dimension. For example, they set up shop or create a product without much consideration for aesthetics, by opening a diner and choosing to put harsh fluorescent lighting overhead, or blaring music so loudly throughout the establishment that nobody can carry on a conversation. If you've ever sat in a booth that was uncomfortable or enjoyed a great meal and then found the restroom to be filthy, you know what I am talking about. Little wonder that 56 percent of businesses don't survive past their fourth year, even after putting no small effort and substantial dollars into their creation.[1]

The branding of any business, like a theater production, takes place in a multisensory environment. Lights, sets, and sound—and even the audience seats and the beverages at intermission—are all part of staging a play. Unarguably, these elements must be carefully constructed or strategically managed. When you try to put on a show without having all of the elements in place, it is much more difficult to impress the audience and get them to buy in to the story you want to tell. When you attend a theatrical production that involves cheap props, dim lighting, and poor sound, you don't expect much from the performance. How much better would the same show be if it had a great stage and high quality production values? How much better would your brand be?

In reality, when marketing your product, service, or brand you're scripting and staging it. And you need to evaluate how well the stage is set for you to tell your story. You may have a well-performing product, but sales could be lagging due to your lack of diligence in setting the stage with multisensory designs for your product, packaging, and service. If you already have a product that is a star performer, how much additional revenue are you missing with the absence of these important elements? What are you doing in order to elicit a strong, positive, emotional response from customers?

The specific keys to branding with scent are to know the exact message that you are attempting to communicate about who you are (your brand identity), the habits and interests of the people with whom you are attempting to communicate (your target consumers), and the response that you desire to trigger in them (an experience). Once these elements have been thoroughly considered and are clearly defined, then you're ready to choose a signature fragrance and put it into service through an integrated plan (your scent script). We'll explore all four elements of branding a scent in this chapter.

Of course, there are other uses of scent for marketing that are not branding *per se*. Branded signature scents are merely one type and use of aromas. You can also strategically utilize selective aromas to trigger nostalgia or cravings, elevate mood, create a relaxed atmosphere, or to influence the perception of a particular product, service, or environment. Selective scents may be incorporated into your overall signature brand or be deployed within the areas of an environment to delineate separate product categories. Understand that even when you use scent in one spot, one time, the four keys apply.

In a retail environment where all the products are similar in nature, such as an electronics store, a jewelry boutique, or a car dealership, a branded signature scent would be more preferable. However, in a department store or a grocery store, where products differ from aisle to aisle, section to section, or department to department, you may wish to deploy a variety of aromas, matching the scents in each area of the retail environment to the products displayed there or to the demographics of the consumers that shop there. In a store like Wal-Mart, for example, you might scent the home repair area differently than the pharmacy or women's apparel area. In a supermarket, the baked goods aisle should smell different than the aisle for pasta sauces. Selective uses for scent will be touched upon here, and covered in greater detail in Part Four, "Winning Strategies for a New Century."

Your ultimate choice of scent can be reached by means of a testing process, by employing the aroma that generates the best sales during a trial period. You may also make your scent design choices by the feelings or inferences that they invoke, as you would with the architectural design elements, such as flooring, lighting, and displays, and the ambient music. Whatever the decision you make regarding the scent of your environment, realize that no decision is an absolute decision in itself—and here's an example of what I am talking about.

Naturally Occurring Signature Scents

When I was a teenager, my parents fulfilled a lifelong dream after moving to Florida in the 1970s. They bought a small bait and tackle shop on the beach that also carried souvenirs, beach accessories, jewelry, and ice cream. The whole family worked in the store. The shop had a large water tank in the back filled with live shrimp, a necessity for avid local and visiting fishermen. (Smelly frozen squid were kept in a freezer and only brought out upon request.) After buying the business, we quickly learned that a given number of bait shrimp would meet their maker during the night. This was a fact of doing business with the little crustaceans. Upon opening the doors in the morning we could tell how severe the loss was, for a whiff of smelly, dead shrimp would meet us at the door. In the bait tank, the healthy shrimp displayed their translucent forms, while the dead shrimp littered the water with their lifeless pink bodies. Hence our family's memorable adage: The more the pink, the more the stink.

We spent time each morning dedicated to boxing the dead carcasses into white cardboard Chinese carryout containers, thus converting the losses into profitable frozen bait. Then we took out oversized fans, which we used to blow the nasty smell onto the sidewalk, as we brewed fresh coffee to battle the pervasive effluvium inside the store. Needless to say, we didn't sell much ice cream most mornings (nor many souvenirs), and yet by the time the tourists rolled in, in the afternoon, the store had returned to its original salty-air signature smell.

Upon entering a bakery, we expect to be immersed in a mixture of recognizable smells, such as baking bread, cinnamon, chocolate, and butter. Combined, these scents identify the *branded* scent experience of a bakery. No matter where we are, the aroma reminds us of why we are there. Likewise, upon entering an automotive repair shop's waiting room, we expect to encounter smells of oil, rubber, and grease. Familiar, easily identifiable smells like these represent the naturally occurring *signature* scents of particular businesses.

Of course, if naturally-scented businesses choose to, they can enhance or alter their expected aromas, for instance by piping a continual bakery scent into the bakery's sales area to cover oven down-times, or by adding another, more pleasing fragrance to the mix of gas fumes and oil already pervading the air of the automotive repair shop. General Motors rolled out a scent marketing program to be deployed in their work bays and waiting rooms in early 2008.

Unlike bakeries, garages, nurseries (which smell of damp soil, plants, and moss), and pottery studios (which smell like clay, glaze, and firing kilns), most other types of businesses do not have familiar inherent scents. Perhaps more pointedly, most retail businesses, including the ones that have pleasant natural aromas, entirely ignore managing the scent dimension of their environments. These retailers do have a scent policy, they just don't realize it.

It's no surprise that 63 percent of convenience store customers felt that aroma played a significant part in the stores they chose to visit.[2] Have you ever walked into a 7-11 and gagged at the smell of bleach or dirty mop water? No doubt you have visited some pretty rancid smelling shops for the purpose of their convenience—I know I have. Did you return again when you didn't have to? Not unless it was an absolute necessity.

It's important to note that scent marketing may not enhance your environment without a clean working space to start. Every business has some sort of smell or another, and these are not always pleasing.

Many businesses, including restaurants and food stores, share a distinct odor reminiscent of a rarely used mop and scrub brush. Many hotel hallways smell of Carpet Fresh layered over stale cigarette smoke and mildew. That's why it is especially refreshing to enter a business that smells clean and pleasant.

One of the factors you need to consider when contemplating a scent strategy is the condition of the atmosphere. How does your business environment presently smell? What aromas, if any, does the customer encounter? If you are like most businesspeople, you haven't tackled these two questions or developed a planned scent strategy. Your official scent policy is literally left up to the trailing odors of the last strong smelling event that took place in the space.

Retail and business environments are merely one facet of scent marketing and branding. Products such as tools, electronics, and household items, services such as insurance, security, and repair, along with the entire industry of packaging, are all subject to developing a scent strategy similar to environmental scenting. No matter what your product or service entails, it either has an inherent smell or not, and the object is to examine and manage your aromatic image.

Developing Your Scent Strategy

There are four main factors to consider in choosing the right scent for your brand.

1. *Your Message:* Who are you? What's your human story? What do you have to offer to the consumer?
2. *Your Target Audience:* What are the demographics of your average customers? What are their habits and interests? What makes them tick?
3. *Your Triggered Response:* What experience do you want your target consumers to have? What's the image/emotion/sensation you desire to evoke? What's the best fragrance to send your message and trigger the desired response?
4. *Your Integrated Delivery Plan:* What's your organization's Whiff Factor? What different times, places, and occasions, and which mediums will you use to deliver your scent?

   Let's consider each of the four factors in turn.

Key #1: Your Message (Your Brand Identity)

Your message is the most fundamental factor in any brand marketing activity, and this includes your scent message, the language that speaks to the instincts and emotions of your customer. Unlike conventional branding strategies where you might develop your message subsequent to identifying your target market, scent marketing applications enter the picture long after your brand identity has been established.

You will need to know who you are and what you offer in order to create your scented message. For the language of scent carries as much meaning and nuance as the written word. And it must be consistent with your brand identity and its intended message. Identifying your message can establish a set of parameters that you can return to, and measure against, while formulating your scent script. Whether your product involves consumer electronics, fashion, the auto industry, or farm equipment, your formulated scent must be consistent with your message.

Let's take a look at how you can define your message as it relates to the language of scent.

- Do you see your brand as hip, edgy, solid, fun, luxurious, homey, trendy, stately, sensible, frivolous, necessary, or unique? What adjectives describe your brand?
- Do you wish to relay that your product is backed by a large organization or that your business is a small and irreverent startup? What are the qualities of your culture?
- Do you wish to portray a relaxed and soothing image, or a happy, upbeat, busy, with-it company portrait?
- Are you planning to illustrate a countrified company or maybe a big city image?
- Does your brand have a flavor of France, Asia, or Latin America?

All of these messages can be relayed through your choice of fragrance, because of the emotional resonance and cognitive power of scent communication.

You may find it relatively easy to relay your brand message through scent. Think of Dunkin' Donuts, Godiva Chocolates, Starbucks, Home

Depot, or Blockbuster Video. You can imagine what types of scents would communicate the image of these types of brands (I'd go with doughnuts, chocolate, coffee, sawdust or cedar wood, and popcorn).

Now think about Midas Muffler, Pottery Barn, the Geek Squad, Rooms To Go, and H&R Block. These brands are a bit more difficult to communicate with scent. But with a little bit of reflection, we can imagine how Midas Muffler would like to relay a message of safety and honesty. Pottery Barn might like to communicate a nostalgic message of a vintage home atmosphere. The Geek Squad may want to convey a feeling of efficiency and being *au courant*. Rooms To Go may emanate the comfort of home. And finally, H&R Block might want to be recognized for its accuracy and expediency.

These are merely guesses on my part, but no doubt you catch my drift. I'm suggesting that every business has a message of some kind to relay about who it is and what it does, one that can be conveyed through scent as well as other physical senses.

Emotional bonds inspire loyalty. The more "human" that your brand, product, or service appears, the stronger the emotional bond you can create with your customers. By human, I mean two things. First, a description of qualities that a person could possess, such as being "friendly," "funny," "intelligent," "sophisticated," "avant-garde," "well-connected," or "efficient," to name only a few, which are applied to the product, the company that stands behind the product, or the user of the product.

Second, I mean a story related to your organization. Humanization of a brand must involve the consumers' senses: sight, sound, taste, touch, and smell. It also needs to include human stories. The televised Olympic Games demonstrate the power of storytelling. Viewership rose dramatically after the producers made a conscious decision to tell in-depth stories about the athletes competing in the Games. They guessed that if we understood the athletes' strife, struggles, and triumphs, we would feel that we knew them. We would become emotionally bonded to these little figures on the screen. And they were right. The same goes for humanizing a brand. Think of AFLAC's quacking duck and GEICO's gecko. Who knew that insurance could be humanized?

Dozens of screenplays are tossed into trashcans every day in Hollywood. Writers pour their hearts out in attempts to tell good stories, but most never make the mark. Why? For many reasons—but I'll boil them down to a few. One reason is that characters in these stories lack emotional depth. A story may have a fairly good plot with the right mix of struggle, good, and evil, and yet the audience can't relate to the wooden descriptions or the dialogue of the participants.

It is imperative that the message you create as your brand identity is short, sweet, and to the point. A promotable storyline is one that the listener can easily repeat to others in 30 seconds, much like what has come to be known as the elevator pitch. Such stories have the potential to spread virally. Think of the two Steves. You know, the ones who started a company out of their garage. The first, a genius, was eventually spurned by the other. The second, being temperamental, was turned out to pasture, but eventually returned to grow the biggest piece of fruit the world has ever seen. He's now thought of as a genius. "Of course," you answer, "you're talking about Steve Wozniak and Steve Jobs from Apple—of iPod, iPhone, and laptop fame." Now that's a promotable story! Of course, each product also has its own story to tell.

Successful storylines are endless, from the one about the college dropout who became the richest man in the world, to the nefarious beginnings of Coca-Cola, to the humorous shenanigans and adventures of the founder of Virgin Records and Airlines, and so on. These stories contribute a human element to a product or brand identity.

With the important sensory addition of scent, your brand's personality and storyline are brought to a higher dimension. You can increase the volume of your message with scent's extraordinary ability to penetrate the emotions and leave a lasting impression.

These are merely the foundational parameters, to be established before moving on to the target market. And with the assistance of a competent scent marketing strategist, you can establish the parameters of your scented message.

Key #2: Your Target Audience (Your Paying Customer)

The next factor in choosing the right scent for your business—and perhaps the most important one—is the identity of your target consumer. Successful entrepreneurs aim to know as much as possible about their customers. Larger companies spend a lot of time and effort to determine who their customers are, what their motivations may be, and how they live their lives: homes, hobbies, cultural background, abilities, tastes, and interests. No matter what size your business is, doing a bit of market research surely will prove profitable in the process of choosing your signature scent and in determining the best media to reach out to consumers.

Market researchers generally categorize target consumers using three modes of analysis: demographics, market segmentation, and psychographics.

Demographics: Perhaps the most obvious way of evaluating consumers is by assessing age, gender, marital status, sexual preference, cultural background, education level, occupation, and income. Statistics such as these can be helpful in developing a scent strategy, for biological and social reasons. We know, for instance, that women are more sensitized to aroma than men,[3] and that we lose some of our smelling capabilities as we age. Age also matters, because nostalgic scents are directly related to experiential periods in our childhood and younger years.[4] Education, occupation, and income could establish where targeted consumers fall on the luxury goods scale, and possibly could intimate a bit about childhood nostalgic smells, too.

Demographics also help to identify and assess the size of the target market. You should aim to choose scents that will influence a majority of potential consumers.

Market Segmentation: Even within a single demographic, you may find distinct subsets of consumers with common needs or characteristics. For instance, some women prefer to exercise alone with weights, others prefer group fitness classes. Having clarified your message (e.g., "I am a personal trainer specializing in weights and kickboxing"), you may select one or more segments of consumers to target with a distinct mix.[5] Businesses have different capabilities that enable them to serve their target market better than any other, which is why they choose to focus upon the segments they do.

Psychographics: Based upon the consumer's activities, interests, attitudes, and opinions, when we look at psychographics we are studying the behavior of our average consumers, their priorities and preferences, how they spend their time, and how they "feel" about specific issues and events. Psychographics reveal a bit more about consumer emotions than segmentation and demographics do. Psychological research is a valuable marketing tool because it helps us to identify the segments of the consumer population that are likely to be most responsive to specific types of marketing messages.[6]

In essence, psychographics interweaves demographics with psychology to create an in-depth profile of the lifestyle of the average customer. Some notable companies that have successfully followed this approach are Apple, Coke, Nike, Sony, and Starbucks. These companies exude a "cool, hip, tuned-in" image, selling their products to a certain segment of the population as a lifestyle choice. Devotees can be easily identified as they sit drinking their venti nonfat lattes while surfing the web on their MacBook laptops, jabbering on their Sony phones in the comfort of their custom-made Nike iD sneakers.

Using a multisensory approach, Starbucks has created a style and ambience with scent, lighting, music, design, and location that has no barriers when it comes to age, sex, or income (even struggling college kids will plunk down four bucks for a latte every day).

Like this leading brand, the more attuned you are to the lifestyle of your customers, the more you will be able to determine what makes them tick. By making smart guesses about their emotional hot buttons, you will be able to better strategize the specific essence or essences that will complement their decision-making process or enhance their mood.

Along these lines, Dominos Pizza's promise years ago to deliver fresh, hot pizza to your door in 30 minutes or less—or you would get your pizza for free—won the brand a huge amount of business on college campuses across the nation.

When considering your audience, you should consider the following questions:

- What is the demographic profile of your target consumer?
- What are your customers' hot button issues?
- What do they love? What gives them pleasure?
- What do they hate? What causes them pain?

- What are the real reasons your customers are already buying your product (speed, price, privacy, assistance, and the like)?
- What are consumers' current perceptions of your business, products, services, and environments?
- In what context will your customers experience the product or service (for example, while shopping, at home, in the morning, afternoon, or at night, attending an event, and so on)?

Knowing as much about your customers as possible will make all the difference when matching the consumer science with your specific message. Knowing what motivates your customers and how to respond to that motivation is also key.

It doesn't take a braniac to understand what makes us get out of bed each day to take on the world in our own individual ways. The human condition that drives us and motivates our actions is joy. We work hard in anticipation of the joy of feeding our families, going on holiday, and bequeathing a legacy to our progeny. We read books and see movies to enjoy them. We eat, sleep, and have sex in anticipation of joy (or some semblance thereof). Of course, many times we fail to hit the mark. But the promise of joy is the carrot in front of us. No matter the reality, it is the anticipation of receiving joy (or reducing the pain that comes from the absence of joy) that motivates us.

Why do consumers consume? Why do we consume foods, beverages, cars, purses, perfumes, watches, clothing, and myriad services? Because we consider that these products will bring us joy. Period. Yes, we may feel that we need them for survival, but we choose one over another for the intended purpose of the joy that they will bring us, however fleeting it may be. If we understand this underlying motivational factor of the consumer, and how to speak to it in the language of scent, we have a winner.

Once you understand your customers, you can appeal to them. That's where the next step comes in, of devising a response triggered by scent. For instance, on a recent trip to Puerto Rico, I took a horseback ride through the rain forest. On entering the foothills, the exotic smells of the tropical flowers immediately transported me back to my very first visit to this lush terrain, and all of the excitement and adventure that occurred at the time. The tourist board of Puerto Rico might target exotic destination travelers by evoking the essence of that experience with a scent that triggers the feeling, memory, or picture of "Rain Forest" in the mind's eye.

Key #3: Your Triggered Response (An Image/Emotion/Sensation)

Upon establishing the qualities of the brand image that you wish to portray—in other words, your message—and subsequently determining the attitudes, feelings, needs, and motivations of potential customers, you can then identify a specific response that you would care to trigger in the consumer. Your choices are varied and broad in scope.

Let's revisit the different kinds of influences that scent can have upon the human brain and, by extension, the ways these subtle influences can enhance your business. Upon identifying the response or set of responses that you desire to trigger, you possess the necessary information to formulate your scent strategy.

Trigger responses induced by your product or service may include:

- Memory/mental pictures
- Nostalgia
- Learning
- Comprehension
- Mood elevation/relaxing
- Pain reduction
- Alertness
- Hunger
- Sexual arousal/sensuality
- Perception
- Behavior modification
- Directional aid
- Danger/warning
- Authentication/identification

Could the waft of an ocean breeze or a field of flowers, or the scent of roasted turkey or an orange grove relate to your product? Might these scents, reminiscent of childhood experiences, bring your target consumers—for a moment—into a dreamy state of mind where a sudden memory of a place and time could trigger an impulse purchase? Maybe an aroma of fine leather or wood would assist in evoking the desired response?

Nostalgia is a potent scent response. With what story would a wide cross-section of your consumers connect—perhaps building sand castles on the beach? Maybe they'd relate to a happy Christmas in the country with jolly carolers singing as they crossed a snowy field—even if they were raised in the tropics? The nostalgic imagination is active.

Most advertising focuses on stimulating emotions through pictures, words, and music. But while we can easily pass by or look away from a photographic image, and we can just as easily turn down or tune out music, scent simply wafts into the nether regions of the brain, as if whispering in the mind's ear, completing its task as a stealthy messenger.

As you consider the list of triggered responses, keep your product or service in mind. Think of your entire brand experience while you review the list. In order to decide on an appropriate story line, try to imagine where your brand qualities and target customers' lifestyle intersect. Not all scents are good matches. We know that pumpkin and lavender trigger a sensual feeling in many men, [7] but does that particular response jibe with selling Ferraris—or with your product or service? Maybe.

Here are a few more questions to consider while developing your scent:

- What is the expected general mood of your intended audience just prior to encountering the scent (for example, upbeat, excited, calm, cautious, nervous, distrustful, and so on)?
- What reaction are you looking to trigger in response to the scent? Would you like to enhance their mood, change their mood, keep the mood the same, or affect some other kind of result?
- What will your target audience's activities entail directly after encountering the scent?

- Will they immediately experience another scent or a line of scents?
- Will you follow up with a scented product, mailing, or gift?
- Will they have the opportunity to purchase a scented product?
- How does your chosen scent interact with other sensory elements already in place (including other scents) in the target environment?
- Considering the environment's lighting, music, and décor, does your chosen scent complement and enhance the overall ambiance, or does it contrast?
- Are there thematic elements to your scent?
- Are you complementing a specific theme in relation to time period, geographical location, music style, colors, other product groupings, or seasonal buying periods?

The First Moment of Truth

From what research studies have taught us so far, scent offers us a direct route to the consumer's emotions that is more effective than a slick graphic, witty slogan, or cleverly shaped packaging. As scent enters the brain's emotional centers—communicating, influencing, and enhancing the message—it arrives in advance of the other sensory perceptions and lays the foundation for the ultimate buying decision.

Corporate giant Proctor & Gamble, the $68 billion grand master of packaged goods, has coined a phrase that you should commit to memory: the first moment of truth (FMOT, pronounced EFF-mot), which refers to the first three to five seconds after a shopper initially encounters a product on the store shelf. In these few impressionable moments, by appealing to their physical senses, as well as their values and emotions, P&G contends that marketers have the best chance of persuading browsers to buy.[8]

If consumer perceptions and purchasing decisions are so heavily influenced during the first seconds of encountering a product on the shelf, shouldn't the same wisdom apply to the consumer's entire experience of a product: from placement, through opening and use?

In addition, when a consumer is entering a hotel, a dealership, a waiting room, a bank, or an airplane, wouldn't it be prudent to enhance those initial encounters through the introduction of a pleasant yet strategic aroma? Of course it would.

Known as a world leader in the art of innovation, P&G touches the lives of two billion people around the world every day with over 300 brands that include Pampers, Tide, Bounty, Pringles, and Folgers. P&G feels FMOT is so important that the company has a 15-person FMOT department in its Ohio headquarters, as well as 50 FMOT leaders stationed around the world—led by a global director of FMOT.

As the old adage goes, you never get a second chance to make a first impression. So it only makes sense, whatever your product or service may be, to load the deck as favorably as possible when it comes to your FMOT. As P&G's director of FMOT, Dina Howell, has stated, "There are actually two moments of truth. The first is when a browser initially encounters a product (and hopefully decides to make a purchase). The second moment of truth happens each time the customer uses the product." [9]

In other words, you can put lipstick on a pig, dab sweet perfume behind its ears, and take it to market, but when the customer gets home they'll still know they bought a pig. Its true value will shine forth during the "second" (at-home, in-use) moment of truth.

Beware. If you do not have a quality product, and you market it with scent, consumers may form a negative connection between their experience of your product and the aroma with which you choose to market it. Every time they take a whiff, a feeling of disappointment or irritation could be reinforced. Scent marketing can mean more emotionally based buying decisions. If the overall second moment of truth is an unpleasant one, you may inadvertently ostracize your customers.

Hence Key #4: planning a sequence of marketing initiatives to implement your scent strategy.

Key #4: Your Integrated Delivery Plan (Your Scent Script)

The best branding efforts take a holistic approach, and include the product itself, its packaging, its placement on the shelf, and ambiance of the overall environment in which the product is sold, as well as every other point where the consumer has brand contact. All of your touch points, from FMOT on down the line, need to convey the story of your brand, which is done most powerfully and emotionally—albeit not *exclusively*—through the vehicle of scent. Those interactions are how you script the consumer's perceptions and ultimate experience of your product, service, or brand.

Scripting in the fields of fragrance design, marketing, branding, and theater is relatively similar. A story has a through-line that contains a series of well-placed and interesting events that the audience accepts. Events can be described as a series of happenings. Ask yourself what's happening in your scripted story. These events/happenings make the world go around. They cause us to react and command our emotions. Therefore they are memorable.

When scent scripting a product or brand, you need to know two things: What's happening in your story line? And what actually happens when the consumer encounters your product, opens it, or uses it? After ensuring that you have a great product or service, your goal should be to showcase its talents as best as possible.

Here's a simple formula that I've used for years in creating a successful and engaging script: anticipation, progression, and surprise (APS). By using these simple elements, you will be able to attract and hold the attention of your target audience.

Reflect for a moment upon your favorite movie, book, TV program, or play. Were you eager to find out what would happen when a pair of would-be lovers confessed their feelings to one another, or the identity of a murderer was revealed in an open courtroom? Did you delight in the progression of scenes and discoveries that brought you closer to the moment or outcome you were anticipating? And wasn't it especially thrilling if there were a series of surprising twists and turns along the way?

Anticipation builds emotion. Progression keeps it coming. Surprise triggers a rush of adrenaline. When these elements of telling a story are missing, we don't really notice what went wrong or why—only that it was a dud. Knowing what's going to happen at the end makes for a lousy script. It's those things that we don't know that create excitement in an event or even in a product. Without the element of surprise, we feel let down.

The APS proposition applies to successfully scripting virtually every product, service, or human event. All you need to do is reflect upon some of your most memorable experiences of the past and you will find these elements were always present. From popular theme park rides to parties, sporting events, dating, and even sensual encounters, every memorable event contains the elements of anticipation, progression, and surprise.

You can apply the APS principal to create an enthralling scent script for your own product, service, or brand. As consumers, we live an APS way of life. A perfect example is the mega-event called Christmas—or to be politically correct, the Holiday Season. We work overtime, spend endless hours online and in malls, strategically plan the perfect gifts and meals, arduously labor in the kitchen, meticulously wrap gifts, and decorate—all in anticipation of a few hours of joy with loved ones. The annual celebration is a marketer's delight. Not to be underestimated, the APS proposition is recycled throughout the year in every other consumer holiday or event from Mother's Day, to Father's Day, Valentine's Day, Thanksgiving, Halloween, Easter, Yom Kippur, Kwanzaa, and even "back to school" in the fall. You name it, there's an APS event somewhere near you—right on schedule.

We are indoctrinated early on. As tiny children we eat, sleep, and dream of the coming holidays. What gift will I get? How many eggs will I find? How many candy bars will be tossed in my bag for trick-or-treat? Anticipation, progression, and surprise, all wrapped up in a consumer holiday package.

APS applies to every product. Think of the childhood experience of eating a box of Cracker Jack. Besides the multisensory experience of opening the box, smelling the caramel covered popcorn and peanuts, and crunching on the snack, a little toy in the box was really the surprise you were anticipating. Nowadays, that toy has transformed into a paper puzzle or a riddle in the middle of a plastic bag, but the concept is the same.

People also love to travel because of the APS proposition. We anticipate the trip for months—dreaming, envisioning, perceiving the joy and revelations it will bring. Then we pack our bags, jump onto a plane or a ship, and leave our regular lives behind for destinations unknown, and surprises to be experienced.

Another popular pastime is watching sports: baseball, soccer, golf, NASCAR racing, the Tour de France, and more. Why are so many people fanatic about sports? Think APS. Sporting events contain all of the elements for the journey to joy—and engage our senses. Long beforehand, we anticipate the game. Throughout the game we anticipate the next move, as we smell the smells, eat the familiar fare, see the sights, hear the roar of the crowd, and feel a surge of emotion within us.

Does your marketing include the APS proposition? Does your package or product contain the elements of a good script? Does the act of seeing, hearing, smelling, tasting, or touching your product create anticipation or contain the element of surprise? What's the toy in your Cracker Jack box? What's the story line that lends a humanizing emotional bond to your brand? What's your brand's personality? What's the event or happening that is taking place? What sort of stage have you set to make your product a star performer?

Once you've developed a strategic scent for your business, it is time to create your scent strategy—exactly how and where you will be employing your olfactory marketing. What fragrance media will you be using? Some companies may only wish to diffuse scent into their offices or retail locations, while others may completely script their scent brand strategy to include aroma anywhere they would display their logo.

After creating your scent script, you will need to put it to use in order to evaluate and adjust it. It is important that you make evaluation a part of your scent development process. In other forms of brand messaging, such as advertising, environmental design, and even product and package design, there is a substantial cost to creating a message and evaluating it. Fortunately, developing and testing your scent script is significantly less expensive than any of these other mediums.

Of all the media involved in advertising and marketing, fragrance media offers the most bang for your buck. But just like buying any other form of media, you'll need to know the supplier's motivations and the basics of what they have to offer, so that you can choose your provider and negotiate wisely.

Chapter 12
Fragrance Media

By now you have surmised that nearly every industry can benefit from the strategic use of fragrances in the presentation of its products and services. However, it is important that you do not jump on the scent bandwagon just because it exists. Some companies—even the largest and seemingly smartest companies—have already leapt on board without understanding the full cognitive powers of scent. They may have heard a report on the evening news about scenting or read some of the published research, and impatiently gone ahead to deliver an ineffective scent through an equally ineffective delivery system, with less than admirable results—because they lacked sufficient insight.

At Whiff Solutions, we have talked with some of these companies and listened to their woes. One chain delivered a chocolate scent that doesn't really smell like chocolate. Another fast food chain dispensed a stale imitation of coffee aroma into the environment, which did little to boost sales (if not depressing them). All opted for second-rate scents based on financial considerations or out of the excitement of trying a new strategy—unfortunately they picked the wrong system. As you'll soon learn, the quality of the aroma you use for your scent branding is imperative, as is the appropriate nature and efficiency of the delivery system.

Much like the liquor industry, where one can find a bottle of cheap scotch for a few dollars or a premium bottle of Glennfidditch down the aisle for a few hundred, the field of fragrance has its low-grade and top-shelf aromas. Inexpensive aroma oils can be mustered up for as little as $10 or $20 per liter, and top-of-the-market aromas for as much as $500 or $1,000 per liter. Lower grade aromas often pass in the market when cost concerns exceed the concern for product quality. Bargain imitations can offer somewhat pleasant smells, but do they achieve the effect desired? Will they align with the studies?

In your foray into scent-related branding, manufacturing, and marketing, the quality of the aroma you use is of the utmost concern, for you will be employing a designated fragrance with the intent to trigger a specific response from the consumer. In your analysis of aroma-marketing costs, it is a mistake to be penny-wise and pound-foolish. Using a low-grade fragrance in an efficient delivery system may save you money, but it could fail to produce the intended effect. When weighing the cost of scenting a 3,000 square foot retail location cheaply for $100 per month against using a higher quality aroma for 50 or 100 percent more, your decision should be determined by your anticipated return on the investment (ROI). Don't make a foolish penny-wise choice of a few dollars if it could mean missing out on a double-digit increase in floor sales.

In terms of effectiveness, a small extra expenditure for a higher-grade oil could mean a 10 to 30 percent increase in positive reactions from customers and ultimately in sales. If spending an extra $100 generates thousands of dollars of additional revenue, then it is clearly worth the expense for the better quality oil. Scent marketing typically is an insignificant cost compared to your other business and advertising expenses, making it literally one of the least expensive ways to dramatically increase your sales.

Quality does not necessarily mean *expensive*. Although there may be a 20 to 50 percent difference in cost between a low-grade and a high-grade fragrance, you may be arguing about pennies. If scenting a printed ad with a cheap aroma costs a penny a unit and the higher quality fragrance you would prefer to use costs 30 percent more, you may easily be able to justify the cost of 1.3 cents in terms of the return that's likely to be generated by a better smelling advertisement. Again, what really matters is always the ROI.

The cost of a scent marketing initiative will often have as much to do with the fragrance media and delivery system, as it does with the cost of the oil. Regardless of the quality of the oil, one type of delivery system may use double the amount of oil that another uses, resulting in a different price tag. Use the same discernment that you would when buying a car. The difference here is that no one will ever actually see the gas-guzzler or the more efficient economy model.

Frankly, not enough can be said about the importance of using quality aromas and efficient delivery systems (which we will discuss further on in this chapter). Those of us in the scent marketing industry are quite concerned about these two issues, for poor quality and poor delivery can tarnish the results for many eager clients. In the information age, there's no reason to go to the party wafting the smell of cheap perfume.

As you will find in any field of endeavor, there are those who hype the benefits that can be obtained by using a product, then sell you a bill of goods with no results. Therefore, I highly recommend that you hire an expert to educate and guide you through the process. Also do your homework and take the time to study the components. If you wish to take full advantage of the proven benefits of scent, make informed decisions. A consultant can help you navigate the hidden dangers and difficulties of the industry, but your good judgment and common sense also have to come into play.

Hiring a Scent Marketing Expert

A lot of manufacturers offer scent marketing consultation as part of their customer service efforts. While this can be fruitful, it is like shopping for a car and asking a Ford dealer whether he would recommend a Toyota. There is a growing field of independent experts, who are also assisting manufacturers and offering objective advice. The New York based Scent Marketing Institute (SMI), the industry's mouthpiece and trade organization, offers a list of its members to the general public with a delineation of their expertise (for contact information, see Resources at the back of the book). According to

SMI, "A good scent marketing consultant will lead you through the full process of defining your marketing goal, finding the right scent, and the appropriate scent delivery systems, and help you evaluate the results of your campaign." Independents, who facilitate communication on the creative and technical sides, are paid in a number of ways, from project-based fees to a small percentage of the media-buying budget.

Cofounded in 2004 with noted chemoreception scientist Avery Gilbert, SMI is the brainchild of Harald H. Vogt, a German-born New Yorker with a flair for networking, diplomacy, and leadership. A former advertising executive, Vogt started out in production, coordinating suppliers and managing projects. Emigrating to the U.S. in the late '90s to work for an American branch of a German advertising firm, he eventually found himself working with a then-new scent delivery company that was collaborating with IFF. Meeting the same fate as many early generations of scent delivery systems, the project was eventually abandoned. But Vogt was only more intrigued, for he found that he was fortunately placed in the middle of an approaching boom in this new industry because he had relationships with most of the players in the industry. Vogt went on to bring together the industry, offering educational forums, conferences, and public relations effort through the auspices of SMI.

Members of SMI come from all walks of the fragrance business from scent developers, to media suppliers, to advertising agencies, among other interested parties. The educational forums include one- and three-day seminars. Designers, architects, marketers, and entrepreneurs are eligible to receive certification from these seminars, which Vogt plans to expand into partnerships with accredited universities and design schools. He also expects that the manufacturers will soon team up with SMI and other brain trust organizations like Whiff Solutions in order to add credence and substance to the strategies they offer clients.

When hiring a scent marketing consultant, look for an individual or firm with credentials in consumer science or marketing. Ask for references, testimonials, and verify the relationships in the field and professional partnerships. Find out if the consultant is a member of professional organizations, such as the Fragrance Foundation (the non-profit educational arm of the fragrance industry) and SMI. Ask:

- How long have you been in this business?
- What principles are you adhering to (for example, quality of oil, guarantee of products, ongoing service)?
- How will you charge for your services?
- Do you offer free trials?
- What are the timelines involved?
- What are your recommended testing processes?
- Could you describe the results that your past campaigns have generated?

Basic Relationships in the Industry

Developing a fragrance is a creative and scientific process that takes a lot of resources. Thus, most scent delivery companies have a relationship with a fragrance house with perfumers and chemists on staff. Due to the nature of business and the dollars involved, partnering with a fragrance house is often their best option. Other scent delivery companies get their fragrances from several different fragrance houses, in accordance with their price needs and various objectives. So far, the market has been driven by the delivery system manufacturers with the primary intent of selling their proprietary systems and a secondary, albeit important focus of sourcing the fragrance material.

When approaching a potential customer, a delivery system company will tout the benefits of scent, describe some of the research that we have noted, and then launch into a sales process that includes finding a scent with which the client is happy. For example, the client may wish to deliver the scent of coffee, cinnamon, or lavender. Because there are scores of aroma oils offered in these categories by various fragrance houses—and they all smell slightly different—the abilities of the source supplier must be evaluated.

Many applications of fragrance are ongoing. If a delivery company has limited relationships in the marketplace, occasionally it might experience a shortage of the customer's oil. Due to an industry standard that dictates minimum order quantities, sometimes a delivery system company may be forced to buy 100 kilos of a fragrance that a customer desires, despite the customer only needing 30 kilos for the entire year.

How might this affect you as a customer? This financial dynamic can inhibit the number of samples made available to you in your selection process. If you have smelled five samples of coffee from your delivery system vendor and you still aren't satisfied with the quality of the fragrance, the most likely reason is that the vendor has limited relationships and is facing strict purchasing requirements. It could interrupt the flow of your chosen oil. And it could elevate the price of the oil unnaturally. Understanding helps you to make informed decisions. You'll need to find a solution that works for you.

Realize that whatever company you are dealing with has expertise with its specific delivery system and is amply prepared to share that expertise. Technology has come a long way, but it is still developing—and to date there is no industry standard.

As you enter the scent dimension for your marketing and communications, I suggest that you look at the industry as a whole and study the entire array of available fragrance media. It is important to create a scent marketing strategy—which may include product manufacturing and packaging, as well as retailing and advertising—rather than just jumping into one type of media. As previously stated, I suggest that you at least get advice from an objective third party expert.

Expect Clear Results

If your scent marketing results don't mirror the results I've been describing throughout this book, don't blame the messenger. Go back and take a fresh look at the components of your efforts: aroma selection, quality, and delivery. Somewhere in the process you may need to upgrade your choices or your aroma implementation team.

Many retail chains have experimented with scent, and many more are currently anticipating the move. Some in-store tests have been no more than the equivalent of using a five-dollar air freshener wall plug-in for a trial and not surprisingly, the results were not worth a mention. Some stores receive their only education about scent from a single provider of low quality discounted aromas and, not surprisingly, they achieve lackluster results.

If you are truly interested in entering the scent dimension to improve your brand, product, space, or service, pay close attention to the details of the research. If you choose specific aromas in order to mimic the results of studies you've read, you must ensure that you deliver the selected scent in the same manner as the researchers did when performing the research. To emulate someone else's results, you must select a delivery system that will diffuse your essence in a comparable manner.

The Fragrance Media

Scent can be delivered by many different kinds of technology. For simplification, I define a fragrance medium as a specific delivery system within a designated category: inks, varnish, plastic, rubber, textile, environmental, or digitally enabled. In a moment, we're going to look at each of these categories in turn. Fragrance houses can deliver an essence designed for use in any of these specified media. The forms that essences can take include liquids, solids, gases, gels, beads, ceramics, pastes, and microencapsulation. In the latter, a fragrance is captured in minute capsules. Such capsules can release fragrance by the mechanisms of touch, rub, scratch, time-release, and other emerging release applications.

Environmental and digitally enabled media are most frequently delivered either in liquid form, or through a gel, polymer bead, or paste medium, whereas the other fragrance media mostly use microencapsulation as a mode of delivery. While suppliers can argue variables in the vehicles of delivery, my goal is to simplify the topic for you. Although other emerging technologies will be added to the mix in coming years, the biggest strides to date have been made in microencapsulation technology.

Please note that the term fragrance media can mean either the *specific* medium employed or the *entire* fragrance delivery field in relation to the advertising media . In creating your branding strategy, your fragrance media will take its position as just one among several elements in an integrated multisensory plan. In this book, unless otherwise noted, I use the term *fragrance media* as a general designation alongside other traditional marketing media, such as billboards, television, radio, print, digital signage, the Internet, and so on.

Now, let's go ahead and study the varieties of fragrance media one at a time.

Paper or Plastic?

We'll start with paper, or, more to the point, scented inks, varnishes, and printing materials. Scented paper has been around for a long time. Popular among perfume companies that want to offer samples of their latest creations to readers of fashion magazines like *Vogue* and *Glamour,* this type of delivery system goes by names such as LiquiTouch, ScentSeal, and DiscCover. This style of scenting has been big business for the few companies who created the technology—most notably Arcade Marketing, the leader in scented advertising products, especially since it swallowed its biggest competitor, Vertis, in 2006.

Arcade uses traditional methods of scent advertising like the ScentStrip, which releases the aroma when you peel it open, and Scratch 'n' Sniff, where you work your thumbnail to reveal the sample aroma. These products have been around for quite a few years, and have been virtually the only method for retailers to showcase their products in a scented magazine ad. Their expense has limited use of the products mostly to high-end perfumers.

But the times they are a-changin', according to Bob Bernstein, president of up-and-coming player Scentisphere, a printed ink supplier. The New York based company is making waves and creating new markets for the scent marketing industry. Bernstein, a mild mannered "nice guy" runs the firm with his partner Jim Berard. Bernstein, who comes from the printing business, made his first fortune by selling patented technology of peel-away labels like the ones you see on medicine bottles. Berard is a former marketing executive in the cosmetics industry, and has worked with companies like Revlon and Benetton. Bernstein is the brain behind perfecting a microencapsulation process called Rub 'n' Smell. Berard created a strategy to immerse the company in the printing industry from the ground up: They educated and empowered every major printer first, and the printers subsequently have become their sales force. Advertisers used to have to go to a company like Arcade for scented ads, but now they can work directly with their local printer.

"We can produce a scented ad for less than half of what the others cost," Bernstein proudly asserted when we spoke. How and why? He explained his claim with a real-life example. In a traditionally scented perfume ad, you have several compulsory costs. First, you must not only buy the page that you are scenting, but, because of the application process, you are required to buy the back side of the page, resulting in a two-ad purchase. "Say a full-page ad costs $80,000 in a major magazine," he hypothesized. "The magazine will offer you the back side at a discount of, say, $50,000. With the price of the costly perfume inserts and graphics, layout, and other ancillary costs, you could pay as much as $250,000 for that ad. With our product, you have no need to purchase an additional page and related artwork, and our per-unit price is substantially less than a stand-alone perfume product insert."

In fact, a Scentisphere Rub 'n' Smell ad can cost from as little as three-quarters of a penny up to two and one-half cents, depending on the size of the scented space on the advertisement. This brings the costs down to a level at which a small company can finally get in the game—and receive the benefits of increased ad awareness. "The scented product is added as a fifth color on the printing press, with literally no effect on the graphics of the ad," Bernstein told me, adding, "The scented varnish comes in quantities as little as one kilo, making it affordable to almost everyone." Additionally, there are no aggressive smells permeating from the magazine, as most of us have experienced with traditional scented magazine ads.

While writing this book, I constantly spoke about its merits to a number of people. One friend told me that she had discontinued her subscription to *O* magazine, because she could not stand the reek of six perfume ads wafting out of her mailbox. "All of these perfume smells emanating from the magazines give me a headache," she said. We hear you, Linda.

"Rub 'n' Smell is a non-aggressive way to advertise," according to Bernstein. "You see the ad and are invited to touch the scented area.

You choose to smell it at your own discretion." And people do choose to smell it. As I mentioned in Chapter 7, a Roper Starch survey found that scented ads increase readership by 136 percent.[1] Another study done by *The New York Times* found that 81 percent of consumers would choose a product that they could see and smell over one that they could only see.[2] Now, those are results!

This is all good news for advertisers, and they know it. Both Kraft Foods and Pepsi used scented ads (supplied by Scentisphere) in *People* magazine in 2006.[3] By 2007, both *The Wall Street Journal* and *USA Today* announced that they would start selling scented ads to their customers.[4] And Bob Bernstein tells us that this is only the beginning. In 2008, scented print ads truly arrived, with many major magazines in the game.

Don't think that magazines and newspapers are the only application—packaging, direct mailers, coupons, CDs, DVDs, and movie and lottery tickets also can be scented. Catalogues are another big area, with a reported 20 percent increase in sales for Yankee Candle (another Scentisphere client) attributed to the scented pages.[5] My partners and I worked with another non-traditional client to create his scent marketing strategy. Brad Schupp of Sportsmith, a leading supplier of health club and workout products, has started integrating signature-scented ads into his quarterly catalogues going out to his 35,000 customers. He has also developed a complimentary line of scented shampoo and body-care products to be used in the gym shower, which are also offered for sale after the workout. Brad comes from a long line of innovators—his father was one of the founders of the Stairmaster brand.

Product design is understood as an integral part of marketing these days, as you'll see when we discuss technology for embedding aromas in plastic and rubber. If not the product's central *raison d' être,* in many cases scent is a highly valued additional feature.

Plastic Please

"I want to say one word to you. Just one word. Are you listening? Plastics." This was a line delivered over 40 years ago by Walter Brooks' character in an exchange with Dustin Hoffman's character, Benjamin, in the movie "The Graduate." That sage advice is no less warranted today, as we see a revolution in the next generation of "intelligent" plastics. The plastics of the future will speak to you—or rather, speak to your nose and, thus, your brain. Much progress has already been made in this area.

Microencapsulation of plastic has been around for many years. IFF created PolyIFF in the 1980s, which is the product involved in the manufacturing of the scented garbage bags you now see for sale in the supermarket. As far as cost goes, Steve Semoff of IFF told me, "If we can afford to scent something as inexpensive as garbage bags, we can afford to scent just about anything." To date, this product has yet to realize its full potential.

One company from the outskirts of Philadelphia is taking scented plastic to where the money is. ScentSational Technologies, a ten-year-old firm, was the clever creation of serial entrepreneur Steven Landau. A former restaurateur, expert chef, marketer, and travel executive, he has identified a big niche in the business of scented plastics—or should we more aptly say, *flavored* plastics. The scents that waft from his plastic products are actually flavorful aromas approved by the Food and Drug Administration.

Like all great ideas, Landau's came tumbling down to him on a lazy afternoon like Newton's apple. He was on a skiing trip in Vale and pulled out a cherry-flavored ChapStick. After smelling the lip balm, he decided to taste it, which is how he noticed that there was no flavor, just the scent of cherry. After protecting his lips, he took a gulp of bottled water, and then immediately got the perception that the water tasted like cherry. As any good entrepreneur would do, he went to his lawyer and they secured a patent for the idea of scenting plastic. ScentSational Technologies was born.

Landau soon opened a lab, and began testing applications for aromatic plastics, including microwaveable plastics and bottle caps. And he found that they worked. He got more excited. During the testing phase, which took him five or six years, he discovered that when flavor aromas are integrated into plastic water containers, the water eventually takes on the aroma. The revelations were pretty amazing. The possibilities seem endless. In 2003, the company finally came to market with a compelling product named CompelAroma™, and it has been steadily growing ever since.

"We are working with some of the biggest brand names in the food and beverage business," he acknowledges. Of course, like just about every other endeavor that is described in this book, the client list remains confidential. But the major food and beverage trade magazines have certainly covered his trail. "At first the big companies didn't get it," he says, "but after about two years there came a major paradigm shift in the thinking." Ever since, he has been very, very busy. Sporting the title Chief Technology Officer, Landau doesn't have to worry about running the company. He would rather be on the creative side. The president and CEO of the company Barry Edelstein is a longtime friend of Landau's and a former successful dot-com impresario. Edelstein keeps the ship running while Landau plays in the land of plastics and aromas.

Landau speaks of the many benefits of his technology, and claims that his is the most cost-effective product on the market. He talks about how aromas can help us by tricking our minds into believing that we are eating or drinking something with fat or sugar in it. He can now add fat and sugar aromas without incorporating a single calorie. For example, a food can smell like butter, and the buttery aromas waft into our nose to mix with the food product, but we don't have any unwanted baggage after the meal. He also makes a case for healthy flavored water. A new product incorporating Landau's technology is called Aroma Water, which claims to be the only flavored bottled water without additives, on the market.

"Traditional flavored waters are really no better than soft drinks," Landau states. "As soon as you add actual flavor ingredients to water, they grow bacteria, so companies then must add all sorts of preservatives, and you end up with another chemical drink." His proposition is that with CompelAroma technology, the flavorful aromas are in the plastic and/or the cap enclosure, thus the flavorful smells mix with the drink without degrading the quality of the water.

Landau has strong opinions about how flavor additives are harming Americans. To me he asserted, "Artificial sweeteners program people to crave sweets. They drink a diet Coke and rationalize, 'Now I can have something loaded with fat or sugar.'" His theory makes sense. (I know this from experience.) He is also among the proponents that believe that the aroma of chocolate can be an appetite suppressant, by making the mind believe that the appetite has been satiated. Although many studies have proven that certain types of chocolate can in fact suppress the appetite, the role of aromas is still under question.

Landau proposes another remarkable theory. He contends that the explosion of obesity in recent years is due, at least in part, to a paradigm shift in American families. In the old days, moms would cook more often, so a home would typically be filled with aromas for hours on end. This, he asserts, helps to lend a feeling of satiation to the appetite before the meal. Now that the major sources of a family's food supply are microwavable meals and fast food, aromas aren't floating around the house inducing satiety. Therefore we are eating more today before we feel satisfied. It's an interesting theory about the role of scent.

Whatever his theories, he's got plenty of business, from diet manufacturers like NutriSystem to the U.S. military, where meals ready to eat (MRE's) could certainly use an upgrade in both flavor and aroma. At the time of this writing, the technology has been undergoing trials with various companies, with projects for aromatic wine corks, beer bottles, microwavable TV dinners, and cookie packaging. In our conversation, he touted what he calls "reminder aromas," meaning scented pillboxes and blister packs for items such as birth control pills. At a recent conference of pharmaceutical executives, he presented the idea of scent-branding pills. He gave an example of Viagra, one of the most successful products that Pfizer has ever had. By itself the little blue pill only has a 20-year patent protection before it goes generic. But, he told the crowd, if it were marketed as the little blueberry pill with a *branded* blueberry aroma, the trademark protection would protect the manufacturer *ad infinitum*. Yes, the times are certainly changing.

In our last conversation, Landau told me that his creative juices have stirred once again and that he is developing an ink-based scent delivery system. It is a natural step for his company to graduate from scent release systems inside the bottle and package to a complementary scent release for the product's label.

There are many new ink, varnish, and plastic delivery systems being developed and sold on the market today, each with its own claims of quality, efficiency, and cost-effectiveness. Many of these systems deliver more than just scent, they deliver everything from antimicrobial and skin care ingredients to insect repellents. This innovative technology will continue to find new applications as savvy entrepreneurs keep looking for the opportunities.

Rubber Scenting

Scent can be embedded in rubber as easily as it can be embedded in plastic. Seoul-based Kuhmo Tire Company, a two billion dollar-plus manufacturer of tires, rolled out a novelty line of scented tires aimed toward the female consumer in 2007.[6] Targeted for sedans such as the Honda Accord, the Chrysler Sebring, and the Ford Taurus, the U.S. market carries a limited number of these tires in the fruity flavors of orange, jasmine, and lavender. This big company at least got it partially right, with the idea of using scent in marketing. But had they been armed with more information and expertise on the strategic power of scent, they might have laid claim to a much bigger goldmine, using scent to alert the consumer of worn tires, triggering replacement sales.

As we have already discussed in Chapter 6, "Danger Will Robinson," embedded marketing triggers can go a long way toward ensuring car safety. Embedded marketing triggers can be placed in almost any product, from tire treads and batteries, to water pipes, water heaters, and electrical conduit products. Anything made of rubber, or plastic for that matter, can be embedded with a comparable warning trigger. We expect to see a slew of embedded marketing trigger products in the coming years.

The biggest strides will be made as product designers and manufacturers begin to apply signature scents as an integrated design feature and an added tool for brand perception and loyalty.

Fragrant Finery and Aromatic Apparel

What will they think of next? Well, how about scent infused clothing that can stand up to 30 washings and still offer a whiff of the original? The process of microencapsulation, and other patented inventions like it, has allowed great thinkers in the fashion business to put out more multisensory textile products than ever before.

The South Koreans deserve kudos for starting a rage of scented clothing in 1999. When LG Fashion launched a line of scented menswear in response to a slow market, their lavender scented suits flew off the racks.[7] Local competitor, Kolon International, immediately followed suit with peppermint scented formal and casual menswear. Essess Heartlist, a fashion house owned by Samsung, stocked its stores with about 8,000 pine-scented suits and jackets soon afterward. In a mere few weeks, the company sold over 3,000 suits without advertising. When patrons were asked why the new fashion was so popular, their responses varied from "keeping the peace at home" to covering up their boozy smell after a long hard night of drinking. The scented nature of the suits is purported to last about three years or up to 20 dry cleanings.

Since the South Korean run on scented suits back then, the field of scented clothing has had a run of its own. Once considered extreme—even weird—fashion designers and clothing engineers have had many breakthroughs in scented textiles. Thus, "emotional" and "smart" clothing designs are now being brought to market.

British fashion visionary, Jenny Tillotson, Ph.D., a senior research fellow of fashion and textiles at Central Saint Martins College of Art and Design, directs the Scentsory Design Initiative. Specializing in printed textiles, she has worked for Unilever, Nike research and development, and fragrance giant IFF, and her work has been studied by NASA, France Telecom, Sony, Nokia, and a long list of scientists and futurists.

Tillotson became interested in "healing clothing" while working with AIDS victims, after seeing their positive mood response from the introduction of smells. She was determined to discover a better way of introducing the smells than scratch 'n' sniff, and hence began her academic career in emotional fashion. She has been working on several projects that will intelligently deliver fragrance within an interactive, synthetic organism woven into the clothing. She calls her design a sort of "wearable technology," a delivery system that picks up on biological information, then responds. If you are sweating, or you are depressed or nervous, your clothing detects that condition and then pulses a fragrance around the fabric to counteract it—with the intention of affecting your brain.

Tillotson is not a lone wolf. Microencapsulation and similar processes have a future in the field of intelligent clothing or, as French fashion company Lytess calls it, cosmetotextiles. This type of clothing incorporates not only scent but also the healing properties of vitamins and moisturizers. Lytess produces a line of holistic garments, such as underwear permeated with caffeine and shea butter, chic tops loaded with aloe vera, and hosiery imbued with ginger and shea butter (this reportedly reduces swelling and invigorates the legs). It all sounds a bit weird or Twilight Zone-ish, but the field is gaining popularity. According to Lytess, this is only the beginning. They confidently claim that intelligent, multi-purpose textiles will represent 80 percent of all fabrics by the year 2020.

Other designers are coming out with lines of clothing that tackle problems like insomnia. If you have trouble sleeping, all you need to do is slip into your lavender nightie or nightshirt before counting sheep. *Caution*: pro or con, this might also ward off middle of the night advances by a feisty spouse.

Speaking of feisty, Reebok now offers the Pulse Scented Short Bra Top for women who exercise. A fresh peppermint scent is released as heat begins to generate during exercise. Peppermint is known to invigorate the user. Using IFF's Celessence technology, [8] Nike also came out with a male version of a peppermint scented tee shirt intended for basketball players. These can be washed up to 20 times without losing the scent. When I asked Nike's public relations department, they didn't answer as to whether scented shoes would be next. But I did locate a product that claims to remove the stink from shoes using a process of ionization: the Shumidor. [9] Target Stores now carries a series of socks that are infused with the smell of "clean" (their description).

As for the future of scent infused fabric, Philadelphia University is working on that. John Pierce, an associate professor at the University, along with two colleagues, has been working on a new technology that simultaneously infuses scent along with color into a strand of yarn. He predicts that we will see an emergence of scented products in the near future: towels, blankets, sheets, and holiday table linens featuring fragrances such as pumpkin pie, gingerbread, peppermint, and pine needle. From what I've seen and heard, he's right.

Something in the Air

The idea of scenting the air has been around since the invention of incense. In the last decade, with the advent of scented candles and different kinds of air fresheners, it has exploded into a multi-billion dollar market. This is not an accident and only proves that, given the opportunity, people will spend scads of cash on products that make them feel good. Now, when they are out and about in their roles as consumers, they don't have to spend a dime to feel good, for a growing list of companies are releasing their "feel good" potions into the atmosphere in public spaces, totally free of charge.

As of this writing, there are less than two-dozen manufacturers producing scent systems for large scale environments that I know of. Most are just gaining a hold in the marketplace, while the few I list in this chapter have grown into the multi-million dollar category. Before I offer an overview of four of the biggest players in the environmental scent delivery market, it is only fair to acknowledge my professional relationship with Air Aroma International and its sister company Air Aroma America. Both authors were initially involved in the start up of Air Aroma America, and we are minor shareholders without active involvement in the management or operations. I do my best to offer you an unbiased opinion of the new technologies noted here.

First let's visit with the most senior of the quartet, a company called AromaSys, from the great white north in Lake Elmo, Minnesota.

The founder of AromaSys, Mark Peltier, had no qualms about stating the obvious. "We are unapologetically the most expensive in the market of scent delivery systems," he remarked in our interview. "Unlike some in the industry, we don't try to be all things to all people. We have a specific type of client in mind, and that is the premiere luxury resorts and casinos." And he has made his mark with that exact client demographic, most notably in Las Vegas. He founded his original company in 1990 with his wife Eileen, specializing in air cleaning ionization systems for heating-ventilation-and-air-conditioning (HVAC) units in large spaces. He soon moved into the relatively unknown field of aroma delivery, and met with a lot of disappointment through most of the 1990s. People at the time just didn't get it.

But after the now-famous study on slot machine usage,[10] discussed in Chapter 2, "Nostalgia, Mood, and Desire," Peltier's company gained a foothold in the Las Vegas casinos, and has profited from the industry ever since. Not disclosing the actual number of locations he services, he did tell me how many individual units he had working in the field. In 2007, he had approximately 1,600 units in the U.S. and 200 in Europe. Understand that there can be many single units working in a massive space—this number does not represent his pool of clients. But his technology does cover vast spaces, and he is definitely covering a lot of ground.

Peltier's systems work to ionize fragrances through a high-voltage process, and his is the only type of its kind in the market. Eileen is the official "nose" for the company. I originally met him in the late '90s during my search for a portable technology. During a brief conversation, he made it clear that he had no designs to enter the portable market. He had invented a portable, but due to its complexity it never took off.

At the opposite end of the spectrum, we look to the provider of the least expensive scent delivery systems in the marketplace: ScentAir based in Charlotte, North Carolina. During its startup phase, the company was managed by a former senior manager from Muzak, the elevator and in-store music company. In 2004, a venture capital group called Alerion Partners funded ScentAir in a deal that included a juicy distribution agreement with Muzak. ScentAir soon established a lead in the market as a result of substantial funding, a great PR campaign, and Muzak's relationships in the retail sector.

Using a small mailbox-sized machine called a ScentWave, the company's primary technology consists of a proprietary scent cartridge and a fan. Coincidentally, this is the technology invented by David Martin and Fragrance Technologies, the company that I encountered in 1997, at the beginning of my scent journey. The technology was eventually acquired and the name was changed to ScentAir in 2000. It is indeed a small world.

Just about everyone in the industry agrees that ScentAir's market push and public relations campaign have helped bring an increased awareness to scent marketing, yet reviews are mixed on the technology's efficacy in delivering a consistent concentration of scent over a period of 30 days. The ScentWave is offered as the most affordable solution and many of ScentAir's customers are satisfied with the solution. But the competition has heated up as potential customers have been exposed to more sophisticated technologies.

ScentAir eventually answered the competition's call with the introduction of an HVAC system that uses what they call "advanced diffusion," but sales of the newer technology have yet to rival the ScentWave or competing HVAC systems.

The initial managing director was eventually replaced by a much more seasoned executive, Tom Conroy, a Villanova University graduate with advanced management training in competition and strategy from Harvard Business School. Conroy cut his teeth as an executive for the Olin Corporation and has had a diverse career that ranges from devising strategies for consumer products companies and private equity investment, to a recent stint as chief executive of a venture capital firm. With an affinity for emerging technologies, Conroy's most recent success resulted in the sale of his VC firm's stake in a digital signage (in-store media) company to CBS for over $70 million. During our discussions he revealed that he intends to expand ScentAir's line of technology products and services, and to rapidly grow the company to meet the rising momentum of the global market. As of this writing, ScentAir claims to be scenting 15,000 environments and expects high double-digit growth in 2008.

In the middle of the road, and purportedly the world's largest manufacturer of commercial scent marketing delivery systems, is Air Aroma International (AAI). The company was founded in 1999 by John Van Roemburg, a native of Holland, who migrated with his family to sunny Melbourne, Australia, in the '90s. A youthful, lifelong vegetarian in his fifties, Van Roemburg is a soft-spoken visionary with an eye for design. In former lives as a mechanical engineer and furniture designer, he learned to assign beautiful aesthetics to functionality. His many scent delivery products as well as his marketing collateral, and even his office environments, are designed to please the senses. His wife Rita runs the day-to-day operations of the business.

Using a cold diffusion-based nebulizing system, his scent machines deliver a leading edge technology along with sleek, high-tech designs. After hitting it big by clearly dominating the discriminating Japanese market, Air Aroma now has distributing partners in 25 countries with an overall annual turnover of $20 million in 2007 revenues. Offering 30 different styles and applications, from localized POP machines to mega-space delivery systems, Van Roemburg finds it difficult to stop designing. A client can choose to put a single scent into the air or to diffuse dozens throughout the day, using remote controls.

They can also deliver pure essential oils, which, according to the research, are imperative in some cases—while many competitors can't diffuse pure essential oils. Business manager Philip D'huij, a humorous, mellow, fellow Dutchman, told me in 2007 that they were approaching a milestone of 1,000 units per month.

When Van Roemburg felt that he was ready to expand into the Americas, he teamed up with an enterprising group of young entrepreneurs to form Air Aroma America (AAA). CEO and president of AAA, Citron Arbel, is an enthusiastic, hard-driving 30-year-old with an aptitude for numbers and networking. He has a successful background in the event and promotion business, and has founded another flourishing company that offers patented audio technology to the nightclub and resort industry. With a serendipitous name for someone in the business of aromas, he teamed up with the Levy brothers, Spence and Marc, self-made entrepreneurs from the beverage and real estate industries.

With the support of Van Roemburg and IFF, Arbel hit the ground running in the U.S. and South American markets. Both Air Aroma and ScentAir have made Charlotte the U.S. capital of scent marketing. Arbel doesn't talk about the competition, but he does talk about quality. "We offer a high quality scent delivery system that can fill the space at any desired concentration. We also use only high-grade, top-quality scents that get real results," Arbel beams. "All we ask is that the client make a side-by-side trial to compare our systems with any that are out there. That's all it takes to prove our product."

Rounding out the quartet is fast exploding, Milwaukee-based, Prolitec, one of the newest players in the industry. Originating not far from fragrance capital Grasse in France, Prolitec's unique technology was introduced in 1997 by engineers from the ink jet printing industry. The patented process converts fragrance liquids into droplets one hundred times smaller than the diameter of a human hair, delivering dry, vapor-like scent molecules into the environment without leaving deposits on surfaces, and without using heat, ionization, or electrostatic energy. After a successful rollout in France, the company's prospects were improved by acquisition and a move to the U.S.

In late 2003, Prolitec was acquired by QUAESTUS & Co., a substantial investment firm run by a very interesting and savvy media industry executive named Richard Weening. With a background as a CEO and investor in publishing, broadcasting, online and software companies, Weening co-founded Cumulus Media in 1997. Taking advantage of the newly de-regulated radio broadcast industry, Cumulus Media began a roller coaster rollup of 250 radio stations in four short years. The company went public in 1998, raising $391 million for new acquisitions. After retiring from the company in 2000 and keeping 28 percent of Cumulus' voting stock, Weening set his sights on his next big hit, Prolitec.

A self-described workaholic with training in chemistry and physics, Weening balances his hard-driving nature by growing olives and producing olive oil during the fall harvest season in the Provence region of France. Scent delivery was a natural progression in the media business for Weening. "We think of scent as media which properly used, can deliver brand messages, sell products, and, not unlike radio and visual media, can target specific demographics, convey information, and influence human behavior," he says.

We'll continue our discussion of Prolitec and other high-tech technologies in just a few pages. First take a look at the following list of questions to ponder if you are considering environmental scent delivery.

....

Points of Consideration for Environmental Scenting

Here are some questions to help you make an environmental scent plan. Use them to evaluate your intentions and the physical space, and to choose the right scent technology for your needs (many of these questions can also be answered by your supplier).

To Evaluate Your Intentions

- How noticeable do you want the scent to be? What is the intended intensity? Will the scent be immersive, filling the whole environment (full coverage), or be localized to a specific area, such as an entryway or near a specific product or display (POP)?
- At what time intervals do you want the scent to be dispersed? Will it be an integral part of the environment, or will it be dispersed at different periods?
- What are your cost considerations? Which departmental budgets will pay for the scent delivery program?

To Evaluate the Physical Space

- What are the physical dimensions of the environment (square feet and ceiling height—total volume)?
- What are the airflow considerations? Airflow is critical to successfully scenting an environment, ergo: You'll need to examine your space's ventilation system, air returns, open doors, windows, and other air-flow factors.
- What are the HVAC considerations? If you will be using your HVAC system to distribute the scent, how is the system configured? Where and how will you need to place the equipment in order to tie-in with the HVAC system? What is the number of air vents and returns—what's the general system layout?
- Are there competing scents in the environment (including cleaning products, scented products, food, proximity to a kitchen, scent from other businesses, proximity to bathrooms, and so forth)?
- Will the diffusion equipment be hidden, or will you need to incorporate it into your design elements?

To Choose the Scent Delivery System

- Will scent be delivered through an existing HVAC system, or will you use an autonomous stand-alone or portable delivery system? As HVAC systems are typically designed to evenly distribute heated or cold air throughout an indoor environment, they can also be a very effective way to disburse scent. However, smaller environments can be scented with more simple portable stand-alone delivery systems.

- What is the technological method of scent delivery? Does the delivery system use cold air diffusion, evaporation, heat, electric stimulation, or other system? As a general rule, in systems that involve fan propelled, scent-infused polymer beads, gels or other dense media, the scent will diminish in intensity over time. Similar to consumer-based home fresheners and plug-ins, these technologies deliver stronger concentrations of scent when the cartridge is first installed, with a noticeable reduction in concentration over a 30-day-period. Systems that diffuse scents by drawing directly from a liquid reservoir are more likely to deliver a consistent concentration. (*Caution:* Systems involving heat elements or flames to disburse the scent are to be cautiously considered due to possible bacteria problems and obvious safety hazards.)

- Is the delivery system portable or can it be wall-mounted? In small environments, or when maximum flexibility is needed, portability may be important for a variety of reasons, including making the best use of air currents to optimize scent dispersion.

- Who will install the equipment? Will there be a cost associated with the installation?

- Does the supplier provide free trials of the system? Will they allow a trial in multiple locations?

- Does the supplier offer a scientific approach to the selection of scent? Do they offer to assist in determining goals and ROI quantifiers, as well as additional assistance in evaluating the trials?

- Service/Maintenance. What procedures are in place to replenish scents and maintain the system in an efficient working order?

Will the machine be easily accessible for maintenance and the replacement of cartridges?

- If the system malfunctions, what is the turnaround time for repair or replacement?
- How long is the subscription program, and what does it cost? The standard in the industry is a contractual one-, two-, or three-year subscription program that includes a monthly replacement of the scent cartridge.
- Support. Is there an easy to follow system manual? Is phone support available? Is there a company technician in your immediate area?
- What types of scents can be used with the technology? Can the system deliver essential oils, aroma oils, and differing viscosities of oils?
- Control features. Does the system have controls to set duration and concentration levels?
- User-friendly. How easy is the system to install, operate and maintain?
- Warranty. What are the warranty and support terms of the equipment?
- Coverage. How many cubic feet of coverage can be obtained evenly throughout the space, and at the desired concentration level? Does the supplier guarantee its coverage claims?
- Cartridge shelf life. In accordance with the quoted costs, how long will the scent cartridge last, and will it be replaced if it is depleted in a shorter time than the company claims? *Note:* Realize that different scents have different consumption rates, according to volatility, accompanying carrier oils, and concentration levels. The industry standard dictates that a cartridge should last about 30 days.

Understanding these different environmental scent delivery systems can be a little bit confusing, but it is good to know the basics so that you can compare apples to apples. Some people love the Red Delicious, while others (like myself) are Granny Smith devotees.

Prolitec's technology as well as its services are somewhat different from its competitors. All of Prolitec's systems use the same computer-controlled technology, from table-top appliances for hotel rooms, to wall mounted systems that cover 20,000 square feet, and HVAC systems that purportedly cover up to 50,000 square feet. The computerized driver of the HVAC system can handle up to 1,000,000 square feet of delivery coverage.

The biggest difference between Prolitec and its present competitors is in its service regimen. While most companies ship the scent cartridge to the customer for handling, Prolitec offers a full-service program that includes technicians who visit the property to change recyclable cartridges and maintain the systems. This aspect of service is being looked at by the other companies and tested in certain markets, but Prolitec has made it one of the core philosophies of its business. Weening insists that his full-service philosophy does not affect Prolitec's price competitiveness, and says that that his wall-mounted unit is cheaper than rival ScentAir's ScentWave unit, and that his HVAC delivery system costs about the same as ScentAir's. As I have repeatedly suggested, until there is an unbiased, third party, evaluating authority in place, only client trials and comparisons can separate the wheat from the chaff.

But Prolitec is taking the market by storm with retail clients like Nordstrom and Diane Von Furstenburg, and major casino players like Harrah's and Las Vegas' New York New York, where they eliminate smoke odors with the smell of apple.

Every bit the entrepreneur and salesman, Weening touts, "We believe Prolitec is the greenest way to scent a public space." He backs up this claim with an in-house toxicology team and, like other systems, his technology volatilizes the scent molecules to a size and concentration that is the generally accepted threshold that will avoid allergic reactions.[11] Like John Van Roemburg of Air Aroma, Weening has a global vision for Prolitec, with resellers in Australia and Latin America, and a very sweet relationship with mega-service company Ambius.

Ambius, a multi-sensory environmental design and service company with 50,000 clients, was formerly known as Tropical Plants, the world's largest environmental plant provider. Owned by $5 billion U.K.-based Rentokil-Initial PLC, Tropical Plants re-branded itself as Ambius in early 2008, and has added graphic wall art and scent delivery to its multi-sensory offerings. Opera buff and international speaker Jeff Mariola runs the behemoth operation from London. With myriad offices throughout the U.S. and Europe, Mariola agreed to carry Prolitec's product line for five years under the brand name Microfresh™. Mariola puts his company's money where its mouth is by saying, "We have made a major commitment to multi-sensorial interiors. Scent, the most powerful of our senses, is a major part of our service offering." And a major commitment and gamble it is, to re-brand such a well established company. Ambius is a great example of the big players who are jumping into the scent game.

Digitally Enabled Scenting

We are at the dawn of digital scent devices in much the same way that computer peripheral devices were in their infancy just a few years ago. In the not-too-distant past, modems, DVD players, speakers, and web cameras were typically exterior components of your computer, creating the tangle of wires that wove their way into the Swiss cheese ports of your desktop machine. These components and many others have quickly been scaled down in size, and now we expect these features as a standard component of even the smallest of portable laptops. Cyber scent delivery systems are now available as add-on devices, but should eventually be folded into the PC as a regular feature in the coming years.

The technology has arrived that will allow us not only to see and hear emails, electronic-cards, PowerPoint pitches, and websites, but to smell them as well. This technology has been around for quite a few years, but the lack of awareness of scent and its powerful influences have stymied its marketability. Companies like Trisenx, Exhalia and NTT Communications are laying the foundation for this field, while a few others are creating scent-enabled exterior components as well.

After many years of trial and error and over $2 million in investment, Savannah-based Trisenx rolled out Scenttv.tv in March 2007, with a digitally enabled, multi-sent delivery system called the Scent Dome.

In 1999, another innovator emerged in France, driven by the possibility of communicating scent digitally through wireless technology and other means. After developing some innovative high-tech tools for his employer, France Telecom, future-minded Yvan Regeard left the company, purchased the rights and patents to his work, and formed Exhalia. This soft-spoken, obviously broad thinking Frenchman speaks in clear and concise concepts. His software and hardware backgrounds have enabled him to continually design scent solutions for basically any type of broadcast medium. He not only created the first software systems in order to be able to synch time-released scents with movie scenes and music cues, he also created easy-to-use editing software that can be learned in five minutes. Now, any Hollywood editor, sound engineer, or music mixer can easily synch up and apply scent cues to any work. The technology can be used in a variety of formats, from cell phones and MP3 players, to PCs and laptops.

Exhalia's unique patented systems have gained quite a bit of attention. A British company has incorporated the company's software programming into another new multi-scent delivery device, and has plans to roll out this new device to the international video gaming industry. Exhalia is working on many different projects for some notable companies. Upon my first meeting with Regeard in September 2007, I realized that he was a genius and visionary, and we have since teamed up on several exciting projects. We will be hearing a lot more about Exhalia in the near future. In December 2000, an emerging Plano, Texas, company called AromaJet announced its success in transmitting fragrance over the Internet.[12] Using an interactive program that allows for the creation of aromas by mixing 16 separate ingredients in 1 percent increments, David B. Wallace, Ph.D., AromaJet's Chief Tech Officer, transmitted several distinct fragrances from Sidney, Australia to AromaJet's offices in Plano. The sending and receiving device connected over the Internet using what AromaJet calls a SmellServer.

The idea behind this smell communication device was to create a platform where a perfumer or fragrance designer from one country could work directly with a customer on the other side of the globe in real time. When I asked Wallace what happened to his technology since it was made public, he explained that the market was not ready for them back in 2000. So AromaJet expanded upon the same technology by creating scent delivery calibration systems for the burgeoning smelling robot detection industry. Now their technology is being used to calibrate and perfect scent sensor systems for drug and bomb detection—the kind being employed in airports. With no active marketing efforts for the scent marketing business, since 9/11, they changed course, and took their technology to where the money is.

For an example of how all of this technology can be used not only functionally but artistically as well, let's take a look at a modern-day space-designing genius who is nothing less than a maestro of orchestrating architectural space.

As a leader in the science of multisensory design, Usman Haque is so much more than a classic architect. This multiple award-winning British designer is in a league of his own. His talents not only include creating interactive environments, but also software and systems that bring them to life. He specializes in the design and research of interactive architectural systems that are considered "dynamic, responsive, and conversant." In simple terms, Haque brings human personality and interaction to buildings and spaces. Even though his craft enlists all of the senses, his work with aromas is truly visionary.

In creating the program "Scents of Space," he teamed up with his former design partner Josephine Pletts and renowned fragrance expert and designer Luca Turin, Ph.D., who was the subject of the 2003 book *The Emperor of Scent* by the eloquent Chandler Burr (see Bibliography). When visitors enter a Scents of Space environment, they are subjected to dynamic three-dimensional fragrance zones that respond to their horizontal and vertical movements with scent diffusions. Within this system, two separate levels of interaction occur. Ingeniously, the system builds up a predictive database, from which it intuits aroma mixes as either "alluring" or "repelling," and responds accordingly. Subsequently, the manufactured aroma brain is constantly evolving. That's the primary level of interchange.

The secondary level of interaction occurs between the visitors and the smells themselves, mixing the patterned scents with the visitor's own smells to create a unique tertiary co-mingled smell. In attempting to visualize this experience, perhaps you are envisioning being zapped from all sides with an invisible scented ray gun. In reality, the Scents of Space system responds to negative avoidance movements by subtly infusing more pleasant aromas in accordance with the visitor's preferences. With this sort of interactive scent-based design, a vivid imagination could dream up a multitude of scenarios.

In the themed entertainment world, for example, Haque's aroma brain could have an interesting application if it was used to recreate an interactive journey through a jungle, a big city, or an animal farm.

The future is now for a lot of the concepts and inventions described above. The market has finally taken hold of the idea. The science has proved what was once considered conjecture and hyperbole. Just observing the sheer number of suppliers entering the market and the big businesses behind these ideas, it is clear that change is imminent in the marketing of products and services. Advertisers have successfully broken through technological barriers to create scented print, POP displays, promotions, and premiums, and the age of scent-enabled computing is waiting in the wings. The only impetus needed now is to equip those who are driving innovation with the education and tools needed to bring them into the mainstream. These concepts and products are true examples of how a revolution of scent communication is taking place in the information age.

Aroma by Design

My colleagues and I believe that the field of design is where the new crop of scent delivery experts will be sewn. Presently the manufacturers of delivery systems and a select group of systems integrators are responsible for retrofitting aroma products into older buildings and spaces. When it comes to residential and commercial construction, merchandising, interior, and product design, however, fragrance lies in the hands of a more educated community of future designers, who will be able to add strategic scent delivery to their expertise, along with efficiency and productivity planning, functionality, and aesthetics.

Design is one of the faster growing professions in the U.S. The U.S. Bureau of Labor and Statistics classified nearly half a million occupations as designer jobs in the year 2000. Over 35 percent of these jobs were classified as graphic designers, a group that includes Andrew Newman, the talented graphic designer of the cover of this book. Another 20 percent were categorized as floral designers—purveyors of scent-induced messages of love, congratulations, and condolences—in the business of packaging and selling nature's own fragrance supply. A much smaller but sizeable field of merchandisers and window decorators came in at 15 percent, while commercial, industrial, and interior designers each represented about 10 percent of the whole.[13]

The 200,000-plus design professionals in the merchandise, decorator, commercial, industrial, and interior design community, and the myriad architects responsible for designing the structures and spaces where scent applications will be made in the future, are the ones who are learning to make full use of the cognitive benefits of scent and, thus, are transforming our world.

Yes, we speak of design in terms of the application and delivery of scent, for aroma in the marketplace must involve measures of a well-conceived design, as opposed to employing an oversized air freshener unit in the corner of a building. We also speak of design as it involves the consideration of aesthetics as well as function and final form.

As a new harvest of scent-educated designers enter different fields, there is no doubt that we'll see many new applications for fragrance in the areas of product design, manufacturing, packaging, and in various types of environments. Inventive minds will take the concepts we've been discussing throughout this book and apply them for as yet undiscovered purposes, incorporating their newfound knowledge and understanding to enhance their vision of what could be.

We've now covered just about every facet of this new industry. You should feel pretty empowered by now, to go out and scent your way to success. But you may still be a bit fuzzy about how to use these applications within your specific line of work. That's why we've added Part 4, "Winning Strategies for a New Century." In this section we cover how selected industries can use scent for their specific needs. Even if you don't see your specialty featured, you'll find some pretty cool applications that you can adapt for your own use. Make sure to check out the interesting strategies we note for use in education, emergency management and prisons.

Part Four

Winning Strategies
for a New Century

Until you walk a mile in another man's moccasins you can't imagine the smell.

—Robert Byrne

As you can see, the wonders and powers of aro- mas can benefit almost any industry or human need imaginable. Our imaginations are the only limitation, and as researchers continue to unravel the mystery of scent and its effects on the brain, new horizons will be identified and conquered. It may take years for some industries to incorporate the concepts and applications I've outlined in this section, but the pressure to grow and the ever-pervading atmosphere of competition and ingenuity will eventually bring scent applications to the fore.

Our knowledge about the incredible cognitive effects of scent is relatively new and its potential application to different industries leaves much to be explored. As the world grows smaller and technology advances in its meteoric marathon to the stars, we will continue to witness seeming miracles of change in the way we do business and live our lives. Of course, each of us has the option to be a passive viewer in this sea of change or an active participant—the captains of our own destinies, if you will.

If knowledge is power, then the knowledge of scent's potential use and impact on business, healthcare, and other areas becomes a powerful tool. I hope that you make this knowledge your own, and assimilate it into your own industry, strengthening your brand, increasing your revenues, and enhancing the lives of your employees and the people you serve. Let's now visit selected industries, identifying some of their specific challenges and motivations, and see how and where communication scents can make an impact.

Chapter 13
What's in Store?

The first goal of any retail operation is to lure the customer into the store's environment, and the second is to create an atmosphere that will entice the customer to stay long enough to make a series of purchases. Initially the customer is attracted to the store by word-of-mouth recommendations, TV, radio, newspaper, magazine and yellow-page ads as well as direct mail coupons, Internet ads, special promotions, discounts and loss-leader offerings, and other creative initiatives. The customer's attention is provoked by strategically placed ads on signs and billboards on the road, in the mall, and in the store environment.

Where does scent fit in to the mix?

Store Exteriors

Immediately outside the front entrance is an optimal place to employ scent triggers to lure the customer inside or to highlight a special promotion. In a busy mall, wafting a scent just outside the front door draws the attention of passersby. Scent triggers can be easily used by brands hawking foodstuffs, sweets, culinary supplies, and household products on the order of Harry and David, Williams-Sonoma, Bed Bath & Beyond, and Godiva Chocolates. Who wouldn't slow down when encountering a whiff of shrimp scampi emanating from the entrance to a cooking store? Yet jewelry, electronics, linens, and clothing stores can also radiate persuasive scents to attract attention to their goods. The key is to select a scent that speaks to the emotions of your targeted demographic.

Even for big box stores and department stores, choosing a promotional scent for the exterior entrance is a viable strategy. Specific scents can be used to promote sales on lawnmowers, barbeque grills, fashion accessories, foliage, flowers, and food items. If the promotion of the day is a seasonal beach item, for example, a delicious coconut oil or pineapple aroma can attract attention. The key is to elicit nostalgia or a pleasing memory as customers enter the store. Holiday and seasonal scents like gingerbread and pumpkin spice are big attention getters.

Store Interiors

While the aesthetics of a store exterior must entice the unfamiliar passerby to enter, the layout of the interior must offer inducements that pull consumers farther inward. Once inside the store, the more strategically the environment is scented, the better the response. A very important key to all retailers is the ability of the shopper to navigate the environment with ease. Navigation can be made easier by separating store departments into identifiable aromas, especially those that evoke nostalgia, assisting the shopper with both a visual and an emotional/memory imprint of that department.

Wouldn't it be easy to remember that the lawn and garden section that smells like fresh-cut grass is to the far left? Or, that the baked apple pie fragrance of the appliances section is in the center toward the back? The imprint of baby powder (infant wear) is to the right just after the Playdough and Crayola crayons in the toy section.

Scent also can lengthen the customer's stay. According to a 2006 *Philadelphia Inquirer* article, specific scents reduce the perception of time and increase the duration of store visits. "[Shoppers] underestimated the amount of time they spent shopping by 26 percent when exposed to the pleasant aromas of clementine and vanilla. They overestimated the time spent by 40 percent when the room smelled of galbanum, a vile aroma..."[1] As we noted in Chapter 8, Samsung's signature scent caused customers to visit three times the number of sections in the store, with two-thirds of their customers expressing a desire to stay longer. Scented POP displays increase localized attention and assist in making a product's FMOT a good one, as well as promoting last-minute impulse purchases.

Designers at Air Aroma International, are presently developing a lightweight, mobile floor model of a 360-degree scent fountain that can be placed anywhere within a store, enabling the management to focus attention more keenly on any store promotion at a moment's notice.

Shopping Malls

Mall rents vary widely based on a variety of factors. Location and area demographics will impact the average revenue per square foot, as will the amount of foot traffic and the length of stay: two key elements that scent can influence. Mall owners go to great lengths to create a pleasant, interesting environment within a mall's confines. Strategically placed food courts, fountains, and seating areas, as well as calming, mood-elevating ambient music and good lighting are key drivers that ensure high traffic volume and longer visits.

Recognizable anchor tenants are also imperative to a mall's success. If a retail store does not have a highly recognizable brand of its own, it benefits from its proximity to a well-known destination store. Radio promotions, valet parking, seasonal promotions, concerts and other types of entertainment are additional elements that bring shoppers to the mall, and these benefits are often the key to keeping people there.

Mall owners should take note of the subtle influence of scent, which can assist in achieving the basic objective of traffic counts and dwelling time. If a wonderful anchor tenant maintains exceptionally high foot traffic, but customers only flow from the parking lot to the anchor store and back, their behavior speaks volumes about their perception of the mall. "Great store, lousy mall." While major aesthetic upgrades seldom occur due to the expense, using scent to create a better impression can be an extremely cost-efficient alternative. A pleasant, comforting scent can go a long way in influencing the customer's perception.

We know that what we feel influences our perceptions. A recent study by the marketing department at West Chester University in West Chester, Pennsylvania, found that good smells cause people to underestimate the amount of time they spend shopping, while bad smells do the opposite. A pleasant smell encourages customers to linger.[2]

Easy navigation is another area that can be tackled aromatically. With some creativity, by using popular or familiar scents, malls may be able to combine navigational SIGN scents with scents that invoke nostalgia. If a mall utilizes scent mapping in this manner, it might enhance the shoppers' experience—people could look forward to a nostalgic walk down memory lane as they travel from the anchor store to another concourse.

Seasonal scents are another easy way to create a positive, memorable atmosphere. The scents of pine, cinnamon, and gingerbread before and during Christmas; pumpkin pie spices and apple cider for Halloween; and roses and chocolate for Valentine's Day: There are nostalgic scents for every occasion. New car promotions could be accompanied by the scent of leather, and kiddy rides by the smell of cotton candy. Every date on the perpetual promotions calendar should incorporate smell, the sense that speaks most loudly to the consumer's brain.

Supermarkets

The advent of homogenization, chemical additives, packaging, food irradiation, cleansing, air conditioning, and a blitzkrieg of other procedures have literally erased the aromatic romance that was once a mainstay of the shopping experience. It may seem a bit unnatural to replace these aromas with artificial ones (kind of like a blood infusion after a vampire attack), yet scent can bring back the sensory experience once again.

Food and staples merchants might return to the days of old when shoppers looked forward to the rich, exotic smells that were an expected pleasure during their shopping experience. Older cultures in various parts of the world still enjoy this tradition. The famous Khan el-Khalili Bazaar in Cairo, Egypt, is a literal mind-invigorating trip through the senses, as are many other Middle Eastern souqs and medinas. Baking breads, candies, chocolates, aged meats, exotic spices, fruits, vegetables, and a wide array of other alimentary delights radiate their essences from covered stalls and stacked displays along the narrow mazes of these ancient marketplaces. This type of scene with its accompanying feast for the senses, can absolutely lay claim to be a place where "shopping is a pleasure."

There is not much doubt that scent marketing works when it comes to edible fare. Every living human can attest to the power that scent can have upon hunger. Many food chains use practical scent marketing minimally today, with motherly types toiling over electric skillets, offering tidbits. This marketing ploy is sponsored by the food vendor of the week, of course—and its increased use is evidence that it must be working.

Robert Mueller-Grunow, managing director of Scent Communications in Cologne, Germany, revealed astounding sales increases reported by a large Italian supermarket chain. Sales increases of 100 and 200 percent for basic staples like meats, cheeses, and other items were reported. In our own experience we have seen substantial, yet smaller increases in food purchases. Culturally ingrained scent triggers, as well as other factors in the environment, all play a part in the results gained from scent marketing. Think of how your own purchasing behaviors would be affected if you entered a marketplace that emitted the smells of fresh baked sweet rolls, brewing coffee, grilling steaks, barbequing ribs, and homemade apple pie. Might you find yourself exiting the store with a few extra T-bones that you hadn't planned on?

What would happen if you walked down the snack aisle and were hit with the aromas of the corn chips, cheese puffs, popcorn, and peanuts? Do you think that the sales of those items might rise dramatically? From breakfast cereals and spaghetti sauce to cake mix and soups, if we could unleash the scents from these cans and tightly sealed containers, sales in these product categories would surely rise. And along with food sellers vying for shelf space and premium displays, they may be also angling for aromatic real estate as well, for without regulation of scented territories, a mishmash of competing flavors could create a less than desirable, odiferous goulash hanging heavy in the air.

Home Improvement Stores

Lawn and garden supplies, appliances, and building materials are all product categories for which a nostalgic scent has the potential to trigger sales. Aromatic POP displays can reach out to touch our emotions, reminding us of the pleasures of planting a garden, or even the guilt of neglected repairs. Smells can remind us of the need for a ladder (walnuts in the gutters?), trimmers (bushes getting bushy?), or a circular saw (ah, the smell of fresh sawdust). Wouldn't an added essence of fragrant seasonal flowers entice us to bring some home for the garden or kitchen? The selection of scent can sway with the seasons.

Department Stores

Many possibilities exist for creating pleasant, nostalgic atmospheres within separate departments or over a store's entire footprint. From baby powder to lavender, to ocean breeze in selected areas, management should test the selling power of scents.

Our suggestion is to scent departments with the weakest sales. Integrate a special promotion with a scent strategy to boost sales of toys or bedding during off-season. We haven't seen any studies yet of this concept; the results might be interesting.

Department store managers are already aware of the lure of the perfume and cosmetics counter. But they may not realize the potential to generate more traffic in the furniture department with a light hint of leather or flowers to recreate the feeling of home.

Clothing and Fashion Accessory Stores

In fashion one must identify the targeted consumer by age, gender, and lifestyle before deciding upon a scent plan. Which scents are more appealing to pre-teens, teens, or young adults? Which scents make women feel sexier or more attractive? Which aromas are more conducive to selling swimwear, lingerie, or jeans? Victoria's Secret has been using scent marketing for years now, getting highly effective results albeit through the relatively unsophisticated media of potpourri. The Gap and Hollister also both use lifestyle scents that appeal to the psychographics of their intended customer base—with good results.

Many branded clothing chains have experimented with scent and many more are anticipating the move. Those that have not seen good results must look at the quality and choice of their delivery systems and scent essences. Some in-store tests have used nothing more than a five-dollar wall plug-in air freshener. Any wonder the results were dismal? Remember, some scents trigger changes of perception and nostalgia, which if used correctly, can be highly influential. Scents used purely for their ambient, aesthetic value, may create a more pleasant atmosphere, but may not necessarily impact sales. Employing a scent without a strategic purpose, just for the sake of having a scent is better than nothing, but it falls far short of the potential.

Drug Stores and Personal Care Stores

Some drug chains are more aromatic than others. Presently most leave their store's aroma in the hands of fate. This can mean that we may get a subtle whiff of photo printing ink, fresh bleach, and possibly the stale smell of medicine, which may induce a negative Proustian Effect because this smell is reminiscent of illness. Small drugstores would be better served by piping out a pleasing floral aroma mix that includes a bit of lavender or rose oil to induce calmer feelings while customers search the shelves for antidotes to their illnesses. Larger drugstores that contain a food section and seasonal merchandise as well as personal care items and medicine can use more targeted localized scents.

Convenience Stores

Convenience stores make up a large percentage of the retail gasoline market. The number of consumers they have and the specific types of products that sell depend on the time of day. In the morning, coffee, breakfast sandwiches, sweet rolls, and doughnuts are the biggest sellers. Later in the day, beer, sodas, sandwiches, hot dogs, salted snacks, and sweets are the preferred fare. Trigger scents can be used to increase sales of coffee, baked goods, hot dogs, and chocolate. An aroma of corn chips and buttered popcorn could possibly initiate an upsurge in beer sales, as smelling salty items often brings up memories and cravings for those items, which need to be washed down with an ice-cold beer or soda. Of these things I know—personally.

Book Stores

Some of us love the dusty smell of old books, while others love the inky scent of the newly printed page. Therefore the question: What should a bookstore smell like? The larger booksellers haven't yet addressed the issue of store aroma, other than the unintentional waft of coffee and snacks from the obligatory coffee bar, as shoppers peruse their newly selected tomes. This is one specific type of retail operation that lures a customer who has already decided on a lengthy visit.

For the most part, customers want to navigate bookstores easily and to find a broad selection. They want to experience the look and feel of the books, as well as to sample their offerings. A strategic scent strategy should therefore incorporate comforting scents that will enhance mood and ensure calmness—leading to a pleasant stay and feeling about the brand. An alternative would be to offer aromas in different sections: cooking, history, travel, religion, for example, could each offer a particular nostalgic trigger scent.

Sporting Goods Retailers

Creating a perception of the outdoors will enhance the customer's positive feelings concerning different categories of sporting goods. Golf, tennis, baseball, football, and other orb-related sports could be associated with a nostalgic scent of fresh cut grass, a field of wheat, or similar outdoor scents. Delicious pine and forest scents might equate to skiing, mountain climbing, and camping. A good old campfire aroma could conjure up a nostalgic craving to buy Coleman products. Every area of the sporting goods store, from diving and fishing equipment to hunting and cycling has a related aroma that can trigger an emotional attachment.

Automobile Dealerships

The FMOT at a car dealership happens upon entering the showroom floor. Admittedly, advertising dollars, sleek designs, and reputations have drawn the customer to the auto dealer's door, but as we all know, creating a pleasant sales experience for the customer is an entirely different ballgame. It's no secret that the auto industry has a less than stellar reputation for high-pressure sales tactics. So much so, that one large car dealer requested a researcher to find a scent that would make their salesmen seem more honest.

Even though the artificially fragranced car interior is truthfully where the sale is often made in the mind of the customer (most of us love "new car" smell), some of us are on edge while perusing the cars, in part from sticker shock, but more probably from the line of salivating salespeople hovering nearby. Personally, I hate buying cars for this reason. And I will walk out of a dealership if I am pestered repeatedly or if the sales person doesn't listen to me. In my youth I had a used car salesman lead me to a remote part of the car lot to deliver an enthusiastic pitch on a rusting, dented junk heap devoid of hubcaps and trim. Much to my astonishment, he commenced to tell me what a stunning, beautiful, flawless, collector's item it was. I couldn't tell if he was blind or stupid, or was convinced that I was. I had grown up hearing and using the term "bold-faced lie," but I came to realize how the term was invented. Since encountering this charlatan, I have ever since been leery of the profession, even after many positive experiences in the ensuing years.

Even the best auto dealers have to battle these types of perceptions and stories. Every manufacturer's recall, publicized defect, and car-purchasing horror story adds to the dealer's difficulties. The dealership's service department is also subject to criticism, as knockoff auto parts companies fuel stories of dealer's price gouging, and mechanics suffer a less than glorious reputation.

Automobile dealerships can employ strategic scents to increase visiting time, induce nostalgia, or to improve how they are perceived. Aromas can directly calm the nerves of a potential buyer, and improve his mood. If the dealership wishes to increase sales to females, specific scents can be geared toward that goal. The overall intention of the designated scent should be to elevate mood and to deliver a nostalgic effect. I would suggest that the bigger the purchase price of an item, the more the need to tap the emotions with a Proustian scent strategy.

A waiting room scent can reduce the perception of a customer's visiting time, and mood-influencing scents could invigorate the workers in the service bays or repair areas.

Obviously the retail trade is diverse in size, scope, and category. I have only touched on specific types of businesses here to offer you a few ideas of practical ways to incorporate scent into your marketing strategies. I suggest that you use these concepts to help you develop your own scent script strategy, with a custom message designed for your own target audience.

The retail trade is a dynamic and fluid industry in the midst of a dramatic foundational change. This is not your mother's market anymore.

As online retailers like eBay and Amazon slowly eat away the revenues and profits of brick and mortar stores, survival will be achieved only by making the in-person shopping experience easier and more enjoyable. Physical retail environments must focus more on the "event" of shopping, with an emphasis on entertainment and emotional value. Enjoyment is the key word. The customer must look forward to an enjoyable experience, one that would sway the consumer's choice between sitting and shopping in the comfort of the home, and dragging herself out of the easy chair, putting on clothes, applying makeup, and battling traffic. The Internet has put the conventional retailer on notice: It is time to do-or-die or die-trying.

In the future, the choice of where to shop will be made between what is easier and what is more enjoyable. And it is the job of the retailer to make the shopping excursion an easy, enjoyable, and entertaining venture. As long as retailers keep doing what they have always been doing, the Internet will continue to nibble away at this lethargic elephantine industry, one piece of wrinkled, leathery, skin at a time, until only a skeletal resemblance remains. Scent marketing in retail by itself is not a panacea to the problem of declining in-store sales, yet it is certainly a part of the multisensory solution.

Chapter 14
Inn Scents

Hotels, resorts, and spas are a booming indus-
try for scent. Many large chains have been releasing a signature scent
in their hotel lobbies over the past couple of years and the trend is
growing.[1] The main strategy, thus far, has been to scent the lobby in
order to enhance the aesthetics of the environment and to offer a wel-
coming atmosphere to the weary traveler. But this strategy stops far
short of the potential that scent could bring in benefiting the brand
and its customer loyalty objectives. The hotelier has many other avenues in which to enhance the emotional bond between the guests
and their experience of the brand. To begin with, why not address the
environment where the guest spends the largest portion of his time?
The guest room experience still leaves much to be desired when it
comes to managing scent and offering personal choices to the guest.
The ballrooms, meeting rooms, bar areas, spa facilities, gym, public
restrooms, and hallways are all part of the guest experience as well.

Seamlessly Branded Public Spaces

A hotel's first obvious option is to expand the range of its signature scent to include foyers, hallways, and ballroom/reception areas,
thus establishing a seamlessly branded atmosphere. A subtle "just
above the radar" aroma in public areas such as these can prolong the
pleasant feelings garnered at the reception desk, and help to sustain

them during the sometimes long and arduous, maze-like journey to the guestroom. The interior design of any common area within the confines of the hotel should be approached in a multisensory fashion, to ensure the brand is represented consistently.

Scent Triggers Near Dining Areas and Lounges

One hotel in England pipes the scent of fresh baked rolls into the hotel lobby in the morning hours, increasing its revenues of full English breakfasts in the adjoining dining room. By allowing aromas to flow from a lounge or bar area, scent can be used to increase beverage sales. From the scent of salty snacks to fruity flavors, cravings can be induced for peanuts and popcorn to a freshly chilled strawberry daiquiri. If ice cream or pastries are the fare, the scent of waffle cones or muffins could enhance revenues at the coffee bar. Even the hotel gift shop can benefit from a strategically released scent.

Hotel Spas and Gyms

A natural place for scenting in a hotel is the spa area and fitness center. A range of scents, whether invigorating or relaxing can be used, to improve a guest's workout or treatment. (See, Chapter 17, "Getting Fit.")

Ballrooms

Events are a significant portion of a hotel's revenues. Meetings, conferences, galas, and weddings can be inexpensively transformed from the mundane to the unique by adding scent. Almost every gala and corporate event is thematically designed to some extent, and scent is an inexpensive, high-profit revenue generator that can offer the finishing touch to any event. Also, from a practical standpoint, after late-night party goers leave the ballroom carpet reeking of stale beer and spilled drinks, the same built-in system can quickly deodorize the space before an early morning breakfast meeting.

Brides can add an extra sensory detail to their weddings, enhancing the floral arrangements with the aroma of a forest, ocean, or a field of flowers. With a delivery system in place, the cost of the actual scent is minimal, being only a few dollars to scent an entire ballroom over three to four hours. And through my own experience as an event professional, I have found that buyers will easily pay several hundred dollars for each scent effect. Why not? They're paying thousands of dollars for lighting and other effects. A simple fog effect costs several hundred dollars. For practical use, you might scent the beginning of the event for affect during the reception, then clear the air (via ceiling air handlers) before the aromas of the meal take over.

Guest Rooms

In terms of aroma, the guest room is probably the most ill-treated space of the entire hotel property. Certainly hoteliers put a great deal of effort into attempting to mask the smells of liquor, cigarettes, and other malodors, as the housekeeping department empties can after can of air freshener into the rooms each day. Some hotels have gone smoke-free to eliminate the problem, turning their back on up to 20 percent of their potential market.[2] But as most road warriors can testify, hotel rooms are pretty stinky more often than not, and the star rating doesn't specifically guarantee a pleasant ambience. No matter the hotel brand, we frequent travelers are often surprised by a room that actually smells nice.

Hoteliers have been fighting an uphill battle with smells for years, integrating less porous materials into the flooring, drapes, and wall coverings, and freeing up the sealed windows to allow Mother Nature to circulate her magic breezes around the room. Getting rid of the smokers, porous surfaces, and improving circulation certainly does help to reduce the impression that 300 sweaty, flatulent guests have shared your bed in the last 12 months—loosening their smelly shoes and socks after a long day at the tradeshow, painting their fingernails with lung clogging polish, or sneaking Cohiba cigars while watching the adult channel. But even for hoteliers who invest in lavish lobbies and common areas, it is quite possible for guests to be charmed at the front desk only to be dismayed upon entering their rooms. Ambiance can effectively reverse all of the hotelier's efforts to induce a positive emotion about the hotel brand.

It is interesting that hotels rarely appear to be invested as much in the air quality of the guest room as in the fine woods and artwork in the common areas. For the relatively small, closed space of the room is where guests actually spend most of their time. In some cases, such as in boutique hotels in Manhattan, the opulence of the lobby and bar areas is over the top, yet when travelers reach the appointed room they find a gussied up coffin-like box that barely accommodates a double bed. Despite elegant fixtures, the bathroom would probably fit into most people's shower stalls back home. The color schemes and tones are chosen with absolute care; nonetheless the claustrophobic box is still a box, at a mere four or five hundred dollars a pop. Can you tell that I speak from experience?

Fortunately, scent offers a solution. When the Smell & Taste Treatment and Research Foundation studied the influence of scent on spatial perception, results showed that when a specific blend of scent is released into the atmosphere, subjects perceive rooms to be larger than they actually are.[3] Architects and interior designers may want to take note of this discovery.

If hoteliers put more thought into the initial impressions of their guests, considering all the senses, they might be more efficient in creating positive guest experiences. Frequently, hotel design seems to focus disproportionately on the visual components of décor for a solution, or to hide a flaw, overlooking the full range of guests' actual experiences once they are immersed in the environment.

As research has revealed, the olfactory path is the most direct to the emotions and can lay a foundation of happiness, nostalgia, relaxation, and comfort more than any 400-thread count bedspread. While hotel designers have come to realize the importance of investment in the actual bed and its accoutrements, most have yet to realize the benefits of controlling the atmosphere that hovers around the bed. Much ado has been made concerning the scented nature of the soaps, shampoos, and lotions offered in the vanity area, but the place where guests sleep has been neglected. With the advent of new delivery system technologies, the idea of the "guest experience" can now easily be brought to the next level.

The next multisensory level of the guest experience transcends the ideal of offering the comforts of home. It also transcends the idea of offering the consumer a choice of room size, club level, bed size, and pillow construction. These offerings have certainly led to repeat customer stays, and undoubtedly help to erase the "move 'em in, move 'em out" perception of the hospitality industry, yet the choice of selecting the ambience in the room is surely one of the most luxurious elements that can be offered.

As the result of my own frequent experiences, and with a new understanding of the possibilities, my colleagues and I teamed up with the French company Exhalia to find the ultimate scent-based solution to offer to the hospitality industry. As we explored the possibilities, we decided to expand our initial concept into an all-encompassing, multisensory solution. The results were pretty remarkable.

We eventually designed and produced a comprehensive scent delivery system called the iMood PMP™, which is driven by a master software program called the Sensory Brain™. Let me explain how it works.

Picture this scenario. Mr. Jones is a valued and frequent guest of a global, multi-branded hospitality chain. Whenever Mr. Jones checks into any property owned by this chain, he will enter a guest room that is customized to his own sensory preferences. His favorite Jazz will be playing, the lighting will be dimmed to his preferred level, and his personally chosen aroma will be wafting in the air.

How does this intelligence come about? Using our patented Sensory Brain, all of the guests' preferences are coded and collected into a database, then sent to a master computer server to be added into his personal customer profile. This intelligent system can code and collect any electronic activity within the guest room from mini bar choices, to movie and video-gaming preferences. We have even partnered with a California-based company called Gold Lantern to add customized digital art that can be displayed on the wall of the room. The guest can touch the screen to bring up a menu of photographic art choices. He could select beach or mountain scenery, character portraits, or even sensual displays as his temporary personal art collection. As a revenue producer, this digital screen can also serve up subtle, intermittent advertising for in-room dining or spa services—complete with complimentary trigger scents.

The iMood PMP offers the guest an opportunity to choose his favorite scent with the push of a button. The menu might include calm-inducing scents to alleviate stress, invigorating scents for in-room work, sensual scents for that out-of-town romance, or a favorite nostalgic scent to remind him of home. An "AirBrush Scent" would clear the room of bacteria and odors. Each of these scented offerings has a specific purpose, and is customized to the guest's own personal mood preference. Air Aroma International has also been developing an advanced multi-scent guest room delivery system that can be driven by the Sensory Brain's intelligent software.

The Sensory Brain uses a software algorithm to predict the popularity of scents according to the regional culture, tastes, and habits of the guests, and also ensures real-time ordering and maintenance for operational staff and suppliers. It is basically a TiVo for the senses and a single system can control over one million hotel guest rooms. It will also prove invaluable in determining scent preferences and trends in select market segments.

With these new cutting edge products, we have now introduced the next generation of emotional branding with multisensory solutions. We can speak to the customers emotions with a message that says "they remember me, they know me, and they care about me." All of this can be implemented for about the cost of a hotel's shampoo bill. Now how's that for an effective brand loyalty program?

Chapter 15
Loading the Dice

Casinos have been players in the aroma game ever since the results of one study in 1994 revealed that scenting the air increased slot machine revenues.[1] It can be argued that, of course, consumers like to spend time in a scented atmosphere more than a non-scented atmosphere. But in fact there may be a little more to the equation. Due to the scent-brain connection, specifically as scent relates to emotional imprinting and adrenaline release, we need to ask: Does scent intensify emotional experiences associated with gambling? Or does scent itself act as an adrenaline-pumping mechanism? Perhaps both. Perhaps neither. It is definitely food for thought. What we do know is that the research to date has revealed that certain scents can reduce the perception of time spent, and increase a gambler's play. Any activity that employs the APS proposition is a suitable candidate for establishing a branded scent marketing imprint on the customer.

Scent marketing could be effectively implemented at racetracks, bingo halls, lottery dispensing areas, and video gaming centers, anywhere that people have a personal involvement in an activity, especially if it stimulates excitement or an adrenaline rush. Gaming is a fact of life and a very popular activity. Scent marketing at a casino or race track may seem Machiavellian to some people. However, it is really no different than the other sensory components of this form of entertainment, such as plush carpets, flashing lights, (simulated) sounds of coins falling in slot machines, and scantily clad waitresses supplying patrons with free drinks, all proven to increase business?

Chapter 16
A Scentsational Performance

Since the advent of the talking picture, enterprising people have experimented with smells, for the most part as a novelty. Now technology and science have caught up with these fertile minds.

Live Entertainment

Live theater, cinema, concerts, and traveling spectaculars all share the common intention to elicit emotion from the viewer. The creator initially sits at his desk, drafting board, computer, or piano, with the intention to move his audience—to make them smile, laugh, or cry on cue. Carefully honed words, musical notes, hues, and settings are crafted synergistically to create the intended emotional response.

What is missing, of course, is the creative tool that has more emotional power than any other. Although the Walt Disney Company incorporates scent in some of its theme park attractions, until recently the use of scent as a dramatic element has been minimal. By adding the quality of scent to a scene, producers of theater or film (or other arts) may be able to create a condition approaching that of synesthesia in audience members. (Synesthesia happens when a person perceives intermingled sensory information in such a way that they might "hear a color" or "smell a sound." It is a sort of cross wiring or melding of the brain's circuitry.)

Movie Theaters

Once movie theaters begin to install scent delivery systems, it will add a whole new dimension to film, allowing enterprising directors with a synesthetic vision to bring multisensory entertainment to audiences. Presenters who can thrill the public by stimulating the emotions and senses to this degree may find a new method of wowing audiences.

Well-made movies are profitable. But it's not where the real money is. As most of us know, there's plenty to be made in eight dollar tubs of buttered popcorn and five dollar fountain drinks. Those of us who struggle with food cravings find it hard to slither by the gigantic snack counter when we enter the theater. The smell of fresh popcorn and candy can murder a diet. If you are like me—a serial dieter—you will hold resolute and bravely pass the counter with nary a purchase. Once in our seats, we are safe from the enticing smells, until, that is, a guiltless patron beside us has purchases one of those $8 jumbo tubs of butter-flavored popcorn.

A theater-chain owner revealed to me that purchases made after the movie starts are only 1 percent of his revenues. Well, that's surprising. I guess most people do have the willpower to stay in their seats. But what would be the result if we intermittently dispersed a buttered popcorn scent inside the theater during the movie? What if we also whiffed up a little teaser of chocolate? You tell me if you think this scent marketing strategy might cause a lift in sales.

The other neglected territory in the theater is the outside ticket line and the front entrance. What better way to jack up sales volume than pumping freshly buttered popcorn smells outside the front entrance? And if you feel that inciting cravings sounds a little evil, why not sell a healthy alternative? Orville Redenbacher sells 94 percent fat free popcorn that only takes up one Weight Watcher's point per five cups, making it an affordable decadence upon occasion. Use scent for good, not for evil!

The implementation of scent delivery systems in theaters could be paid for by the enhanced revenues of the snack counter, as well as by income from screen advertisers for perfumes, foods and scented products. With this technology in place, it can start an entire new trend for the entertainment industry.

Chapter 17
Getting Fit

The local health club or gym can be a place to prance and flex, and impress the opposite sex, but the quick oxidization of healthy bench-pressing sweat can turn any Adonis or Aphrodite into a reject and the surrounding environment into an unpleasant smelling stew of body odors. Another culprit is the multitude of odiferous sports bras and jockstraps hidden inside changing room lockers for months on end—forgotten possessions of those who haven't been very disciplined or diligent in their workout regimens. All gyms suffer from the side effects of perspiration, and the severity is commensurate with the efficiency and quality of the air conditioning, fresh air ventilation, and cleanliness.

Regardless of the cause, club managers are quite aware that undesirable smells are an inevitable byproduct of fitness clubs. They do their best to eliminate porous surfaces and often scent the atmosphere with plug-in or handheld spray air fresheners. Specific scents can be used to mask odors or infuse an aroma of freshness. However, the delivery of scent through the HVAC system is the most efficient way to battle odors.

Plenty of gyms are using scent today in steam rooms, workout areas, and locker rooms. But many gym owners are not using the correct types of scent, and they are ignorant of the fact that certain aromas make bad odors more pronounced. The result? It makes conditions worse. If this is your situation, get expert advice.

Scents can also be used to invigorate those using the gym. The steam room can be infused with peppermint, pine, or eucalyptus, all of which would simultaneously clean the air and create a zestful, uplifting atmosphere.

Dirty Clubs

In the past couple of years, incidents of infections from dangerous microbes have climbed significantly within the nation's 35,000 health clubs. Dirty clubs (at a microbial level), where Staph infection outbreaks are prevalent are losing customers in droves. This Superbug epidemic can be stopped at the gym door with a diffusion of antibacterial essential oils into the environment. After speaking with some major players in the industry, I have a feeling that we will see and smell these air-cleansing scents in our local health club in the very near future.

Spas

When it comes to environmental scenting in the spa, aromatherapy oils and candles have long-been used to provide a strategic blend of fragrances to complement many massages and other procedures.

Here's another, highly efficient and more cost-effective solution. Instead of using costly candles and bottles to scent the various areas of the spa, management releases a controlled concentration of scent into the common areas and separate massage rooms, and interchanges different scents for specific treatments and procedures. Sales for specialty procedures, such as hot stone massages, body wraps, or aromatherapy could be enhanced by a themed scent that's released in the main spa lobby.

The Exhalia Company has developed a system that delivers custom scents via Mp3 players, to accompany the theme of the music being played during massage services in many high-end spas in France.

Chapter 18
Bon Appetit

Fine dining and casual restaurants are already in the business of aromatic marketing, for the dining room is constantly barraged with sizzling, steaming dishes from the kitchen. It might not be a good idea to try to compete with these aromas, unless the surroundings are sterile and relatively odorless, like we might find in hospitals or school cafeterias, or in isolated dining rooms. In this case, strategic scenting may become your most potent ally. As everyone knows, aromas can induce cravings even when we think we aren't hungry. Aromas trip desire triggers that are much more emotional and psychological than they are physiological.

Stand-alone restaurants with pedestrian traffic nearby could employ the magic of scent triggers to draw in customers from right outside their doors. These establishments might be multi-choice eateries along a restaurant row or hotel restaurants with adjoining bars or lobby lounges where guests may be enjoying a cocktail. The wafting aroma of grilled meat, pasta sauce, or roasted garlic can be delivered out onto the sidewalk or doorway of the eatery, alerting the customers' senses and beckoning them to sample the goods, even if it is not the lunch or dinner hour. In certain large cities, one can amble by dozens of cafés, ignoring the menus prominently placed on stands and in windows, and even the hawkers and greeters placed strategically at the door. But aroma cannot be ignored. It seeps out, hungry to perform its seductive magic. It can do what other long-standing marketing measures cannot.

Food courts are another venue ripe for scent marketing. Located primarily in retail malls, these establishments line up fast food brands side-by-side, to compete for customers on the lookout for a quick fix. Asian, southwestern, vegetarian, Italian, and bakery chains vie for customers competing with mega-brands like McDonald's, Burger King, and Roy Rogers. Some consumers have their favorite brand and will make a beeline for that counter. Yet, in consideration of the consumer who really doesn't know what he's in the mood for, aromas can make all of the difference. For the deliberating customer, the pleasing smell of a slice of pizza, barbeque, or a mango-banana smoothie can serve as the tasty tiebreaker of his spur-of-the-moment, gastronomic selection.

Many baked goods chains have strict protocols to fire up the ovens every 30 or 60 minutes. This tactic applies to selling cinnamon rolls, pretzels, popcorn, pizza, or even cookies. The home office knows that there is an up-tick in sales when the customer has the opportunity to sample the product with his nose. But headquarters also knows that when policies are left to human hands, procedures may not be carried out consistently, and sales will suffer as a result.

A time-released scent delivery system overcomes the natural inconsistencies of human nature, including forgetfulness, misguided thrift, and just plain laziness, by ensuring the preordained release of desire triggers on a regimented basis throughout the day.

I spoke with a large chain of South American cafeterias that bakes the day's quota of cookies in the morning hours and then, for cost efficiency, turns the ovens off for the rest of the day. Not surprisingly, cookie sales were great in the mornings, and then decreased drastically later in the day. It was a perfect scenario in which to employ a scheduled scent strategy to keep the chocolate chip cookies moving throughout the day.

From hot dog stands to coffee shops and chophouses, aromas are an integral part of the sales process. And, in using scent to enhance revenues, this is one of the easiest areas to evaluate the resulting ROI. One set of trials in a few locations will be all that it takes to identify the value for your own restaurant business.

Chapter 19
Nine-to-five

Every day, millions of us battle our way through frustrating traffic to offices where we spend an inordinate amount of time. For many, office time far exceeds time spent with our friends, spouse, children, and, more importantly, time to regenerate. With this in mind, it makes sense that we invest the time wisely—in a comfortable, pleasant atmosphere. Of course, many of us find our already difficult jobs burdened by the stress of insurmountable emails, reports, calls, and overflowing in-baskets. Add to this the human equation: the fluctuating moods of coworkers, demanding bosses, and the cutthroat atmosphere of career advancement, and you can see how the place that we spend most of our adult lives can sometimes become unbearable.

Fortunately, there are scent-based solutions that can be used in the workplace to elevate mood and decrease stress. The research also shows that we can increase alertness, comprehension, and recall, and effectively decrease clerical errors. Certain Japanese companies have employed different scents throughout the day, targeting the creation of a relaxed atmosphere in the morning and much needed alertness after the lunch hour.[1] As any employer knows, productivity generally decreases after lunch, and even more so as the day wears on. Furthermore, the results of pheromone studies conducted by David Berliner, M.D.,[2] indicate that certain chemicals may produce a warm and fuzzy atmosphere in the workplace. There are many objectives that can be met with a scent-based solution.

As the digital revolution and the information age unfold, our lives are becoming more hectic (not easier, as we once conceived), so anything we can do to create positive attitudes in the workplace should be done. The implementation of aromas in the office can help to accomplish this goal.

Factories

Much like the environment in an office, the industrial environment of the factory is subject to politics, quotas, delays, and pressures which can cause stress. Fatigue can also be a factor, the result of long hours or the monotony of working on an assembly line. Mistakes can be costly during production, and devastating once the product has been delivered. If you want to increase alertness and minimize error, the same specific aromas that do the trick in offices can deliver their benefits to the factory floor.

Chapter 20
It's Academic

From kindergarten to college—and beyond—education is a natural application for scent. Among other cognitive benefits, aroma can increase comprehension, learning, and recall. In the classroom, for instance, if students smell the same scent mix while being tested as they did while studying subject material, they are more apt to recall the correct answers.[1] Also we know that specific scents can assist in reducing errors, most likely due to higher alertness levels. As you learned in Chapter 3, "Thinking and Perception," scent boosts alertness.[2]

Traditional classrooms represent merely a portion of where instruction and learning take place. Corporate and governmental training programs, trade school courses, business seminars, and personal growth workshops are conducted each day throughout the world. Anywhere that information is being disseminated is a scenario that can benefit from the use of CAT Scents™ and mood-altering aromas.

Aromas can be used to identify information and separate it into categories. In the course of a three-day seminar with a lot of material to be covered, a signature scent can be introduced during each segment or session. Recall of the material can be stimulated through odor-based recognition. For example, the Day 1 presentation would be fragranced with orange blossom, the Day 2 presentation with lemon, and the Day 3 presentation with peppermint. Besides the specific effects that each scent's properties have upon learning, the participants will recall each class with odor-based recognition. Instead of identifying the first or second day's class in terms of date or title, the participant is bound to identify it as the "orange or lemon seminar."

If you are one of the many people who claim to have poor recall after studying, try an experiment by scenting your space with lavender, rose, or patchouli oil during the course of studying one chapter of a book, then at a different time, study another chapter in an unscented environment. You may just be surprised at the results.

Eliminating the Superbug from Schools

Since 2003, the MRSA microbe has mutated into a new strain of Superbug. Where once it was fatal only to those with weakened immune systems, this stronger variety of MRSA is now killing healthy adults and, most startlingly, teenagers. Due to its recent migration into the general population, this new strain is called Community Associated MRSA (CA-MRSA).

Since 2003, U.S. schools have become acutely aware of the problem of MRSA, as numerous students contracted the deadly Staph infection. Over three school seasons, 276 Texas high school football players contracted the virulent infection as a result of turf burns they acquired while playing the game. [3]

Across the country, state governments from New York to Washington responded to outbreaks with multiple school closures in 2007. In October 2007, 21 Virginia schools were closed after an MRSA outbreak caused the death of an otherwise healthy 17-year-old student. Total student death counts have not been tallied thus far, but local headlines across the country have shown that these types of the deaths are mounting and communities are reacting with a resounding outcry.

A school is the prime example of an environment that can be made safer through the dispersion of antimicrobial essential oils. The discoveries made to battle the MRSA epidemic aren't a panacea, but these measures can assure parents that their children's schools are doing everything possible to overcome the problem.

Emergency Drills and Danger Notifications

Scent can be used for practical training for crisis situations. For instance, an aroma can be released during a fire drill to help reinforce the training, and subsequently facilitate the recall of specific protocols. The scent can then be employed for use in the case of a real fire. Interestingly, in the course of learning a particular alarm response, the more anxiety that is felt by the trainee during the process of odor-based training, the more ability the trainee will have to recall the training later on. This has to do with the scent-memory connection. Of course, I am not suggesting we want to cause children to panic during school drills, but teachers and emergency personnel should use a serious tone and demeanor. The following concept came to mind during an event that took place while I was writing this book. On that early spring day in April 2007, when chaos put the sleepy town of Blacksburg, Virginia, on the world map forever, and the U.S. record was surpassed for "most massive serial killing spree," officials blamed the two-hour delay in notifying the students that a killer was on the loose, on communication problems. It seems that text messaging 25,000 students would have jammed the telecommunications systems, and emails (less than an instant signal) would have been inefficient. Alarm bells could have helped, but after scores of years of exposure to fire drills, most people deliberate whether or not an alarm is real (and doubt it). Furthermore, they would have no idea that the alarm was related to anything other than a fire.

After one singular practical drill with an identifiable branded scent, every student on campus could be made aware that a killer was on the loose within minutes, if not seconds. A scent release system within each building and upon the perimeters of a campus could be the quickest signal of any currently in place. The emotional intensity of scent has the power to trigger an additional "inner" alarm. This form of communication signal is how many other animals relay danger to others of their species, yet we have been slow to adopt it. We are biologically designed for this organic alarm system to be effective.

In addition, an installed delivery system could warn of different types of dangers, by simply training the students to identify and acknowledge associated communication scents. The entire student population could immediately be warned, and be able to distinguish between a riot, fire, flood, or earthquake, and respond instantly with appropriate measures to ensure their safety. Another communication scent would denote an "all clear" or "everything is safe" signal. These types of systems could be implemented in classrooms all over the nation.

With scent becoming a multi-faceted solution for many problems in today's school systems, the cost of implementation would be insignificant when weighed against the safety, security, and well-being of the student population. Scent delivery systems could serve a dual purpose in protecting the students. An antibacterial program could eradicate the infectious microbes in the atmosphere on a daily basis, while the same technology could serve as a backup emergency warning communication system.

These concepts and solutions may seem far out of reach as you read this book. But we have only just begun to discover how scent and its effects can offer state-of-the-art solutions to modern day problems.

Chapter 21
Dial 9-1-1

In the last chapter, I wrote about the benefits of warning students of danger through the use of scent communication signals. Governments should not turn up their noses at this concept, which could be of tremendous benefit to the general public. Terrorism is a real threat, as are other man-made and natural disasters. For example, whether you subscribe to global warming theories or global climate cycle theories, one thing is sure; our planet is going through some major climate adjustments. Record strength hurricanes, massive earthquakes, and mega-tornadoes are no longer the stuff of legend. And many people who get caught in disasters die or are wounded by making ignorant or misinformed decisions.

When disaster has struck, communications are usually obliterated. This is the time when our caveman sensory radars can be put to use. Will there be more severe tremors? Has the storm passed, or are we in the calm of the eye? Is the danger over, or is there more to come? Is help on the way, or will we need to fend for ourselves? All these types of questions that occur in the midst of disaster can be answered with a scent strategy disaster plan.

We can be trained to interpret any specific scent in the form of a message. Where monotone alarms speak to us without communicating the nature of the danger, scent offers us more exacting information. A deaf or blind person knows this intimately.

Fire and burglar alarms should be doubly equipped with scent for the very reason that the deaf cannot hear them. Geographically placed sensory alarms can inform a blind person in the midst of a burglary at home. In 1991, 8.6 percent of the population was either deaf or hard of hearing.[1] That is a whopping 25 million-plus people in the U.S. alone. And standards to protect these people in a time of emergency are lacking.

Ignorance is a common disability. Even with all of the publicity and warnings about the deadly dangers of carbon monoxide poisoning, still dozens of Americans die each year after operating a gasoline generator in their home or garage. Finally, in 2007, government regulators stipulated that a warning label must be attached to the generator, alerting the user that he may die if he uses the product indoors.

While these warnings are a step in the right direction, safeguards should go further. Scent warning signals could provide the answer to this problem. If a warning scent were emitted whenever a generator is being used, then the user can be alerted that if he can smell the scent, he is in danger. This application can be achieved through the use of scented fuels in custom containers, forcing the consumer to use only the regulated fuels, or by attaching a small scent delivery system to the generator that emits the scent any time that the generator is in use.

In what could be called a gift of nature, humans are hard-wired with a built-in emotional mechanism to respond to danger signals relayed by scent. We are also gifted with the memory imprinting that scent affords, so that we can quickly respond in a vital and appropriate manner, without delay or debate. With our new understanding of this age-old purpose of scent communication, we can develop new safety systems that can truly benefit mankind.

Chapter 22
Open to the Public

Scent can improve the public spaces in which people gather, such as airports, seaports, banks, and court buildings. Calm-inducing scents could be utilized in locations where there is a tendency for frustration. Airports are a prime candidate, due to cancellations, scheduling delays, security hassles, and seemingly sadistic machinations of many of the airlines. Speaking of the airline industry, wouldn't it be a good idea to use scents as a measure to combat air traffic controller and pilot fatigue, and to reduce stress and error?

Tax, auto tag, and driver's license offices—and any other government mecca where the public is forced to show up, take a number, and wait—can benefit from the use of fragrance. Any customer service area or complaints/return department also should have a relaxing, pleasantly scented atmosphere.

Banks and lending institutions can not only create a branded signature scent (one that offers customers a feeling of security, trust, and empowerment), but also expand that message through mailing out scented bank statements and promotional offers.

These institutions can also employ danger-warning scents to be released in times of incident and crisis. Scent can be used as an alarm when a secure area is breached, warning those outside (or inside) the space of the situation. Aromas can be used to signal the public of any abnormal situation better and more efficiently than sound alarms or other means. As I have noted in previous chapters, the same scent delivery system can be used to emit cleansing or relaxing scents, and also be used to deploy warning scents in cases of emergency.

Chapter 23
All Aboard

Even though we are bombarded by smells while traveling in any form of public transportation, combating these smells is not the primary reason for the use of scents on trains, planes, buses, and in stations and terminals. If anything, we expect to have to put up with exhaust fumes, smelly people, heavy perfumes, and the stale smell of cigarette smokers while traveling en mass. While aromas can enhance the ambient air, there is a more concerning issue.

Plane travel can be frustrating to say the least, with its lines, overstuffed crowds in undersized seats, delays, bad attitudes, and poor service. But the number one concern today while traveling on planes, subways, cruise ships and other forms of mass transit, is germs: infectious airborne microbes.

On the fateful day of March 15, 2003, 120 passengers on Air China flight 112 navigated their way onto a Boeing 737-300 for a three-hour flight from Hong Kong to Beijing.[1] The flight went without incident, as snacks and beverages were served, and little notice was given to the soon-to-be-famous person that was sitting in seat 14E. No one gave much thought to what seemed to be just a fellow traveler suffering from a chronic cough.

The passengers deplaned and went about their lives, oblivious to the ticking time bomb that was released on this notable day, the

Ides of March. Within eight days, 20 of the passengers and two flight attendants became infected by the SARS virus. People sitting as far as seven rows away from the man carrying the virus were infected. Five of them eventually died as a result of the trip.

The CDC and World Health Organization say that you are only at risk of infection if you are sitting within two rows of someone who has a contagious flu—and only if you are in the vicinity for eight hours. But this information directly conflicts with the Flight 112 scenario, and another documented case: a 1979 commercial airliner that sat on the tarmac for three hours with its ventilation system shut down. In that case, a passenger with the flu transmitted the virus to 75 percent of the fellow passengers.[2]

Although most airlines do their level best to inhibit airborne viruses by changing the cabin air 15 to 20 times an hour, and circulating the air through high efficiency particulate air (HEPA) filters, air travelers are still under constant exposure. As of 2005, 15 percent of U.S. commercial airlines carrying more than 100 passengers still weren't using HEPA filters.[3] I would also venture to guess that the majority of the American public doesn't feel that these filters are too efficient. With my own multi-year history of 100,000-mile-per-year travel, I have attributed many cases of the flu to being enclosed in an aluminum tube, sharing the air with the dozens of passengers around me.

Manufacturers of HEPA filters specifically designed for today's commercial aircraft claim that their products can reduce up to 99.99 percent of the airborne particles including bacteria and viruses, and are effective in trapping the SARS and Avian Flu viruses, with the caveat that the products must be "true" HEPA filters.[4] The disparaging news is that there are currently no airworthiness standards or regulations which specify the level of filtration removal efficiency that must be used on board aircraft. And an equally ominous revelation is that there are no standards to dictate when these filters must be changed. In essence, it's up to the airline's maintenance schedule and budgeting guidelines. Some types of aircraft have filters with lower efficiencies, and still other, older planes have no filtration systems at all.

The idea of these filters is noble, but the lack of standards and regulation is disheartening. Additionally, these filters only work when the air is re-circulated through the system. So if you are sitting in the vicinity of a tuberculosis victim, good luck. Furthermore, due to the pressurization of the sealed cabin—in which air is heated then cooled through the plane's engines—the moisture of the air is all but removed. The longer you fly in this dry atmosphere, the drier your mucous membranes become. And the drier your mucous membranes become, the more susceptible you are to infections. There's no wonder why we catch nasty bugs on airplanes.

The use of aromas to eliminate microbes in airplanes is not as simple as one might think. The results of the studies to combat microbes have mostly involved the use of pure essential oils. High concentrations of essential oils can be detrimental to plastic parts, but studies show that only very low concentrations are needed to be effective. Laboratories are working on this issue presently, for the benefits of antimicrobial aromas are numerous.

At the time of this writing, Air Aroma International was in discussions with two non-U.S. based airlines, and an Indian railway company who were considering aroma delivery systems for use in their passenger compartments. Other sources have told me that Delta Airlines is also in the process of developing a scent marketing program.

Other modes of public transportation can benefit from antimicrobial prophylaxis. For instance, the steely nature and design of cruise ships is not as sensitive to essential oils, yet they are just as germ-laden below deck. Not a season goes by without newspaper headlines noting a ship or two full of nauseated, trotting passengers, threatening to jump ship unless they are returned to port.

Chapter 24
Health Care

Nowhere does an industry need to change
its image and the consumer's preconceived notions more than in the
impersonal settings that are so prevalent in health care. A vast number of patients experience undue stress when visiting care providers because of the setting as much as the treatment. My late father
hated hospitals and taking trips to the doctor. After a sickly childhood with polio, some very negative experiences were ingrained in
his memory. The thought of hospitals unsettled him, and their disinfectant smell only made it worse. As a result, he would sometimes
receive false blood pressure readings (the result of what is known as
white coat syndrome) during his visits, only to have his pulse rate
return to normal at home.

Many of us have experienced an unsettling foreboding of danger
in a doctor's office, dentist's office, hospital, or medical testing facility, for obvious reasons. Uncertainty, pain, fear, and the contemplation of our own or a loved one's mortality, can be very stressful.
The advent of HMOs, super short visits, and cattle call waiting lines
do absolutely nothing to calm the nerves. In fact, the modern-day
health care system only exacerbates tension and dread during the
most stressful of times.

A complex set of factors enters the mix when we seek health care
and, amazingly, whoever designs the systems and settings, with a

few exceptions, often seem to neglect the feelings of patients. While even medical professionals can do relatively little about the policies and bureaucracy of the mainstream medical system, the experience within a practitioner's office and other medical environments can be improved through the use of aromas that promote relaxation and lower anxiety.

Here, we're going to look at scent strategies that may be employed in waiting rooms, diagnostic clinics, examination rooms, and operating rooms to soothe and improve the moods of patients and medical staff alike, as well as to combat hospital germs.

Waiting Rooms

The waiting room of a physician, a dentist, or a diagnostic laboratory presents a prime opportunity to provide a soothing atmosphere for patients. Perceiving a pleasant, mood-elevating scent can take the edge off of worry, and possibly reduce the blood pressure and pulse rate of the patient. The traditional waiting room supplies patients with magazines, newspapers, spiritual books, and daytime television programming in order to occupy their time while waiting, and take patients' minds off the clock. If you manage a medical office, make a note to try out scents known to shorten the perception of waiting times.[1]

Diagnostic Clinics

Any diagnostic procedure, with its obligatory series of pokes and prods and cold metal gadgets wielded by often fatigued or disengaged technicians can be an anxiety-provoking experience. As with waiting rooms, scenting the testing areas can induce calming effects. MRI's, treadmill tests, blood tests, X-rays, CAT Scans, colonoscopies, mammograms, pulmonary function tests, and an endless array of other diagnostic procedures can each be made less frightening if soothing aromas are released directly into the testing area.

During a recent MRI, I noticed a serene mural hanging on the wall of the testing room. Clearly the large panel was placed there in an effort to reduce patients' anxiety. Claustrophobia is the primary issue. Anxiety from the procedure is created by the coffin-like tube into which the body is fed. But the technician joked, "The artwork doesn't do too much good when the entire procedure takes place *inside* the machine." With a specific mix of scents, spatial perception can be improved and calm alpha waves induced in the brain, relieving claustrophobia.[2] Some clinics that have employed these scents have not only seen a drastic reduction in anxiety levels, but also a reduction in MRI cancellations.[3]

Facilities can strategically release scent in order to induce calm, trigger a positive nostalgic moment, or affect the patients' perceptions of time and space. It's a wonder that they also don't use calming music during diagnostic procedures. The combination of scent and sound could make a world of difference in the patient experience.

The Examination Room

Anywhere a patient is examined, from the obstetrics table to the psychiatrist's couch, calming aromas can help to relax the patient and lead to a more efficient procedure. The dentist's chair is a medical icon that produces the "sweats" in some people, even though modern dentistry has come a long way in terms of patient comfort. The whirring sound of the drill and the scraping of metal instruments against the teeth may send chills down your spine, as may the indignity of your own slobbering numbed-face, and obtrusive interrogation lamp blinding your eyes. Women do not look forward to assuming the position for gynecologists. The optometrist's exam room is also a place that could be more comforting for patients who are anticipating a tire hose-like blast in the eye or attempting to learn the application and removal of contact lenses. In all of these settings, scent can help to reduce apprehension in the patient as well as the technician.

The Operating Room

In pre-op, post-op, and within the actual confines of the operating theater, mild calming scents can be used to relax the patient. Where only local anesthetics are used and the patient is awake, scent could possibly assist in reducing the quantity of tranquilizers required during the procedure. And, as the latest research shows, an infection-cleansing, microbe-smashing scent could help to reduce the high percentage of infections contracted during invasive procedures in the healthcare environment.

The Hospital Environment

With two million hospital-acquired infections and almost 100,000 resulting deaths each year, the Manchester Metropolitan University study showing a 90 percent reduction in airborne bugs is critically important.[5] It is important to note that this study used a blend of essential oils drawn from a variety of plants.

Not coincidentally, plant derivatives are the foundation of most pharmaceutical medications. If life-saving pills and liquid remedies can be derived from the roots and leaves of plants, it is easy to understand that their fragrant essences could also contain potent healing powers. And as the studies continue to deliver astounding results, the case for essential oils becomes stronger. Our planet is a source of wonder, with an amazingly complex network of intertwined systems. The elegant system of machines we call plants is beautifully and delicately balanced. These miraculous green machines continuously pump oxygen, the life-blood of our existence, into the atmosphere, while simultaneously drawing in our waste product of carbon dioxide, in a perfectly orchestrated exchange. It would be more fitting to say that plants, not dogs, are man's best friend.

It isn't difficult to conjure up images of an omnipotent, otherworldly genius, creating the ultimate design called life. And it would be easy to conceive that this maestro would incorporate a wide range of design features into the extraordinary plant-machines, including benefits for their fellow organisms, such as shade from the sun, nutrition, and a host of medications and fragrant remedies.

Psychiatric Facilities

Psychiatric hospitals are especially tension-filled institutions, because wards are frequently subjected to sudden outbreaks of dramatic or aggressive behavior. During an 18-month tenure working in a locked ward in a large psychiatric facility early in my life, I noticed that when a group of patients became agitated it was usually attributed to a single source. One distressed and hallucinating patient could inflame a small, angry mob of other confused inhabitants. In addition, all hell would break loose if we ran out of cigarettes. Smoking was rampant because many patients found comfort in the medicating effects of nicotine.

And, yes, tensions ran higher on the nights of full moons. During those nights, we would nix smoking limits, increase permitted meds, and prepare for the anticipated string of troubled souls who would be dropped off by the police right on cue.

While I have not discovered any research to show that aromas can directly influence serotonin, hallucinations, delusions, or effects of astrological transits, we have certainly seen proof that agitation and anxiety can be mitigated with fragrance.

The Staff

So far, we have covered many key elements of the healthcare industry, mostly showing locations where aromas can be implemented to enhance the aesthetic quality of the environment and reduce anxiety. Yet the most important factor in the entire industry actually lies in patient contact, the human element. From receptionists, to nurses and technicians, to physicians, right down the line, professionals of all kinds must interact with the horde of patients that flow through the system. If they feel good, we all benefit.

Healthcare workers are merely human, and they face stressful conditions. Often they are overworked, underpaid, and underappreciated. Theirs is the lot of continual encounters with fearful, anxious, sad, moody, and cantankerous (not to mention sick) people throughout the day. I know this intimately from several years spent working in the emergency medicine and mental health fields. Most healthcare workers are truly compassionate and professional. But when it's been a hard day and they have had to confront one too many incorrigible patients, or they are in need of a caffeine or nicotine fix, human nature will take over.

In essence, calming fragrances in the workplace can work on the most important element in the process—the healthcare worker. From the waiting room to the billing department or the records room, aromas make for a happier workforce.

Chapter 25
Scent to the Slammer

Correctional facilities of all types, from jail cells to maximum-security lockups, can benefit from the properties of scent. As music soothes the savage beast, so can fragrance calm the convict. Prison is said to be a pretty horrible place, with bad food, heat, humidity, and "Bubbas" who want to get to know you more intimately. Racial tensions, gang scores to settle, and more than a few people in a bad mood do not make for a comfortable residence. Although there are no aroma studies to show behavioral changes in serial rapists and murderers exposed to different scents, shouldn't we at least make an attempt to mellow the mood inside these nerve-strained steel fortresses?

Here's a novel idea. When the tension of a prison population builds—and it has been noted that guards can intuitively feel this happening—a calming balm of a fine lavender mist could immerse the building, both settling nerves and signaling the convicts that the authorities know that something is up. As on the battlefield (see Chapter 6, "Danger Will Robinson"), dispersal of different scents could be used to coordinate security tactics throughout the prison if the traditional communication methods failed, as might happen during an inmate uprising.

Nostalgic scents might be used as a sort of behavioral modification reward system. Fresh cut grass, hay, Playdough, leather, ocean breeze, summer rain, women's perfume, and any number of reminders of happier times could be offered as rewards for good behavior amongst the prisoners in a specific cellblock. These would be emotion-laden behavioral rewards in a place where the reward options are otherwise quite limited.

Finally, in lieu of rubber bullets, billy clubs, tasers and tear gas, a more humanitarian solution to prisoner uprisings and bad behavior could possibly be provided with an approach that I call smell behavioral therapy. If inmates refuse to respond to more traditional procedures, they could be more easily persuaded to get along if the consequences included the lingering stench of, for example, rotting fish.

And they said that life on the inside was already rough.

Afterword: A Final Whiff Note

In creating this book and its related elements, James Goldney and I have taken our teachings to heart. For example, I'm sure you quickly discovered the little surprise embedded in the cover of this book—the subtle aromatic essence. Would you have expected anything less from a book about scent? This simple element serves as a messenger whose story, we hope, will be retold and spread by others around the globe. ("A" students of this book will not forget to add a healthy dose of anticipation, progression, and surprise when communicating the story.)

Due to the trendsetting nature of the subject, this is most likely the first book about scent communication you have ever read, and almost certainly the first scented book you have ever read. I hope that you now have a new appreciation and understanding of scent and its vast possibilities. We have gone to great lengths to bring our message to life by featuring stories, research and real life examples of the events taking place in this field. I hope that some of the discoveries described in this book were as fascinating for you as they were for me when I first came across them.

Scent can be a powerful and eloquent emissary, and I hope that after reading this book you will be inspired to adopt some form of scent initiative, no matter how small, to enhance your business or personal life. Once you begin, you will soon discover that there are countless applications for scent that are only limited by the imagination.

To attain a deeper understanding of this subject, I invite you to visit one of our seminars, where you will find that we practice what we preach, incorporating many of the multisensory philosophies described in *Whiff!* If you are fortunate enough to attend one of these scented sessions, you might discover that your comprehension and recall improve, for we endeavor to use scent as an integral communication tool when delivering our message. And for a taste of the *Whiff!* brand, you'll receive a delicious gift of chocolate.

To receive updated information on the themes, technologies and industries covered in *Whiff!* visit www.whiffbook.com.

For more information about our scent related consulting services and educational seminars, visit our website www.whiffsolutions.com. You can *Get Whiff the Program!*™, with access to informative videos, industry-specific instructional DVDs, and check out our calendar of upcoming seminars, teleseminars and events.

Finally, I invite you to submit your specific queries and questions by visiting www.askthewhiffguys.com.

Having read *Whiff!*, you will recognize that all of our promotional elements combine to make a strong "Whiff Factor," and are designed to create a bond with you through sight, sound, scent, taste, and touch. I encourage you to increase your "Whiff Factor," and to do the same for your customers or clients.

We would love to hear how you are using scent communication to enhance your business, and how you are implementing any other techniques you may have learned from *Whiff!'*

Now go out and tell your friends to get *Get Whiff the Program*!

Whiff Solutions
135 West 26th Street
New York, NY 10001-6833
Direct Inquiries to:
4415 Serena Circle
St. Augustine, FL 32084
Tel: (866) 779-4433
www.whiffsolutions.com
www.askthewhiffguys.com

Scent Marketing Institute
7 Fox Meadow Road
Scarsdale, NY 10583
Tel: (646) 236-4606
www.scentmarketing.org

Monell Chemical Senses Center
3500 Market Street
Philadelphia, PA 19104-3308
Tel: (267) 519-4700
www.monell.org

The Fragrance Foundation
145 East 32 Street
New York, NY 10016-6002
Tel: (212) 725-2755
www.fragrance.org

SOSI–Sense of Smell Institute
145 East 32nd Street
New York, NY 10016-6002
Tel: (212) 725-2755
www.senseofsmell.org

Smell & Taste Treatment and Research Foundation
845 North Michigan Avenue
Suite 990W
Chicago, IL 60611
Tel: (312) 938-1047
www.smellandtaste.org

IFRA–International Fragrance Association
Avenue des Arts, 6
1210 Brussels
Belgium
Tel: 011 32 214 20 60
www.ifraorg.org

RIFM–Research Institute for Fragrance Materials
50 Tice Boulevard
Woodcliff Lake, NJ 07677
Tel: (201) 689-8089
www.rifm.org

FMA–Fragrance Materials Association of the United States

1620 I Street NW, Suite 925
Washington, DC 20006
Tel: (202) 293-5800
www.fmafragrance.org

International Flavors and Fragrances

USA Sales
521 West 57th Street
New York, NY 10019-2960
Tel. 212-765-5500
www.iff.com

Introduction

1. *Epcot Center Today,* vol. 1, no. 2 (1981).
2. Diane Ackerman, *A Natural History of the Senses.* (New York: Vintage, 1991): p. 1.

Chapter 1

1. Tristram D. Wyatt, *Pheromones and Animal Behaviour: Communication by Smell and Taste* (Cambridge, UK: Cambridge University Press, 2003).
2. N.J. Vickers, "Winging It: Moth Flight Behavior and Responses of Olfactory Neurons Are Shaped by Pheromone Plume Dynamics," *Chemical Senses,* vol. 31, no. 2 (February 2006): pp. 155–66.
3. E.J. Robinson, D.E. Jackson, M. Holcombe F.L. Ratnieks, "Insect Communication: 'No Entry' Signal in Ant Foraging," *Nature,* vol. 438, no. 7067 (November 24, 2005): p. 442.
4. Diane Ackerman, *A Natural History of the Senses* (New York: Vintage, 1991): p. 11.
5. Richard Axel, "The Molecular Logic of Smell," *Scientific American,* vol. 273 (October 1995): p.154.
6. *The Writings of Henry David Thoreau,* Volume 8: 1854, edited by Sandra Harbert Petrulionis (Princeton, N.J: Princeton University Press, 2002): p. 179.
7. "How Does the Sense of Smell Work?" Lesson #1 from the section Smell 101 on the Sense of Smell Institute Website: www.senseofsmell.org, and E.B. Goldstein, *Sensation and Perception,* 5th Edition (London, UK: Pacific Grove, 1999).
8. M. Spehr, G. Gisselmann, A. Poplawski, J.A. Riffel, C.H. Wetzel, R.K. Zimmer, and H. Hatt, "Identification of a Testicular Odorant Receptor Mediating Human Sperm Chemotaxis," *Science,* vol. 299, no. 5615 (March 28, 2003): pp. 2054–8.
9. K. Mizuno, N. Mizuno, T. Shinohara, and M. Noda, "Mother-infant Skin-to-skin Contact after Delivery Results in Early Recognition of Own Mother's Milk Odour," *Acta Paediatrica,* vol. 93, no. 12 (December 2004): pp.1560–2.
10. M. Kaitz, A. Good, A.M. Rokem, and A.I. Eidelman, "Mothers Learn to Recognise the Smell of Their Own Infant within Two Days," *Developmental Psychobiology,* vol. 20, no. 6 (November 1987): pp. 587–91.
11. G.E. Weisfeld, T. Czilli, K.A. Phillips, J.A. Gall, and C.M. Lichtman, "Possible Olfaction-based Mechanisms in Human Kin Recognition and Inbreeding

Avoidance," *Journal of Experimental Child Psychology*, vol. 85, no. 3 (July 2003): pp. 279–95.

12. R. L. Doty, P. Shaman, S.L. Applebaum, R. Giberson, L. Siksorski, and L. Rosenberg, "Smell Identification Ability: Changes with Age," *Science*, vol. 226, no. 4681 (December 21, 1984): pp. 1441–43.

13. E. Navarrete-Palacios, R. Hudson, G. Reyes-Guerrero, and R. Guevara-Guzmán, "Lower Olfactory Threshold during the Ovulatory Phase of the Menstrual Cycle." *Biological Psychology*, vol. 63, no. 3 (July 2003): pp. 269–79; also N. Ochsenbein-Kölble, R. von Mering, R. Zimmermann, and T. Hummel, "Changes in Olfactory Function in Pregnancy and Postpartum," *International Journal of Gynaecology and Obstetrics*, vol. 97, no. 1 (April 2007): pp. 10–14.

14. S. Carusol, C. Grillo, C. Agnello, L. Maiolino, G. Intelisano, and A. Serra, "A Prospective Study Evidencing Rhinomanometric and Olfactometric Outcomes in Women Taking Oral Contraceptives," *Human Reproduction*, vol. 16, no. 11 (November 2001): pp. 2288–94.

15. K. Ackerl, M. Atzmueller, and K. Grammer, "The Scent of Fear," *Neuroendocrinology Letters*, vol. 23, no. 2 (April 2002): pp. 79–84.

16. J.J. Leyden, K.J. McGinley, E. Holzle, J.N. Labows, and A.M. Kligman, "The Microbiology of the Human Axilla and Its Relationship to Axillary Odor," *The Journal of Investigative Dermatology*, vol. 77 (October 31, 1981): pp. 413–16; also X.N. Zeng, J.J. Leyden, and G. Preti, "Analysis of Characteristic Human Female Axillary Odors: Quantitative Comparison to Males," *Journal of Chemical Ecology*, vol. 22 (1996): pp. 237–57.

17. April Armstrong, "How Well Can You Smell?" *ABC News Online* (December 18, 2006). Website: http://abcnews.go.com.

18. R.L. Doty, et al: pp. 1441–43.

19. Ibid.

20. R.I. Mesholam, P.J. Moberg, R.N. Mahr, R.L. Doty, "Olfaction in Neurodegenerative Disease: A Meta-analysis of Olfactory Functioning in Alzheimer's and Parkinson's diseases," *Archives of Neurology*, vol. 55, no. 1 (January 1998): pp. 84–90.

21. S. Nordin, C. Murphy, T.M. Davidson, C. Quiñonez, A.A. Jalowayski, and D.W. Ellison, "Prevalence and Assessment of Qualitative Olfactory Dysfunction in Different Age Groups," *The Laryngoscope*, vol. 106, no. 6 (June 1996): pp. 739–44.

22. Robert S. Wilson, PhD; Julie A. Schneider, MD; Steven E. Arnold, MD; Yuxiao Tang, PhD; Patricia A. Boyle, PhD; David A. Bennett, MD, "Olfactory Identification and Incidence of Mild Cognitive Impairment in Older Age." *Archives of General Psychiatry* 2007; 64:802–808.

23. O. Schwenn, I. Hundorf, B. Moll, S. Pitz, and W.J. Mann, "Do Blind Persons Have a Better Sense of Smell than Normal Sighted People?" *Klinische Monatsblatter fur Augenheilkunde*, vol. 219, no. 9 (September 2002): pp. 649–54.

24. Website: http://dictionary.reference.com/browse/influence.

25. Danny Hakim, "New Luxury-Car Specifications: Styling. Performance. Aroma." *The New York Times* (October 25, 2003): p. A1.

26. Ibid.

27. Russ Mason, "Exploring the Potentials of Human Olfaction," *Alternative and Complimentary Therapies*, vol. 2, no. 3 (June 2005). In an interview, Alan Hirsch is quoted: "We looked at 989 people from 45 states and 39 countries, and found that the number-one odor that made people nostalgic for childhood was baked goods."

28. R.W. Moncreiff, *Odour Preferences* (New York: John Wiley, 1966); also W.S. Cain and F. Johnson, Jr., "Lability of Odor Pleasantness: Influence of Mere Exposure," *Perception*, vol. 7, no. 4 (1978): pp. 459–65.

29. S. Ayabe-Kanamura, S. Saito, H. Distel, M. Martínez-Gómez, and R. Hudson, "Differences and Similarities in the Perception of Everyday Odors: A Japanese-

German Cross-cultural Study," *Annals of the New York Academy of Sciences*, vol. 855, no. 1 (November 30, 1998): pp. 694–700.

30. David Michael Stoddart, *The Scented Ape: The Biology and Culture of Human Odour* (Cambridge, UK: Cambridge University Press, 1990): p. 61.

31. Lyall Watson, *Jacobson's Organ: And the Remarkable Nature of Smell* (New York: Norton, 2000).

32. Constan Classen, *Aroma: The Cultural History of Smell* (Oxford, UK: Routledge, 1994).

33. Ibid.

34. Ibid.

35. Ibid.

36. Edwin T. Morris, *Fragrance: The Story of Perfume from Cleopatra to Chanel* (New York: Scribner, 1984).

37. B. Rasch, C. Büchel, S. Gais, and J. Born, "Odor Cues During Slow-wave Sleep Prompt Declarative Memory Consolidation," *Science*, vol. 315 (March 9, 2007): pp. 1426–9; also Benedict Carey, "Study Uncovers Memory Aid: A Scent During Sleep," *The New York Times* (March 9, 2007): p. A1.

38. "Science of Fragrance Honorees 2006." Sense of Smell Institute Website: www.senseofsmell.org.

39. A.R. Hirsch and C. Kane, "The Effects of Green Apple Fragrance on Migraine Headache," *Headache*, vol. 37, no. 5 (May 1997): p. 312.

40. S. Haze, K. Sakai, and Y. Gozu, "Effects of Fragrance Inhalation on Sympathetic Activity in Normal Adults." *Japanese Journal of Pharmacology*, vol. 90, no. 3 (November 2002): pp. 247–53.

41. U. Stockhorst, E. Gritzmann, K. Klopp, Y. Schottenfeld-Naor, A. Hübinger, H. Berresheim, H. Steingrüber, and F.A. Gries, "Classical Conditioning of Insulin Effects in Healthy Humans." *Psychosomatic Medicine*, vol. 61 (1999): pp. 424–35.

42. "Average Daily Package Volume for FedEx Express and FedEx Ground was 5.868 Million Packages," *FedEx 2006 Annual Report.*

43. FedEx Kinkos Press Release (January 2007), "FedEx Kinko's Adds Direct Mail, Print Online to Portfolio."

44. R. Colin Johnson, "Star Trek's 'Tricorder' Realized," *EE Times* (March 7, 2007). Website: http://www.eetimes.com.

45. I. Cotte-Rodriguez and R.G. Cooks, "Non-proximate Detection of Explosives and Chemical Warfare Agent Stimulants by Desorption Electrospray Ionization Mass Spectrometry," *Chemical Communications*, vol. 28 (July 28, 2006): pp. 2968–70.

46. L. Nyadong, M.D. Green, V.R. DeJesus, P.N. Newton, and F.M. Fernandez, "Reactive Desorption Electrospray Ionization Linear Ion Trap Mass Spectrometry of Latest-generation Counterfeit Animalarials via Noncovalent Complex Formation," *Analytical Chemistry*, vol. 79, no. 5 (March 1, 2007): pp. 2150–7.

47. "A Brief Overview of Counterfeiting," International Chamber of Commerce (August 28, 2004). Website: http://www.iccwbo.org.

Chapter 2

1. Originally published in 1913 as *Du Côté de Chez Swann*, the first volume of *A la recherche du temps perdu (In Search of Lost Time)* by Bernard Grasset. The English translation by C.K. Scott Moncrieff was first published by Chatto & Windus (London) and Henry Holt (New York) in 1922.

2. Samuel Beckett, *Proust* (New York: Grove, 1994).

3. R.S. Herz, "A Naturalistic Analysis of Autobiographical Memories Triggered by Olfactory Visual and Auditory Stimuli," *Chemical Senses*, vol. 29, no. 3 (March 2004): pp. 217–24.

4. R.S. Herz and G.C. Cupchik, "The Emotional Distinctiveness of Odor-evoked Memories," *Chemical Senses,* vol. 20, no. 5 (January 1995): pp. 517–28.

5. C. Warren and S. Warrenburg, "Mood Benefits of Fragrance," from a speech by Dr. Warren at the November 12, 1991 symposium "Aroma-Chology: The Impact of Science on the Future of Fragrance" sponsored by the Olfactory Research Fund.

6. D. Michael Stoddart, "Follow Your Nose: The History, Physiology, and Psychology of Smell," *The New York Times on the Web* (September 28, 1997). Accessed online: http://www.nytimes.com/books/97/09/28/reviews/970928.28stoddat. html?_r=1&oref=slogin.

7. Robert A. Baron, "Of Cookies, Coffee and Kindness: Pleasant Odors and the Tendency to Help Strangers in a Shopping Mall," *Aroma-Chology Review,* vol. 6, no. 1 (January 1997).

8. "Studies Reveal that Scents of Flowers Can Influence the Mood in a Room," Procter & Gamble/Tide press release posted November 29, 2006 on Hispanic PR Wire Website: http://www.hispanicprwire.com.

9. Kara Newman, "Gas Pumps that Smell like Coffee," *Business 2.0* (March 26, 2007). Accessed online: http://money.cnn.com/magazines/business2/business2_arc hive/2007/04/01/8403354/index.htm.

10. Envirodine Studios Website: http://www.enviroscent.com/research.php.

11. A.R. Hirsch, "Preliminary Results of Olfaction Nike Study," report distributed November 16, 1990, by the Smell & Taste Treatment and Research Foundation.

12. A.R. Hirsch, "Effects of Ambient Odors on Slot-Machine Usage in a Las Vegas Casino," *Psychology & Marketing,* vol. 12, no. 7 (October 1995): pp. 585–94; and N. R. Kleinfield, "The Smell of Money," *The New York Times* (October 25, 1992): Style section, p. 1.

13. P.F. Bone and P.S Ellen, "Scents in the Marketplace: Explaining a Fraction of Olfaction," *Journal of Retailing,* vol. 75, no. 2 (1999): p. 243–263.

14. Nanette Varian, "Dollars and Scents: Find Your Fortune by Following Your Nose," *Success* (December 1997).

15. Ibid.

16. Eric R. Spangenberg, David E. Sprotta, Bianca Grohmannb, Daniel L. Tracy, "Gender-congruent ambient scent influences on approach and avoidance behaviors in a retail store," *Journal of Business Research,* vol. 59, no. 12 (November 2006) pp: 1281–1287

17. Suzanne Hoppough, "Dollars and Scents. What's That Smell?" *Forbes* (October 2, 2006).

18. "Hershey's ScentAir Boost Sales with Chocolate Aroma," *Vending Times,* vol. 43, no. 11 (November 2003).

19. Fabien Deglise, "The Nose Knows," *enRoute* (February 2003). Website: http://www.enroutemag.com.

20. Martin Lindstrom, *Brand Sense: Build Powerful Brands Through Touch, Taste, Smell, Sight, and Sound* (New York: Free Press, 2005): p. 15.

21. Jeremy Smith, "Sweet Smell of Excess," *The Ecologist* (January 11, 2002).

22. "Westin Hotels Stirs the Senses with New Multi-million Global Ad Campaign, Experiential Campaign Brings to Life Westin's New Brand Positioning of Personal Renewal," Starwood Hotels press release (March 14, 2006).

Chapter 3

1. "Women Can 'Smell' Thin to Men," *USA Today-Magazine* (June 1, 2003).

2. Charlene Laino, "Smell of Grapefruit Helps Women Look Younger," *WebMD Medical News* (March 24, 2005). Website: http://www.webmd.com.

3. M.L. Demattè, R. Osterbauer, C. Spence, "Olfactory Cues Modulate Facial Attractiveness," *Chemical Senses*, vol. 32, no. 6 (July 2007): pp. 603–10.M.L.

4. Ibid.

5. R.S. Herz, J.W. Schooler, "A Naturalistic Study of Autobiographical Memories Evoked by Olfactory and Visual Cues: Testing the Proustian Hypothesis," *The America Journal of Psychology*, vol. 115, no. 1 (Spring 2002): pp. 21–32.

6. R. Herz, C. Schankler, and S. Beland, "Olfaction, Emotion and Associative Learning: Effects on Motivated Behavior," *Motivation and Emotion*, vol. 28, no. 4 (December 2004): pp. 363–83.

7. R.A. Osterbauer, P.M. Matthews, M. Jenkinson, C.F. Beckmann, P.C. Hansen, and G.A. Calvert, "Color of Scents: Chromatic Stimuli Modulate Odor Responses in the Human Brain," *Journal of Neurophysiology*, vol. 93, no. 6 (June 2005): pp. 3434–41.

8. "As much as 80 percent of what we call 'taste' actually is aroma," Dr. Susan Schiffman, as quoted in *Chicago Tribune* (May 3, 1990). "Ninety percent of what is perceived as taste is actually smell," Dr. Alan Hirsch, as quoted in *MX* (Melbourne, Australia: January 28, 2003).

9. "The Smell Report," Social Issues Research Center Website: www.sirc.org.

10. Kathi Keville and Peter Korn, *Herbs for Health and Healing* (Emmaus, PA: Rodale Press, 1996).

11. Valerie Ann Worwood, *The Fragrant Mind: Aromatherapy for Personality, Mind, Mood, and Emotion* (Novato, CA: New World Library, 1996): p. 58.

12. Keville and Korn.

Chapter 4

1. Gina Hyams and Susie Cushner, *Incense: Rituals* (San Francisco, CA: Chronicle Books, 2003).

2. Ibid.

3. Sheikh Muslih-uddin Sa'di Shirazi, *The Gulistan* (Whitefish, NT: Kessinger Publishing, 2004).

4. Nancy L. Nickell, *Nature's Aphrodisiacs* (Berkeley, CA: Crossing Press, 1999): p. 72.

5. "Chemical Communication," *Young Naturalist*, The Louise Lindsey Merrick Texas Environment Series (College Station, TX: Texas A&M University Press, 1983), no. 6: pp. 55–8, as reprinted on the Texas Parks and Wildlife Department Website: http://www.tpwd.state.tx.us/learning/young_naturalist.

6. Danek S. Kaus, "Realm of the Senses. Fremont Firm Follows Retail Scent, but Returns to Research Roots," *San Francisco Business Times* (October 27, 2000).

7. "It's What You Don't Smell that Makes It Incredible: Inner Realm and the New Pheromone Phenomenon," EROX Corporation press release (April 1, 1997).

8. Website: http://www.erox.com/SixthSense/pheromones.html.

9. C. Wyart, W.W. Webster, J.H. Chen, S.R. Wilson, A. McClary, R.M. Khan, and N. Sobel, "Smelling a Single Component of Male Sweat Alters Levels of Cortisol in Women," *The Journal of Neuroscience*, vol. 27, no. 6 (February 7, 2007): pp. 1261–65.

10. M. Bensafi, W.M. Brown, R. Khan, B. Levenson, and N. Sobel, "Sniffing Human Sex-steroid Derived Compounds Modulates Mood, Memory and Autonomic Nervous System Function in Specific Behavioral Contexts." *Behavioural Brain Research*, vol. 152, no. 1 (June 4, 2004): pp. 11–22.

11. G. Preti, C.J. Wysocki, K.T. Barnhart, S.J. Sondheimer, J.J. Leyden, "Male Axillary Extracts Contain Pheromones that Affect Pulsatile Secretion of Luteinizing Hormone and Mood in Women Recipients," *Biology of Reproduction*, vol. 68, no. 6 (June 2003): pp. 2107–13.

12. K. Stern and M. K. McClintock, "Regulation of Ovulation by Human Pheromones," *Nature*, vol. 392 (March 12, 1998): pp. 177–9.

13. B.I. Grosser, L. Monti-Bloch, C. Jennings-White, D.L. Berliner, "Behavioral and Electrophysiological Effects of Androstadienone, a Human Pheromone," *Psychoneuroendocrinology*, vol. 25, no. 3 (April 2000): pp. 289–99; and Catherine Zandonella, "Pheromones Can Banish Premenstrual Syndrome," *New Scientist*, (July 18, 2001).

14. D. Singh, P.M. Bronstad, "Female Body Odour Is a Potential Cue to Ovulation," *Proceedings of the Royal Society, Biological Sciences*, vol. 268, no. 1469 (April 22, 2001): pp. 797–801.

15. I.S. Penton-Voak, D.I. Perrett, D.L. Castles, T. Kobayashi, D.M. Burt, L.K. Murray, and R. Minamisawa, "Menstrual Cycle Alters Face Preference," *Nature*, vol. 399, no. 6738 (June 24, 1999): pp. 741–2.

16. Y. Martins, G. Preti, C.R. Crabtree, T. Runyan, A.A. Vainius, and C.J. Wysocki, "Preference for Human Body Odors Is Influenced by Gender and Sexual Orientation," *Psychological Science*, vol. 16, no. 9 (September 2005): pp. 694–701.

17. A.R. Hirsch, and J.J. Gruss, "Human Male Sexual Response to Olfactory Stimuli," *Journal of Neurological and Orthopaedic Medicine and Surgery*, vol. 19, no. 1 (Spring 1999): pp. 14–19.

18. Alan Hirsch, *Life's a Smelling Success: Using Scent to Empower Your Memory and Learning* (New York: Authors of Unity Publishing, 2003).

19. A.R. Hirsch, "The Effects of Odors on Female Sexual Arousal," *Psychosomatic Medicine*, vol. 60 (1998): p. 95.

20. Scent researcher George Dodd, PhD, as co-director of the University of Warwick Olfaction Research Group from 1971–1994, in reporting on a possible progenitor of androstenone, a steroid called Osmone 1, claimed that "women are 1,000 times more sensitive than men to these steroid musk molecules," from Caitlin Costello, "Sexual or sexist? Replication of human pheromones" available online at: http://serendip.brynmawr.edu/exchange/node/1865. Also referenced in Anabelle Birchall, "A Whiff of Happiness," *New Scientist* (August 25, 1990), available online at: http://www.newscientist.com/article/mg12717314.700.

21. V. Gudziol, M. Muck-Weymann, O. Seizinger, R. Rauh, W. Siffert, and T. Hummel, "Sildenafil Affects Olfactory Function," *Journal of Urology*, vol. 177, no. 1 (Month 2007): pp. 258–61.

22. Tetsuro Shingo et al., "Pregnancy-stimulated Neurogenesis in the Adult Female Forebrain Mediated by Prolactin," *Science*, vol. 299, no. 5603 (January 3, 2003): pp. 117–20; and Alan Farnham, "Is Sex Necessary?" Website: www.Forbes.com (posted October 8, 2003).

Chapter 5

1. Piet A. Vroon, *Smell: The Secret Seducer.* Translated by Paul Vincent (Farrar, Straus & Giroux, 1997).

2. Lois N. Magner, *A History of Medicine, Second Edition* (London, UK: Informa Healthcare, 2005).

3. H. Grundmann, M. Aires-de-Sousa, J. Boyce, E. Tiemersma, "Emergence and resurgence of meticillin-resistant Staphylococcus aureus as a public-health threat." *The Lancet*, Volume 368, Issue 9538, pp. 874–885. Published online June 21, 2006

4. Charles Graham, "Infection Fight Breakthrough," *Wigan Observer* (February 16, 2007).

5. Jet Propulsion Laboratory, California Institute of Technology, Press Release, "Electronic Nose: Nothing to Sniff at" (June 6, 2000). Website: http://www.jpl.nasa.gov/releases/2000/e-nose.html.

6. Smiths Detection News Release, "Smiths Group Acquisition Expands Detection Technology Base" (March 10, 2004). Website: www.smithsdetection.com.

7. C.M. Willis, S.M. Church, C.M. Guest, W.A. Cook, N. McCarthy, A.J. Bransbury, M.R. Church, and J.C. Church, "Olfactory Detection of Human Bladder Cancer by Dogs: Proof of Principle Study," *BMJ*, vol. 329, no. 7468 (September 25, 2004): p. 712; and M. McCulloch, T. Jezierski, M. Broffman, A. Hubbard, K. Turner, and T. Janecki, "Diagnostic Accuracy of Canine Scent Detection in Early- and Late-stage Lung and Breast Cancers," *Integrative Cancer Therapies*, vol. 5, no. 1 (March 2006): pp. 30–9.

8. A.R. Hirsch and C. Kane, "The Effects of Green Apple Fragrance on Migraine Headache," *Headache*, vol. 37, no. 5 (1997): p. 312.

9. Center for Medicines in the Public Interest press release (September 13, 2005).

10. "Counterfeit Medicines," World Health Organization Fact Sheet 275 (Revised November 14, 2006). Website: http://www.who.int/mediacentre/factsheets/fs275/en/.

Chapter 6

1. Piet A. Vroon, *Smell: The Secret Seducer*. Translated by Paul Vincent (Farrar, Straus & Giroux, 1997).

2. Ibid. p 41.

3. W.L. Silver and J.A. Maruniak, "Trigeminal Chemoreception in the Nasal and Oral Cavities," *Chemical Senses*, vol. 6, no. 4 (1981): pp. 295–305.

4. Lyall Watson, *Jacobson's Organ: And the Remarkable Nature of Smell* (New York: Norton, 2000).

5. D. Chen, A. Katdare, and N. Lucas, "Chemosignals of Fear Enhance Cognitive Performance in Humans," *Chemical Senses*, vol. 31, no. 5 (June 2006): pp. 415–23.

6. K. Ackerl, M. Atzmueller and K. Grammer, "The Scent of Fear," *Neuroendocrinology Letters*, vol. 23, no. 2 (April 2002): pp. 79–84.

7. S.S. Schiffman, "Use of Olfaction as an Alarm Mechanism to Arouse and Alert Sleeping Individuals," *Aroma-Chology Review*, vol. 4, no. 1 (1995): pp. 2–5.

8. Sewell Chan, "A Rotten Smell in Manhattan Raises Alarms and Questions," *The New York Times* (January 9, 2007).

9. Kareem Fahim, "Good Smell Perplexes New Yorkers," *New York Times* (October 28, 2005).

10. Aaron Zitner, "Foul Odors Tantalize in Quest for Non-lethal Weapons: Pentagon Believes Awful Smells Might Be a Way to Disperse Hostile Crowds," *Los Angeles Times* (November 28, 2002).

11. Lyall Watson, *Jacobson's Organ: And the Remarkable Nature of Smell* (New York: Norton, 2000).

12. U.S. Department of Health and Human Services, "Terrorism And Other Public Health Emergencies: A Reference Guide for Media," (September 2005): pp. 32–42.

Chapter 7

1. Lazlo Unger, an economist at Givaudan, reported by Leffingwell & Associates. Website: http://www.leffingwell.com/top_10.htm.

2. "The U.S. Market for Home Fragrances," (Packaged Facts, 1 June 2002).

3. Unity Marketing, "Home Fragrance & Candle Market, 2005: Understanding and Predicting Consumers' Passion for Candles and Home Fragrances" (April 1, 2005).

4. Leffingwell & Associates Website: http://www.leffingwell.com/top_10.htm.

5. Rich Thomaselli, "Trends to Watch in 2007," *Advertising Age* (December 18, 2006).

6. Martin J. Smith, Patrick J. Kiger, "OOPS: 20 Life Lessons from the Fiascoes That Shaped America," *Collins,* (Feb 20, 2007).

7. Ibid.

8. Ibid.

9. Ibid.

10. Janet Maslin, "'Polyester,' An Offbeat Comedy," *The New York Times* (May 29, 1981).

11. "Rugrats Go Wild," an animated movie by Klasky-Csupo, released June 13, 2003.

12. *TV Guide,* vol. 55, no. 18, issue 2822 (April 30, 2007): pp. 22–5.

13. "The New World," a film written and directed by Terrence Malick, and distributed by New Line Cinema (2005).

14. Al Ries and Laura Ries, *The Fall of Advertising and the Rise of PR* (New York: Harper Collins, 2002).

15. "Online Advertising to Grow Seven Times Faster than Offline Advertising in 2007" (December 4, 2006). ZenithOptimedia Group press release. Website: www.zenithoptimedia.com.

16. Martin Lindstrom, *Brand Sense: Build Powerful Brands through Touch, Taste, Smell, Sight, and Sound* (New York: Free Press, 2005).

17. Amy Corr, "All That Jazz," *Media Post* (October 9, 2006).

18. Brian Steinberg, "Kraft Vies for Eyes—and Noses: Ad Play in *People* Magazine Uses Some Scented Spots to Tickle Readers' Fancy," *The Wall Street Journal* (November 13, 2006).

19. Erik Sass, "Study Finds Spectacular Print Ads Get Spectacular Recall," *Marketing Daily* (February 23, 2007).

20. In the 1930s, Garnet Carter hired sign painter Clark Byers to promote his now famous Georgia attraction. Byers traveled the nation's highways and offered to paint farmers' barns in exchange for letting him paint three simple words: "See Rock City."

Chapter 8

1. These two houses are International Flavors & Fragrances (IFF) and Givaudan.

2. Chandler Burr, "Sniff, and Scratch Your Head," *The New York Times* (August 28, 2005).

3. Ibid.

4. Kathi Keville, *Aromatherapy: Healing for Body and Soul* (Publications International, 1999): pp. 47–50. Accessed online at "How Essential Oils Are Produced." Website: http://health.howstuffworks.com/how-essential-oils-work1.htm.

5. Leffingwell & Associates, "2002–2006 Flavor & Fragrance Industry Leaders." Website: www.leffingwell.com.

6. International Flavors & Fragrances, 2006 Annual Report.

7. K. Miller and T. Phillips, "Space Scents: Researchers Hunting for New and Profitable Fragrances Will Soon Send a Pair of Flowers into Earth Orbit," NASA (December 18, 2002). Website: http://science.nasa.gov/headlines/y2002/18dec_scents.htm.

8. S.M. McClure, J. Li, D. Tomlin, K.S. Cypert, L.M. Montague, and P.R. Montague, "Neural Correlates of Behavioral Preference for Culturally Familiar Drinks," *Neuron* vol. 44 (October 14, 2004): pp. 379–87.

9. S. Warrenburg, "The Consumer Fragrance Thesaurus: Putting Consumer Insights into the Perfumer's Hands." *The Aroma-Chology Review,* vol. 8, no. 2 (1999): pp. 4–5, 7.

Chapter 9

1. Rachel Gordon, "Ad Firm with a First—but Will It Whiff by Mixing Cookies, Muni?" *San Francisco Chronicle* (November 30, 2006); and Rachel Gordon, "Cookie Smell Didn't Pass Muster with the Scent-sensitive," *San Francisco Chronicle* (December 6, 2006).

2. Lee Hudson Teslik, "Candy Clash: Mars Is Opening a Times Square Megastore across from Archrival Hershey's Somewhat Less Mega Store," *Newsweek* (December 7, 2006); and Tara Weiss, "Marketing Innovations: Marketing Milk" Forbes online (December 1, 2006). Website: www.forbes.com.

3. Fragrance Materials Association of the United States, "Fragrance Safety Evaluation" Website: www.fmafragrance.org.

4. James Hannah, "Bomb-sniffing Robots Put to Test in Iraq," *MSNBC* (March 30, 2007). Website: http://www.msnbc.msn.com/id/17874529.

5. Ibid.

6. Michael Crichton, *Runaway* (TriStar Pictures, December 1984).

7. Erik Kirschbaum, "Germans Outraged by 'Scent Profiling' ahead of G8," *Reuters* (May 23, 2007). Website: http://www.reuters.com/article/worldNews/idUSL2349413320070523.

8. Spencer Tebrich, "Human Scent and Its Detection," Central Intelligence Agency Historical Review Program (September 22,1993). Website: https://www.cia.gov/library/center-for-the-study-of-intelligence/kent-csi/docs/v05i2a04p_0001.htm.

9. Gary Beauchamp, director of the Monell Chemical Senses Center, as quoted in an article by David Cohn, "Scent of a Terrorist" (posted June 5, 2006) *Seed Magazine.* Website: www.seedmagazine.com.

10. "The Whole Story on Skin" (posted March 2007) on www.KidsHealth.com.

Chapter 10

1. Valpak "Corporate Overview" Website: www.valpak.com.

2. GlobalShop2007. Website: www.globalshop.org.

Chapter 11

1. Amy E. Knaup "Survival and Longevity in the Business Employment Dynamics Database," *Monthly Labor Review,* vol. 128, no. 5 (May 2005): pp. 50–6; and Brian Headd, "Redefining Business Success: Distinguishing Between Closure and Failure," *Small Business Economics,* vol. 21, no. 1 (August 2003): pp. 51–61.

2. Hakuhodo, Inc. Press Release, "Hakuhodo's Sensory Branding Study: The Importance of the Senses to Sei-katsu-sha" (April 24, 2006). http://www.hakuhodo.jp

3. R.L. Doty, S. Applebaum, H. Zusho, and R.G. Settle, "Sex Differences in Odor Identification Ability: A Cross-cultural Analysis." *Neuropsychologia,* vol. 23, no. 5 (1985): pp. 667–72.

4. R.L. Doty, "Influence of Age and Age-related Diseases on Olfactory Function," *Annals of the New York Academy of Sciences,* vol. 561, no. 1 (1989): pp. 76–86; and E.A. Maylor, S.M. Carter, E.L. Hallett, "Preserved Olfactory Cuing of Autobiographical Memories in Old Age," *The Journals of Gerontology, Series B Psychological Sciences and Social Sciences,* vol. 57, no. 1 (January 2002): pp. 41–6.

5. L. Schiffman, D. Bednall, E. Cowley, A.O. Cass, J. Watson, and L. Kanuk, *Consumer Behaviour*, second edition (Victoria, AU: Prentice Hall, 2001).

6. Ibid.

7. A.R. Hirsch and J.J. Gruss, "Human Male Sexual Response to Olfactory Stimuli." *Journal of Neurological Orthopaedic Medicine and Surgery*, vol. 19, no. 1 (Spring 1999): pp. 14–9.

8. Emily Nelson and Sarah Ellison, "In a Shift, Marketers Beef Up Ad Spending Inside Stores," *The Wall Street Journal* (September 21, 2005): p. A1.

9. Ibid.

Chapter 12

1. Erik Sass, "Study Finds Spectacular Print Ads Get Spectacular Recall," *Marketing Daily* (February 23, 2007).

2. Tamar Charry, N.Y. Times News Service, "Marketers Hope to Win Customers by a Nose with Use of Scented Ads." *The Oklahoma City Journal Record* (July 11, 1996).

3. Brian Steinberg, "Kraft Vies for Eyes—and Noses," *The Wall Street Journal* (November 13, 2006).

4. Thomas Claburn, "Newspapers Smell Profit in Scented Ads: Scentisphere Will Give *The Wall Street Journal* and *USA Today* an Odiferous Experience," *InformationWeek* (January 29, 2007).

5. Margaret Webb Pressler, "Appealing to the Senses: Aromatic Packaging Is Just the Start of Futuristic Sales Ploys," *The Washington Post* (February 19, 2006): p. F1.

6. "KUMHO Introduces World's First 'Aroma Tire' for Select Passenger Vehicles," KUMHO Tire USA press release (December 21, 2006).

7. South African Press Association-Associated Press, "Sweet-smelling Suits Throw Wives off Scent," *Dispatch Online* (April 5, 1999). Website: www.dispatch. co.za.

8. Michael McCoy, "Getting Fragrance onto Clothes Presents a Challenge for Detergent Companies and Their Suppliers," *Chemical and Engineering News*, vol. 85, no. 5 (January 29, 2007): pp. 21–23; and Celessence International Website: **www.celessence.com**.

9. Website: www.michaelkritzer.com.

10. Alan R. Hirsch, "Effects of Ambient Odors on Slot-machine Usage in a Las Vegas Casino," *Psychology and Marketing*, vol. 12, no. 7 (October 1995): pp. 585–94.

11. Prolitec "Technology Advantage." **www.prolitec.com.**

12. "AromaJet.com Announces Fragrance Synthesis Over the Internet," AromaJet press release (December 21, 2000).

13. U.S. Department of Labor, Bureau of Labor Statistics. Website: www.bls.gov.

Chapter 13

1. Stacey Burling, "Shopper Study: Do Smells Sell?" *Philadelphia Inquirer* (October 30, 2006): p. D1.

2. Ibid.

Chapter 14

1. Harvey Chipkin, "Brands Say Scents Make Sense in the Guest Experience," *Hotel and Motel Management* (June 4, 2007); and Barbara De Lollis, "Hotels Wish Guests a Nice-smelling Stay," *USA Today* (May 30, 2006).

2. Hospitality Management and Development Exchange, "Marriott Stubs Out Cigarettes" (July 24, 2006). Website: www.hotelinteractive.com.

3. Speech given by Alan Hirsch, "Odors and Perception of Room Size." The 148th Annual Meeting of the American Psychiatric Association in Miami, FL, on May 24, 1995.

4. Charles Graham, "Infection Fight Breakthrough," *Wigan Observer* (February 16, 2007).

Chapter 15

1. Alan R. Hirsch, "Effects of Ambient Odors on Slot-machine Usage in a Las Vegas Casino," *Psychology and Marketing*, vol. 12, no. 7 (October 1995): pp. 585–94.

Chapter 19

1. K. Keville and P. Korn, *Herbs for Health and Healing* (Emmaus, PA: Rodale, 1996).

2. "It's What You Don't Smell that Makes It Incredible: Inner Realm and the New Pheromone Phenomenon," EROX Corporation press release (April 1, 1997).

Chapter 20

1. C.L. Morgan, "Odors as Cues for the Recall of Words Unrelated to Odor," *Perceptual and Motor Skills*, vol. 83, no. 3, pt. 2 (December 1996): pp. 1227–34.

2. Valerie Ann Worwood, *The Fragrant Mind: Aromatherapy for Personality, Mind, Mood, and Emotion* (Novato, CA: New World Library, 1996): p. 58.

3. Victor Epstein, "Texas Football Succumbs to Virulent Staph Infection From Turf," *Bloomberg.com* (December 21, 2007).

Chapter 21

1. National Center for Health Statistics, National Health Interview Survey, series 10, no. 188, table 1 (1994). Centers for Disease Control Website: http://www.cdc.gov/nchs/nhis.htm.

Chapter 23

1. Daniel J. DeNoon, "Planes, Trains, and …Germs? Travel Health Risks You Can—and Can't—Avoid," *WebMD* (October 1, 2006). Website: www.webmd.com.

2. Ibid.

3. Ibid.

4. Pall Corporation Website: www.pall.com.

Chapter 24

1. Stacey Burling, "Shopper Study: Do Smells Sell?" *Philadelphia Inquirer* (October 30, 2006): p. D1.

2. Speech given by Alan Hirsch, "Odors and Perception of Room Size." The 148th Annual Meeting of the American Psychiatric Association in Miami, FL, on May 24, 1995.

3. Linda Tischler, "Smells Like Brand Spirit: In the Battle for Consumers' Attention, Some Innovative Companies Are Exploring a New Branding Frontier," *Fast Company*, issue 97 (August 2005).

4. "CDC Invests $10 million for Research to Reduce Infections in Health Care Settings," U.S. Centers for Disease Control press release (May 4, 2006). Website: http://www.cdc.gov.

5. Charles Graham, "Infection Fight Breakthrough," *Wigan Observer* (February 16, 2007).

Bibliography

Ackerman, Diane. *A Natural History of the Senses.* New York: Vintage, 1991.

Ackerman, Diane. *An Alchemy of Mind.* New York: Scribner, 2004.

Barbara, Anna and Perliss, Anthony. *Invisible Architecture: Experiencing Places Through the Sense of Smell.* Milan, Italy: Skira, 2006.

Bradbury, Ray. *Fahrenheit 451.* New York: Ballantine Books, 1953.

Burr, Chandler. *The Emperor of Scent: A Story of Perfume, Obsession, and the Last Mystery of the Senses.* New York: Random House, 2003.

Burr, Chandler. *The Perfect Scent: A Year Inside the Perfume Industry in Paris and New York.* New York: Henry Holt and Company, 2008.

Clark, Rosemary. *The Sacred Tradition in Ancient Egypt: The Esoteric Wisdom Revealed.* Woodbury, MN: Llewellyn Publications, 2000.

Classen, Constance, Howes, David, and Synnott, Anthony. *Aroma: The Cultural History of Smell.* New York: Routledge, 1994.

Damian, Peter and Damian, Kate. *Aromatherapy: Scent Psyche.* Rochester, VT: Healing Arts Press, 1995.

Drobnick, Jim. *The Smell Culture Reader.* New York: Berg, 2006.

Gobe, Marc and Zymann, Sergio. *Emotional Branding: The New Paradigm for Connecting Brands to People.* New York: Allworth Press, 2001.

Hawkes, Christopher. *Disorders of Smell and Taste: The Most Common Complaints.* Boston, MA: Butterworth-Heinemann, 2007.

Herz, Rachel, Ph.D. *The Scent of Desire: Discovering Our Enigmatic Sense of Smell.* New York: William Morrow, 2007.

Hirsch, Alan, M.D. *Life's a Smelling Success: Using Scent to Empower Your Memory and Learning.* Mt. Shasta, CA: Authors of Unity, 2003.

Hirsch, Alan, M.D. *Scentsational Sex: The Secret to Using Aroma for Arousal.* Boston, MA: Element Books, 1998.

Johnston, Robert D. *The Politics of Healing: Histories of Alternative Medicine in Twentieth-Century North America.* New York: Routledge, 2003.

Le Guerer, Annick and Miller, Richard. *Scent: The Mysterious and Essential Powers of Smell.* New York: Kodansha America, 1994.

Lindstrom, Martin. *Brand Sense: Build Powerful Brands through Touch, Taste, Smell, Sight, and Sound.* New York: Free Press, 2005.

Lowry, Tina. *Brick & Mortar Shopping in the 21st Century.* Mahwah, NJ: Lawrence Erlbaum, 2007.

Morris, Desmond. *The Human Zoo: A Zoologist's Study of the Urban Animal.* Tokyo, Japan: Kodshana Globe, 1996.

Morris, Edwin. *Scents of Time: Perfume From Ancient Egypt to the 21st Century.* New York: Bulfinch Press, 2000.

Morris, Edwin T. *Fragrance: The Story of Perfume from Cleopatra to Chanel.* New York: Scribner, 1984.

Pine, Joseph B. and Gilmore, James H. *The Experience Economy: Work Is Theater and Every Business a Stage.* Cambridge, MA: Harvard Business School Press, 1999.

Proust, Marcel. *Remembrance of Things Past.* Ware, UK: Wordsworth Editions Ltd., 2006.

Rindisbacher, Hans J. *The Smell of Books: A Cultural-Historical Study of Olfactory Perception in Literature.* Ann Arbor, MI: University of Michigan Press, 1993.

Rippin, Joanee. *The Power of Aroma: Using Essential Oils for Health and Healing.* London, UK: Southwater Publishing, 2001.

Roberts, Kevin. *Lovemarks: The Future Beyond Brands.* New York: PowerHouseBooks, 2004.

Sachs, Jessica Snyder. *Good Germs, Bad Germs: Health and Survival in a Bacterial World.* New York: Hill and Wang, 2007.

Schmitt, Bernd. *Experiential Marketing: How to Get Customers to Sense, Feel, Think, Act, Relate To Your Company and Brands.* New York: Free Press, 1999.

Solomon, Michael R. *Conquering Consumerspace: Marketing Strategies for a Branded World.* New York: AMACOM, 2003.

Stoddart, David Michael. *The Scented Ape: The Biology and Culture of Human Odour.* Cambridge, UK: Cambridge University Press, 1990.

Suskind, Patrick. *Perfume: The Story of a Murder.* New York: Vintage, 2001.

Vroon, Piet A. *Smell: The Secret Seducer.* Translated by Paul Vincent. New York: Farrar, Straus & Giroux, 1997.

Watson, Lyall. *Jacobson's Organ: And the Remarkable Nature of Smell.* New York: Plume, 2001.

Wilson, Donald A. and Stevenson, Richard J. *Learning to Smell: Olfactory Perception from Neurobiology to Behavior.* Baltimore, MD: The Johns Hopkins University Press, 2006.

Worwood, Valerie Ann. *The Fragrant Mind: Aromatherapy for Personality, Mind, Mood, and Emotion.* Novato, CA: New World Press, 1996.

Wyatt, Tristam D. *Pheromones and Animal Behavior: Communication by Smell and Taste.* Cambridge, England: Cambridge University Press, 2003.

Index

C. Russell Brumfield is a classic entrepreneur with a keen ability to identify upcoming trends and to harness their potential. With an endless curiosity that is as diverse as his career, he is a student of science, technology, business, marketing, philosophy, religion and metaphysics. His interests and experience have afforded him the insight to grasp the nature and potential of the pioneering field of scent communication. He is continually involved in new start-up ventures, and has built several multi-million dollar companies. His most notable venture has been Wizard Studios, an entertainment, event, and experiential design company catering to the Fortune 500. With clients like Chrysler, Lexus, Motorola, FedEx, Pfizer, Colgate, MTV, Disney, and the NFL, he became a trailblazer in the industry.

With partner James Goldney, he founded Whiff Solutions, the world's leading scent marketing and branding company, providing leading edge companies with expertise and advice in the science, technology and the application of scent marketing and communication.

Over the course of his career, Brumfield has conceived and honed many revolutionary concepts in his fields of endeavor. Now, with a laser focus on the amazing powers of scent, he has formulated new and exciting strategies and applications to benefit business and society.

Delivering his message with clarity and wit, he is a sought after speaker for international audiences, and an entertaining teacher for seminars and workshops.

When he's not traveling, Brumfield spends his time in Clearwater Beach, Florida. You can visit him at www.whiffbook.com or www.whiffsolutions.com.

James Goldney is a leading expert in the field of scent marketing and communication. An entrepreneur and business owner, his career includes working for private and publicly held companies covering a broad range of industries, including real estate, telecommunications, and hospitality. His expertise is in the creation and implementation of business strategies, and implementing new technologies. He has over 15 years of corporate writing, speaking, and presentation experience.

He has served as chief operating officer and marketing VP of a Florida-based real estate company. Earlier in his career, he was in on the forefront of the Internet boom, serving as director of marketing and investor relations for a $300 million public company which grew to the largest of its kind in the Midwest.

Originally from the United Kingdom, he now lives in Odessa, Florida.

Stephanie Gunning is a bestselling author, editor, and publishing consultant. She is the coauthor of more than 18 books and editor of hundreds. Her A-list clientele includes *New York Times* and national bestselling authors Gregg Braden, Hale Dwoskin, Dr. Ruby Payne, and Dr. Frank Lipman, major publishing firms, top caliber literary agencies, and innovative independent publishers.

After graduating with a B.A. from Amherst College in 1984, Gunning launched her publishing career in New York City, rapidly rising through the ranks as an editor at HarperCollins Publishers and then as a senior editor at Bantam Doubleday Dell. She left the ranks and went solo in 1996, and has never looked back. After a full career in the nonfiction genre, she has just completed her first screenplay.

Gunning lives and works in Manhattan, where she runs her consulting firm, Stephanie Gunning Enterprises.